THE HISTORIC ROSWELL COOK BOOK

By:
The Roswell Historical Society, Inc.
Roswell, Georgia

1982

Printed by Williams Printing Company, Atlanta, Georgia
Typography by Alpharetta Print, Alpharetta, Georgia

First Printing, October 1982 — 10,000 copies

Additional copies may be obtained by addressing
The Roswell Historical Society, Inc.
P.O. Box 274
Roswell, Georgia 30077
(404) 992-1665

ACKNOWLEDGEMENTS

Grateful appreciation is expressed to all the members and friends of the Roswell Historical Society who contributed their recipes, shared their memories and volunteered their time to make this book possible. A special thank you to the owners of the historic homes and landmarks for their cooperation.

Darlene Walsh, *Editor*

Historical Text: Clarece Martin

Art: Members of the Roswell Fine Arts Alliance

Cover Design: Dot Beebe

Foreword: Frances Elyea

Assistant Editors

Wanda Bardin
Peggy Bartleson
Marian David
Shirley Deuchler
Harry Doud

Wilma DuVal
Merijoy Rucker
Carolyn Sparks
Patsy Turner

Cook Book Committees

Ellie Brazee
Diana Butler
Martha Coursey
Frances Elyea
Barbara Garrison
Beth Hamilton
Frances Hargrove
Margaret Harris
Carol Hoskinsen
Mary Jane Jarrett

Mildred Kelley
June Lindgren
Juanita Mitchell
Janine Powers
JoAnn Rieger
Dot Ringler
Harry Smith
Tricia Smith
Denny Walsh

ROSWELL MANUFACTURING COMPANY
Vickery or Big Creek

The cotton mills of the Roswell Manufacturing Company, built in 1838, the first in the county, were the life-blood of Roswell and of importance throughout the South. The Ivy Mills, built a few years later, manufactured woolen goods. Grey cloth used in making Confederate uniforms during the Civil War, known as "Roswell Grey," was made in these mills. Though the mills were destroyed by Union Troops during the War in July 1864, and the workers were deported to the North, the mills were rebuilt by 1866. The main building burned in 1929 after being struck by lightning.

Laurie Engel

FOREWORD

The Roswell Historical Society proudly presents *The Historic Roswell Cook Book* with 470 recipes carefully selected, tested and edited by a large committee of excellent cooks. The recipes cover a period in Roswell's history from open-hearth to microwave cooking.

Included are highlights of Roswell's history and pen and ink drawings of its historic structures. Anecdotes which reflect life in Roswell since the turn of the century are also included. A bit of the South shines through in these as well as in its recipes and its history.

The proceeds from the sale of the book will be used in the preservation of historic Roswell. That was the main purpose of the Historical Society when it was organized in the fall of 1971.

With a growing membership (now almost 700) many things have been accomplished. The Society is credited with saving Bulloch Hall, the girlhood home of President Theodore Roosevelt's mother, and also the 1836 Vickery Creek Dam, the oldest historic site in Roswell.

Special projects for educational purposes and to stimulate interest in history and traditions—such as Quilt Shows, Historic Tour of Homes, Family Heritage Day, Youth Art Shows, Holiday Magic at Bulloch Hall, Heritage Auction, et cetera—have been held from time to time. A hard back book, *Roswell—Historic Homes and Landmarks,* has been published. Markers highlighting historic sites have been placed throughout the area. A tour guide program with a professional slide presentation and trained guides has been organized and made available to the public.

So—as we welcome visitors to Roswell, we are delighted to present in *The Historic Roswell Cook Book* a taste of Roswell in history and foods.

THE OLD BRICKS
Sloan Street

Two similar brick apartment buildings known as The Old Bricks, are said to be the oldest in continuous use in the South. Constructed in 1840 for the Roswell mill workers, they were used by Union soldiers as a hospital during the war.

Nancy Collis

CONTENTS

SOUTHERN MILLS
Mill Street

The Southern Mills building near the banks of Vickery Creek, now Big Creek, was built in 1882 to spin the cotton woven at the original cotton mill. The newer two-story rambling structure remained in production until 1975 when it was closed. The Southern Mills building is listed on the National Register of Historic Places.

Linda Bulkley

LIST OF DRAWINGS

COVERED BRIDGE
Chattahoochee River

The original covered bridge spanning the Chattahoochee River at Roswell, built in the early 1850's, was burned by Confederate soldiers in July 1864 in an attempt to delay the Union attack on Atlanta. A toll bridge was constructed on the piers of the first bridge after the Civil War. Fulton County erected a narrow concrete bridge over the river in 1925, widening it in 1965.

Marguerite Cauble

HISTORIC ROSWELL

The warmth of hospitality, the joy of sharing the bounties of the land, are as traditional in Roswell today as they were in the days of campfires and open-hearth cooking. The heritage of hearty satisfying meals dates from the days the Cherokee Indians first harvested crops of maize and reaped the yield of forest and stream in the Blue Ridge foothills of North Georgia.

As pioneer families moved onto the land bringing the cultured manners and refined ways of coastal gentry, fireplaces and beehive ovens replaced campfires. The settlers, as well as the Indians before them, depended on corn as a vital staple. Present-day recipes for corn puddings and bread have Indian origin.

Roswell King, a native New Englander, later manager of the Pierce Butler plantations south of Savannah, rode through the Georgia uplands on banking business to the gold-rush towns of Auraria and Dahlonega. He acquired land just north of the Chattahoochee River along Vickery Creek after the departure of the Cherokee Indians in the late 1830's. With his son, Barrington King, he built a log house and dammed the creek to power the cotton mill they constructed. Homesites were offered to coastal friends who joined the Kings in carving a society from the wilderness frontier.

The early settlers used natural resources in their buildings, at first erecting modest cottages. Later, with the skilled hands of finishers, carvers, and cabinetmakers, they constructed elegant edifices of brick and clapboard, with stately columns towering above broad porticoes. Profits from the mill, shared by the original families, allowed them to enjoy the lifestyle they had known in Savannah and Darien.

Loyal slave families, brought from the coast, tended the homes and fields, minded the babies, and served up sumptuous meals from iron pots and kettles swung over coals of pine knots and ax-hewn logs. Kitchens with massive fireplaces were located in the basement or separated from the main house by a covered walkway. The cook in the "big" house carried within her head traditional family recipes passed on from generation to generation, a treasured heritage with which she was entrusted.

Visitors were welcomed for weeks or months at a time, as homes were large and servants and food plentiful. Christenings and funerals were oc-

casions for lavish food and drink. But weddings were the ultimate of enjoyment, for the bride and groom were entertained for days before and after the ceremony.

As the War Between the States ripped the nation apart, Roswell families and friends were separated, some never to be reunited. Women and children sought refuge in other towns as husbands and sons went off to war. Union soldiers advanced toward Atlanta through Roswell, burning the mills and turning the church and homes into hospitals and officers' quarters. When the soldiers departed, they left a looted village, its mills destroyed, its people gone. And though the mansions were not burned, they did not escape the devastating effects of the war.

At war's end, returning families faced the ordeal of reconstruction, with few tools and seed, no crops or supplies, and no help. Still, the tradition of sharing and hospitality reappeared. Simple social functions again were enjoyed. Picnics, hay rides, dancing, and a new game called, "croquet," as well as sodas, ice cream, and ribbon candy at the drug store, helped dim memories and losses of war.

A new century brought telephones, electricity, and automobiles to Roswell. Kitchen shelves held cook books and canned goods. The handy corner grocery store gave way to the giant supermarket, a store much like the old-fashioned country store where one could buy food, cleaning supplies, utensils, toys, magazines, and clothing. But the cracker barrel and rocking chairs around a pot-bellied stove had disappeared.

Seated six-course dinners served by servants were replaced by cocktail parties, backyard barbecues, and pot-luck dinners. But Roswell retains its distinctive character and heritage, even though it rests in the shadows of the City of Atlanta. The drive from Atlanta takes less than a half an hour. The contrast, however, is startling. A few miles from the bustle of the city lies the historic village that combines the tranquility of the country with the excitement of progress and growth.

The resplendant architectural detailing found in the ancient landmarks of Roswell contribute to the town's unusual charm, as does the fact that most of the historic district can be seen on foot. The cosmopolitan citizenry of Roswell beckons and guides the town toward the future, though never forgetting its appeal lies in its history and heritage, its serenity, its warm hospitality.   —Clarece Martin

BEVERAGES

Primrose Cottage (Circa 1839)
Roswell, Georgia 30075

Laurie Engel

PRIMROSE COTTAGE
MIMOSA BOULEVARD
Circa 1839

PRIMROSE COTTAGE

The home of widowed Eliza King Hand, Primrose Cottage, was the first permanent home built in Roswell. Mrs. Hand and her three children shared the two-storied clapboard cottage with her father, Roswell King. Symmetry defines the facade of the 1839 home, with shutters setting off the 18-pane, triple-hung front windows in parlor and library.

A high hipped roof crowns the exterior. Pilasters flank the columned entry of the classic portico, a later addition to the house. The doorway opens to a central hall running the length of the original structure and opening to large, high-ceiling rooms on either side, with the same basic plan upstairs. This was the most popular floor plan of the day.

An unusual hand-turned balustrade fence of Rosemary pine extends across the front of the house. The fence was constructed by Peter Minhinnet, a carpenter from Plymouth, England, who was to fence other homes in the area, but was forced to return to England by a disgruntled wife. The original kitchen in the basement of the home boasts a large rustic fireplace decked with antique kitchen utensils and features a beehive oven.

The Roswell Presbyterian Church was organized in the parlor of Primrose Cottage on October 20, 1839, by fifteen charter members, with the help and prayers of Dr. Nathaniel A. Pratt, the church's first minister. Mrs. Hand furnished a simple plate of pottery and a crystal goblet, in which the first communion was served, now displayed in the History Room of the Roswell Presbyterian Church.

The home is listed on the National Register of Historic Places.

———

PRIMROSE COTTAGE CHRISTMAS EVE DROP-IN

Christmas Cranberry Punch*

Smoked Turkey   Honey Baked Ham
Biscuits and Assorted Crackers
Mustard - Mayonnaise - Horseradish Sauce
Vegetable Tray with Sour Cream Dip
Variety of Cheeses
Pears, Apples and Grapes
Marinated Mushrooms   Olives
Fruit Cake
Christmas Cookies   Candies

Christmas Cranberry Punch

Yield: 3 gallons

Holiday entertaining idea from Primrose Cottage.

1 gallon plus 12 ounces
  cranberry juice
1 gallon (80 proof) vodka
12 ounces cherry liqueur
48 ounces orange juice
2 teaspoons cinnamon
1 teaspoon allspice
½ teaspoon nutmeg
2 limes, sliced

Make a paste of spices and small amount vodka. Pour over ice mold in punch bowl. Add remaining ingredients. Float slices of lime on top.

Alice King (Mrs. Charles N.)

Champagne Punch

**Yield: 132 ounces
or 125 drinks**

3 bottles champagne (white)
1 fifth brandy
1 small bottle Triple Sec
1 quart seltzer

Chill well all beverages before mixing. Just before serving, place large pieces of ice in punch bowl. Add all ingredients and mix gently. Serve in champagne glasses or punch cups.

Tom Rieger

Fruit Punch Slush

Yield: 6 quarts

Especially good for children's parties!

6 ripe bananas
1 (6 ounce) can frozen lemonade,
  thawed and undiluted
1 (12 ounce) can frozen orange
  juice, thawed and undiluted
1 (46 ounce) can pineapple juice
3 cups water
2 cups sugar
2 (64 ounce) bottles Sprite, chilled

Combine bananas and fruit juice concentrates in electric blender container. Blend until smooth. Combine banana mixture, pineapple juice, water and sugar in large mixing bowl. Mix well. Pour into plastic freezer containers. (May use ½ gallon plastic milk cartons.) Freeze. To serve, thaw until mushy. Add chilled Sprite.

Gloria Barkley Bond (Mrs. Robert)

Hot Buttered Punch

Yield: 24 (4 ounce) cups

¾ cup brown sugar
¼ teaspoon salt
¼ teaspoon nutmeg
½ teaspoon cinnamon
½ teaspoon allspice
¾ teaspoon cloves
4 cups water, divided
2 (1 pound) cans jellied cranberry
  sauce
1 quart unsweetened pineapple
  juice
¼ cup whipped sweet butter

Mix brown sugar, salt and spices with 3 cups water in saucepan; bring to boil to make syrup. Set aside. Add 1 cup water to cranberry sauce; beat with rotary beater until smooth. Add pineapple juice and cranberry mixture to hot syrup; heat almost to boiling. Serve hot with ½ teaspoon butter in each cup.

Mary W. Hawkins (Mrs. Aubrey L.)

Mocha Punch

Yield: 20 servings

3 cups boiling water
4 tablespoons instant coffee
6 tablespoons chocolate syrup
1 quart milk
½ gallon vanilla ice cream,
  softened

Mix together boiling water, instant coffee and chocolate syrup. Let cool. When ready to serve, add milk and ice cream.

Mary Holman (Mrs. Penn G.)

Summer Punch

Serves: 12-15

8 oranges, seeded and juiced
4 lemons, seeded and juiced
2 limes, seeded and juiced
1 quart rum
1 pint Triple Sec
3-4 (quart) bottles sparkling water
orange and lime slices

Chill fruit juices. Combine all ingredients in punch bowl. Float a ring ice mold, orange and lime slices.

Peggy Swenson

Marie's Spiced Cider Punch

Yield: 40 (½ cups)

juice of 5 lemons
brown sugar to taste
1 gallon sweet cider
3 sticks cinnamon
1 tablespoon allspice
1 tablespoon whole cloves

Mix all ingredients. Boil 15 minutes and serve hot.

Lenox T. (Tom) Thornton

Hot Spiced Cider

Yield: 1 gallon

Like Russian Tea, but simpler to prepare.

1 gallon apple juice
peel of 2 lemons, cut in spirals
4 (1-inch) cinnamon sticks
½ cup honey
2 oranges, thinly sliced
8 whole cloves

Combine apple juice, lemon peel, cinnamon sticks, and honey. Simmer 20 minutes. Remove lemon peel. Serve in mugs or tea cups topped with orange slices which have been stuffed with cloves.

R. Luke DeLong

Orange Tea Cooler

Yield: 8 cups

6 cups orange-spice flavored tea
  (double strength)
1 cup honey
½ cup orange juice
¼ cup lemon juice

To freshly brewed hot tea, add honey, orange juice, and lemon juice. Stir to dissolve. Chill.

Beth Stark

Rich Egg Nog

Serves 12

6 eggs, separated
1 cup sugar, divided
3 cups half and half cream
1 cup brandy
1 cup heavy cream
nutmeg

Beat egg yolks with ½ cup sugar. Stir in half and half cream and brandy. Let mixture mellow in refrigerator 2-3 hours. Just before serving, beat egg whites with remaining sugar. Beat heavy cream until it forms soft swirls and fold into meringue. Drop by spoonfuls onto the "nog" and sprinkle with nutmeg.

Merijoy Rucker (Mrs. Rodney)

Buttermilk and Watercress Drink

Serves 4

Nice summer drink.

2½ cups buttermilk
5/8 cup yogurt
1 bunch watercress

Combine buttermilk, yogurt and leaves of watercress in blender or food processor. Pour into glasses and chill.

Ossi Mabry

Frozen Peach Freezy

Yield: 4-6 drinks

1 small can frozen lemonade,
   thawed and undiluted
¾ can water
1 can rum or vodka
1 small package frozen peaches

Mix together in blender. Serve.

Bettie Skaggs

Hurricane

Serves 4

6 ounces rum
12 ounces Hawaiian Punch
4 ounces unsweetened pineapple
   juice
juice of one lime

Combine all ingredients. Shake with ice. Serve on ice.

Bobbie Pridmore

Mint Juleps

Serves 8

Syrup makes the difference! Outstanding Southern sippin'!

2 cups sugar
1 cup water
16 sprigs mint
4 pounds ice, finely crushed
8 (1½ ounce) jiggers bourbon
confectioners' sugar for garnish
mint for garnish

Mix sugar and water; bring to boil, stirring. Cool. Place 2 sprigs of mint in each glass; crush to release mint flavor. Add 2 ounces sugar syrup, stirring gently. Fill glasses with ice. Add 1 jigger bourbon. Stir until glass frosts. Top with sprig of mint and sprinkling of confectioners' sugar.

Gloria Conrad (Mrs. Richard)

Sherry Blossom

Serves 1

Perfect for a ladies' luncheon or bridal shower.

2 ounces sherry
¾ ounce frozen lemonade,
   thawed and undiluted
sprig of mint

Mix together sherry and lemonade. Pour into glass ¾ full of crushed ice. Add sprig of mint. NOTE: Can multiply by number of servings desired and make a punch.

Mary Francis Walker (Mrs. Walter P.)

Amaretto

Yield: one fifth

2 cups water
2 cups sugar
rind of one lemon
⅔ cup (80 proof) vodka
6 teaspoons almond extract
1 teaspoon chocolate extract
2 teaspoons vanilla extract
1 drop green food coloring
4 drops yellow food coloring
3 drops red food coloring

Combine water, sugar and lemon and bring to full boil. Reduce heat and simmer 20-25 minutes. Allow to cool completely. Remove any lemon rind that did not dissolve. Add all other ingredients and stir. Put in decanter and let set for one week. Serve over ice as after dinner drink or over ice cream.

Jill Cheek

Orange Liqueur

Yield: 1 quart

3 navel oranges
3 cups vodka, divided
1½ cups superfine sugar

Pare very thinly the bright colored orange rind from oranges. Blot peel on paper towels to remove excess oil. Put peel in 4-cup screw top jar. Add 2 cups vodka. Close tightly and place in cool, dark place for 2 days, or until vodka has absorbed flavor and color of the peel. Remove peel; add sugar and shake vigorously until sugar has dissolved. Add remaining 1 cup vodka and stir until liquid is clear. Close jar. Store in dark, cool place for one week to age. NOTE: To make daiquiri liqueur, follow same procedure but use 4 large limes and 3 cups light rum.

John E. McGaughey, Jr.

Bob's Mocha Mix

Yield: 1 cup mix

Makes great gift in a pretty cannister.

¾ cup hot cocoa mix
⅓ cup instant coffee
2 tablespoons non-dairy creamer
4 teaspoons sugar
¼ teaspoon cinnamon

Combine all ingredients in food processor and process to a fine powder; or, combine in bowl and stir until well mixed. For each serving measure 2 tablespoons mix into mug. Pour in boiling water. Stir until dissolved.

Bob St. Jean

7

GENERAL STORE TO FAMILY GROCERY

Times were in Roswell when it did not require a major decision WHERE to do the grocery shopping. A single small store in the Lebanon Community on Grimes Bridge Road was the only option open to Roswell King in 1837. It was there he visited and did business while laying the foundation for his planned community. With the establishment of the Roswell Manufacturing Company came the construction of a commissary on the town square where millworkers and their families could shop for supplies. Later, as other buildings were added, folks could purchase luxury items as well as staples. The stores offered tobacco, gunpowder, bonnets, colognes, gumdrops and taffy, ointments and liniments, coffee mills and caskets! Old ledgers from 1909 to 1915 reveal records of some astonishing sales: twenty-five cents for two pounds of butter, thirty-five cents for two pounds of coffee, sixty cents for two chickens, fifty cents for two roosters, and $4.00 for five bushels of potatoes!

The Roswell Store on the square, a true general store, served the community until the 1960's. A one-step shopping excursion took care of grocery, clothing and hardware supplies. Pins and calico were purchased along with eggs and cheese and sometimes a coal bucket or a new plow blade went home with the bread and beef. What you could not carry you could have delivered! At the flour mill next door you could buy nickel burlap bags, perfect for everything from fertilizer to arts and crafts. Old flour sacks made the best kitchen towels!

Long time residents remember the family grocery businesses on Canton Street. Reeve's was a regular shopping stop where under a balcony of lush tropical plants folks shopped for groceries while visiting with their neighbors and catching up on affairs in town.

Giving an ethnic flair to the little street of shops is Feckoury's Groceries and Fresh Meats, a feast for the eyes as well as the stomach with baskets and baskets of colorful blooms spilling over onto the sidewalk and graceful ferns swinging from the small shed roof. Papa Feckoury was for many years Roswell's only bona fide "foreigner", introducing wonderful Lebanese dishes to the community.

For many years people from Atlanta enjoyed driving "out" to Roswell to buy fresh vegetables direct from farmers and gardeners who put signs in their yards advertising the seasonal offerings. Taylor Williams made available for the asking plentiful turnip greens from his farm. A signed guest book is testimony that people from all over the world have taken home some of Taylor's turnip greens as a souvenir of their visit to Georgia. One family developed a produce company as a result of the demand for wholesale vegetables. The Mansells moved a home basement operation to a large store on Alpharetta Street and ran a very successful business for years providing fresh fruits, vegetables, bulk seed and fertilizer for the garden.

APPETIZERS

W. Todd Moore

**MIMOSA HALL
BULLOCH AVENUE
Circa 1840**

MIMOSA HALL

Mimosa Hall was built in the early 1840's by John Dunwody and his wife, Jane Bulloch, sister of Major James Stephens Bulloch, whose home, Bulloch Hall, adjoins the property. The original clapboard home, called Dunwody Hall, burned on the night of the housewarming, but was immediately rebuilt of stucco scored to resemble stone. The home was renamed Phoenix Hall.

Four massive Doric columns support the two-storied portico, approached by a stone driveway bordered with ancient boxwoods. The wide central hall leads to large rooms on either side, graced by crystal chandeliers, ornate pier mirrors, and Victorian furniture of the period.

The Greek Revival mansion was used as a hospital for Union soldiers during the War. It was purchased in 1869 by General Andrew Jackson Hansell, great-great-grandfather of the present owner. Mrs. Hansell renamed the home Mimosa Hall for the numerous mimosa trees on the property. Neel Reid, one of Georgia's outstanding architects, owned the home for several years, laying out gardens and a courtyard. Removing the walls between double parlors, he created a great hall with matching fireplaces.

The house retains much of the original woodwork, sashes, shutters, and hardware saved by loyal servants who fought that first blaze. Paneling, cabinetry, and floors of heart pine cut on the premises, show the exquisite carpentry work of the day. The original kitchen, located in the basement, retains pieces of the orginal 1840 iron cookware.

Mimosa Hall is listed on the National Register of Historic Places.

———

RECEPTION AT MIMOSA HALL FOR SIGNORA MARIA PIA FANFANI, WIFE OF THE PRESIDENT OF THE ITALIAN SENATE
November 1980

Hot Bite-Size Minced Chicken Tarts
Hot Bit-Size Curried Lamb Tarts with Chutney
Tiny Hot Dogs   Assorted Canapes
Fresh Fruit Platter of
Pineapple Spears, Strawberries, and White Grapes
Garnished with Fresh Mint
Rolled Mushroom Sandwiches*
Dainty Chicken Salad Sandwiches
Ginger Cream Served with Carr's Wheatmeal Biscuits*
Tiny Homemade Cream Puffs Filled with
Pumpkin Fluff or Mincemeat
Miniature Pecan Tarts
Hot Spiced Cider   Hot Coffee

Ginger Cream Spread

Yield: 8-cup mold

An original secret recipe from Mimosa Hall!

- 6 (8 ounce) packages cream cheese, softened
- 1 bottle Keiller imported ginger preserve
- ½ cup pecans
- 2 small jars Major Grey's Chutney

Mix softened cream cheese and ginger preserve well. Place in 8-cup mold and freeze. To serve, unmold. Crumble pecans on top and surround with chutney. Serve with Carr's Wheatmeal Biscuits or other plain wholewheat crackers. NOTE: Ginger preserve can be found in most supermarket fine food sections.

Sylvia Hansell (Mrs. C. Edward)

Mushroom Roll-ups

Yield: 300
400° oven

Canapé enjoyed at Mimosa Hall parties.

- 100 thin slices white bread
- 9 large onions, minced
- 14 cups fresh mushrooms, minced
- 27 tablespoons butter
- 18 tablespoons flour
- 4 teaspoons basil
- 4½ teaspoons salt
- 1 cup sour cream
- 1½ cups mayonnaise

Remove crusts from bread and roll each slice flat with rolling pin. Sauté onions and mushrooms in butter until onions are transparent. Add flour, seasonings, sour cream and mayonnaise. Heat, but do not boil. Cool slightly and mix well. Spread evenly on bread and roll up. Brush lightly with melted butter. Place on cookie sheet and chill. May be frozen at this point. Thaw and cut each roll into 3 pieces. Bake on Pam sprayed pan 10 to 15 minutes at 400°.

Sylvia Hansell (Mrs. C. Edward)

Crab Crisps

Yield: 3 dozen
broiler

Great crowd pleaser.

- 1 (6½ ounce) can crab meat, drained and flaked
- 8 ounces sour cream
- ½ cup shredded Swiss cheese
- 2 tablespoons dry onion soup mix
- Melba toast rounds

Combine ingredients and spread on toast rounds. Broil 4 or 5 inches from heat for 2 to 3 minutes.

Marie Mitchler (Mrs. H. G.)

11

Chicken Cream Puffs

Yield: 6 dozen
425° oven

½ cup butter or margarine
1 cup boiling water
1 cup sifted flour
¼ teaspoon salt
4 eggs

Combine butter and boiling water in saucepan. Keep over low heat until butter is melted. Add flour and salt all at once. Stir vigorously over low heat until mixture forms a ball and leaves sides of pan (about 2 minutes). Remove from heat and add eggs one at a time, beating well after each addition. Continue beating until smooth and satiny. Drop level teaspoonful of mixture onto greased baking sheet and bake 18 to 22 minutes. Cool on rack. Slice top from puffs. Fill with warm Chicken Pecan Filling.

Chicken Pecan Filling

4 tablespoons butter or margarine
2 cups finely chopped pecans
3 cups finely minced cooked chicken
½ cup mayonnaise
8 ounces cream cheese
½ teaspoon salt
1 teaspoon ground nutmeg
1 teaspoon grated lemon rind

Filling: Melt butter in skillet. Add pecans and lightly brown over low heat. Cool. Combine with remaining ingredients. Will fill 6 dozen puffs.

Mickey Cox (Mrs. Ralph)

Cucumber Sandwiches

Yield: 48

Rave reviews! Good for tea sandwiches.

2 cucumbers
3 garlic cloves, split
1 tablespoon soy sauce
½ teaspoon salt
1-2 dashes Tabasco
vinegar to cover cucumbers
thinly sliced bread
mayonnaise

Peel cucumbers and slice thin. Place in covered container with all other ingredients. Chill at least 12 hours. (Cucumbers will keep a week in refrigerator.) Spread thinly sliced bread with mayonnaise and arrange cucumbers on top. Cut into triangles.

Thelma Florence

Crispy Cheese Roll-Ups

Yield: 40-48
broiler

Very good as luncheon or dinner rolls too (makes 20-24).

1 cup grated cheese
1 teaspoon mustard
1 teaspoon mayonnaise
dash of salt
1 tablespoon minced onion
¾ teaspoon celery seed
20-24 slices white bread

Combine first six ingredients. Cut crust from white bread. Roll with rolling pin until flat. Spread bread thinly with cheese mixture, roll up and chill. Roll in melted butter and broil until brown. Cut in half if used for hors d' oeuvers. Serve whole as luncheon or dinner rolls.

Wilma Deuel DuVal

Cheese Straws

Yield: 100
350° oven

1 cup butter
1 pound sharp cheese, grated
2 cups flour
1 teaspoon salt
4-5 dashes red pepper or Tabasco

Cream together butter and cheese. Add other ingredients. Mix well with hands. Divide dough in half and make each half into a 13-inch roll. Wrap in waxed paper and chill 3 or 4 hours. Cut into ¼-inch slices and bake at 350° 10 to 12 minutes.

Ann Ledsinger (Mrs. Lewis, Jr.)

Spinach Balls

Yield: 40
350° oven

Good to have in the freezer and bake as needed.

1 package frozen spinach, thawed
  and drained
1 cup Baco Bits
1 cup fresh mushrooms, chopped
1 medium onion, chopped
4 eggs, beaten
¾ cups butter, melted
1 (12 ounce) package Pepperidge
  Farm Herb Seasoned Stuffing
6 ounces Parmesan cheese
¼ teaspoon garlic powder

Mix together all ingredients and refrigerate four hours. Roll into balls. Bake at 350° for 20 minutes.

Barbara Garrison (Mrs. Gary)

Black Eyed Susans

Yield: 100
300° oven

1 pound sharp cheese, grated
½ pound margarine
1 teaspoon salt
½ teaspoon red pepper
3 cups flour
1½ pounds pitted dates
pecan halves
granulated sugar

Cream cheese and margarine. Add salt, pepper and flour. Work dough well. Stuff each date with pecan half. Wrap each date with small portion of dough, leaving each end of date showing. Roll in sugar. Bake at 300° until slightly browned. Store in covered container.

JoAnn M. King

Spinach Balls or Spread

Yield: 70-100
350° oven

2 boxes frozen chopped spinach, cooked and drained
2 cups herb stuffing mix
¾ cup margarine, melted
3 eggs, beaten
2 large onions, chopped fine
½ cup Parmesan cheese
1 teaspoon black pepper
1 teaspoon garlic salt
1 teaspoon thyme

Mix all ingredients. Shape into balls and bake at 350° for 20 minutes. May be forzen before baking. If so, thaw 30 minutes, then bake. May also be served as a spread with crackers.

Barbara Wiggins

Cocktail Meatballs

Yield: 25-30

1 pound ground beef
½ cup dry bread crumbs
⅓ cup chopped onion
¼ cup milk
1 egg
1 tablespoon parsley
1 teaspoon salt
½ teaspoon pepper
½ tablespoon Worcestershire sauce
12 ounces chili sauce
10 ounces grape jelly

Mix first nine ingredients and shape into small balls. Brown in skillet. Combine chili sauce and grape jelly in saucepan. Heat until jelly is melted. Place meatballs in sauce and simmer one hour. Serve in chafing dish.

Mary Ann Wages

14

Sausage Balls

Serves 50

1 pound hot sausage
3 pounds mild sausage
1½ cups stuffing mix
2 teaspoons sage
4 eggs, slightly beaten
1 cup chili sauce
1 cup catsup
8 tablespoons brown sugar
4 tablespoons soy sauce
2 cups water

Combine sausage, stuffing mix, sage and eggs. Form into small balls, fry and drain. Mix remaining ingredients to make sauce and simmer 30 minutes. Add sausage balls to sauce and refrigerate or freeze. Reheat before serving and place in chafing dish. Serve with cocktail picks.

Jean Sentinella (Mrs. Alan)

Barbecued Chicken Wings

Serves 20-30
400° oven

4 to 5 pounds chicken wings
¾ cup soy sauce
¾ cup pineapple juice
3 tablespoons sherry or
   vermouth
1 clove garlic, crushed
1 medium onion, chopped
1½ teaspoons ginger
5 tablespoons brown sugar

Discard tips of wings; cut remaining wing into two pieces. Mix all ingredients well and marinate wings overnight in mixture. To serve, spread evenly in baking pan and bake 1½ hours at 400°. Midway in baking, turn wings and baste with sauce.

Joan Gaeta (Mrs. Richard)

Buffalo Cocktail Chicken Wings

Yield: ¾ pound
300° oven

1 (6 ounce) can frozen orange
   juice
1 (5 ounce) bottle soy sauce
1 (6 ounce) jar prepared mustard
¾ pound chicken wings

In blender, mix together orange juice, soy sauce and mustard. Pour over chicken wings in shallow pan to fit. Wings should rest in approximately ¼ to ½ inch sauce. Place under broiler to brown. When all sides are browned, bake at 300° until all sauce is gone (approximately 1 hour).

Eileen Harbrecht (Mrs. John)

Hot Pecan Spread

Serves 8-10
350° oven

May be frozen before baking.

8 ounces cream cheese
2 tablespoons milk
3 ounces dried chipped beef, chopped fine
4 green onions, finely chopped
¼ cup chopped green pepper
½ cup sour cream
½ teaspoon pepper
½ teaspoon garlic salt
chopped pecans

Mix together all ingredients except pecans and place in casserole dish. Top with pecans. Bake at 350° until thoroughly hot. Serve with crackers.

Dorcas David (Mrs. John H., Sr.)

Hot Artichoke Spread

Serves 10
350° oven

If other hors d'oeuvres are served, this will go first!

2 cans artichoke hearts, well drained
1 cup mayonnaise
1 cup grated Parmesan cheese
cayenne pepper to taste
garlic powder to taste
paprika

Chop artichokes fine. (May use food processor.) Combine with all other ingredients. Place in baking dish and sprinkle with paprika. Bake at 350° for 30 to 40 minutes (until slightly brown on top). Keep hot in chafing dish. Serve with crackers.

Tillie Wood (Mrs. Roy)

Crab Spread

Serves 10-20

2-3 small green onions, chopped (include tops)
½ stick butter
16 ounces cream cheese, room temperature
8 ounces crab meat or 8 ounces boiled shrimp, peeled and deveined

Sauté onions in butter until tender. Remove from heat. Add cream cheese and crab meat. Mix well. May be molded and served on a bed of lettuce with crackers.

Marion Melton (Mrs. Bruce)

Shrimp Spread

Yield: about 4½ cups

1 stick margarine
8 ounces cream cheese
1 small onion, chopped
1 cup finely chopped celery
dash Worcestershire sauce
1 tablespoon lemon juice
2 (4½ ounce) cans shrimp, drained
2 tablespoons mayonnaise
salt and pepper to taste

Cream together margarine and cream cheese. Add remaining ingredients and mix well. Use as spread on crackers or party bread.

Mary Louise Phipps (Mrs. J. M.)

Shrimp Mold

Yield: 1½ quarts

Very pretty for a party!

1 can tomato soup
1 tablespoon unflavored gelatin
½ cup water
8 ounces cream cheese
1 cup mayonnaise
1½ cups diced celery
½ cup minced onion
2 cups (12 ounces frozen) shrimp, chopped
2 spoons pickle relish

Heat soup, but do not boil. Dissolve gelatin in water and add to soup. Stir in cheese and beat until smooth. Cool. Add remaining ingredients and pour into 2-quart mold. Chill until set. Serve with crackers.

Lorrie Berry (Mrs. Roger W.)

Curry Party Dip

Yield: 2 cups

8 ounces cream cheese
¾ cup chopped onions
1 teaspoon salt
1 teaspoon celery salt
2 tablespoons curry powder
milk

Place cream cheese in mixing bowl. Sprinkle all other ingredients over cheese. Pour small quantity of milk into bowl while stirring and mixing, until a smooth, creamy dip is acquired.

Berlin H. Pless

Curry Dip

Yield: 2 cups

1 pint mayonnaise
1 teaspoon grated onion
1 tablespoon garlic salt
1 tablespoon horseradish
1 tablespoon curry powder

Mix all ingredients. Use as a dip with fresh vegetables. Flavors blend well overnight.

Rick Hoskinson

Smoked Oyster Dip

Yield: 3½ cups

8 ounces cream cheese
1½ cups mayonnaise
4 dashes Tabasco
1 tablespoon lemon juice
1 small onion, chopped
1 (4 ounce) can smoked oysters,
    drained and chopped
1 (4 ounce) can black olives,
    chopped

Mix all ingredients. Serve with crackers or fresh vegetables.

Laurie Engel (Mrs. Herbert)

Hot Seafood Dip

Serves 45-50

2 cans cream of mushroom soup
1 can cream of shrimp soup
8 ounces cream cheese
3 (4½ ounce) cans small shrimp,
    rinsed and drained
3 (8 ounce) cans sliced
    mushrooms
1 pound frozen lump crab meat
2 (8 ounce) cans water chestnuts,
    sliced
2 teaspoons lemon-pepper
    seasoning
3 tablespoons Worcestershire
3 tablespoons white wine or
    sherry
2 teaspoons dry mustard
salt and pepper to taste

Heat cream of mushroom and cream of shrimp soups. Add cream cheese and stir until melted. Add remaining ingredients. Serve hot in chafing dish with Melba toast rounds.

Dr. Wendell Phillips

Shrimp Dip

Yield: 3 cups

8 ounces cream cheese
½ bottle Heinz chili sauce
1 teaspoon Lea and Perrin's
1 teaspoon lemon juice
1 teaspoon onion juice
7-8 drops Tabasco
1 cup shrimp, cooked and
    chopped

Mix together all ingredients, except shrimp, with electric mixer. Fold in shrimp. Serve with king size Fritos.

Carolyn Sparks (Mrs. Don)

Steak-Cheese Dip

Serves 50-60

Also makes good grilled sandwiches.

1 pound ground steak
1 pound Velveeta cheese
1 pound sharp cheddar cheese
1 can mushroom soup (undiluted)
1 tablespoon dried onion
Worcestershire sauce to taste
Tabasco sauce to taste
salt and pepper to taste

Broil meat until pink. Put cheese, soup, onion and seasonings in double broiler and melt. Add meat to cheese mixture. Serve warm with Melba toast, crackers or potato chips. Keeps well in refrigerator.

Dottie Picquet (Mrs. Paul)

Sausage in Cheese Dip

Serves 10
275° oven

1 pound smoked sausage, sliced
1 pound Velveeta cheese
1 (8 ounce) can tomato sauce
   with chili peppers

Mix together in baking dish and bake at 275° until hot and bubbly. Serve hot! Keep warm in chafing dish or fondue pot.

Cathy Robinson (Mrs. David E.)

Spinach Dip

Yield: 3 cups

Keeps well for several days if refrigerated.

1 package frozen chopped
   spinach, uncooked
½ cup mayonnaise (scant
   measurement)
½ teaspoon salt
dash coarse ground pepper
½ teaspoon grated onion
   (optional)
3 tablespoons crumbled bleu
   cheese

Thaw and drain spinach well. Combine all ingredients and chill. Serve with large corn chips.

Marva L. Mapp (Mrs. C. A.)

3rd Hole Dip

Yield: 1½ cups

8 ounces cream cheese
1½ tablespoons mayonnasie
½ tablespoon lemon juice
3 green onions, grated
3-4 ounces dried beef, chopped
horseradish to taste
garlic salt to taste

Mix together all ingredients. If necessary, thin with milk. Serve with raw vegetables or fruit.

Phyllis Galloway (Mrs. James)

Jezebel Sauce

Yield: 2 pints

Vary amounts to suit taste.

- 1 (18 ounce) jar peach or pineapple preserves
- 1 (18 ounce) jar apple jelly
- ½ can dry mustard
- 6 tablespoons horseradish

Mix ingredients together. Serve as appetizer with cream cheese and crackers.

Irene D. Howell

Cheese Log

Serves 8-10

- 1 small jar Old English sharp cheese
- 8 ounces cream cheese
- 4 ounces bleu cheese
- 1 clove garlic, minced
- ¼ cup tomato catsup
- ½ teaspoon Worcestershire sauce
- ½ cup crushed pecans

Bring all ingredients to room temperature and mix well. Chill and form into log or ball and roll in crushed pecans. Serve with crackers.

Dorothy Lyons (Mrs. F. E.)

Pineapple Cream Cheese Ball

Yield: one cheese ball

Unusually good!

- 1 pound cream cheese
- ¼ cup chopped green pepper
- 2 tablespoons chopped onion
- 1 teaspoon seasoned salt
- 1 (8 ounce) can crushed pineapple, drained
- ½ cup chopped pecans

Blend all ingredients except nuts and form into ball. Roll in chopped pecans. Wrap and chill.

Anne Bishop

Spiced Pineapple

Yield: 4½ cups

Great served cold at a coffee or as a hot accompaniment to ham. Prepare 1 to 2 days before serving.

- 3 (14 ounce) cans pineapple chunks
- ½ cup tarragon vinegar
- ¾ cup sugar
- dash salt
- 12-14 cloves
- 4-6 pieces stick cinnamon

Drain syrup from pineapple (1½ cups). Add vinegar, sugar and spices to syrup. Heat 10 minutes. Add pineapple and bring to a boil. Store in glass or plastic container in refrigerator. To serve, drain well. Place in glass bowl. Serve with toothpicks.

Marion Davies

Pickled Carrot Sticks

Yield: 2 pints

Hors d'oeuvres or garnish for entree.

1 pound carrots, peeled and
  thinly sliced into sticks
¾ cup vinegar
¾ cup water
½ cup sugar
1 teaspoon mixed whole pickling
  spices

Cook carrots in boiling, salted water 10 minutes. Bring vinegar, water, sugar and spices to boil. Simmer 3 minutes. Drain carrots and pack in hot sterilized pint jars, leaving ½ inch headroom. Cover with hot pickling liquid, seal and process 10 minutes in boiling water bath. Processing may be omitted if carrots are refrigerated and used within two weeks.

**Maxine Overbey
(Mrs. James Bronson)**

Crackerjack

Yield: 8 quarts
250° oven

Won't last long enough to worry about storing!

2 sticks margarine
½ cup white Karo syrup
2 cups brown sugar
½ teaspoon baking soda
pinch cream of tartar
8 quarts popped corn

Cook margarine, Karo syrup and brown sugar until sugar dissolves. Remove from heat. Add baking soda and cream of tartar. Pour over popcorn in large roaster pan and mix well. Bake at 250° for 1 hour. Stir once. Cool and enjoy!

Sarah Valand

Chinese Fried Walnuts

Yield: 4 cups

Super delicious! Great for gift giving.

6 cups water
4 (plus) cups walnuts
½ cup sugar
salad oil
salt

In 4-quart saucepan or wok heat water to boiling. Add walnuts and boil 1 minute. Rinse under hot water and drain. In large bowl gently stir warm walnuts with sugar until sugar is dissolved. (If necessary, let mixture stand 5 minutes to dissolve sugar.) In 4-quart saucepan heat about 1 inch salad oil over medium heat. Add about half the walnuts and fry 5 minutes (until golden), stirring often. With slotted spoon, place walnuts in coarse sieve over bowl to drain and sprinkle very lightly with salt. Toss lightly to keep from sticking together. Transfer to paper towels to cool. Repeat process with remaining walnuts. Store in thightly covered container. NOTE: Can be prepared 1½ hours before serving or up to 2 weeks ahead. Walnuts can be boiled the day before, drained on paper towels and fried the following day.

Lee Ann Rousar (Mrs. Derrill J.)

Oyster Cracker Snacks

Yield: 12 cups
250° oven

½ pound margarine
1½ teaspoons celery salt
1½ teaspoons garlic salt
1½ teaspoons onion salt
1 (12 ounce) box oyster crackers
½ cup grated Parmesan cheese

Melt margarine and stir in salts, then crackers. Add cheese and toss well. Bake at 250° for 45 to 60 minutes, stirring occasionally.

Mildred Holland

SALADS
and
SALAD
DRESSINGS

Loris North

DOLVIN HOUSE
BULLOCH AVENUE
Circa 1880

DOLVIN HOUSE

The Dolvin house, built in the late 1880's, acquired its Victorian additions after the turn of the century. It is one of the few Victorian style houses in Roswell. After the Greek Revival rage reached its zenith before the Civil War, Victorian cottages became the popular style. Extra gables, porches with elaborate posts and bannisters, graceful curves, arches, and scroll work were typical of the houses built in the postwar years of the late nineteenth century.

The porte-cochere and the gazebo-like corner offer added interest to the Dolvin House. Extra gables arching above upper windows, bracketed cornices at the eaves, delicately turned porch bannisters, and slender Doric columns give the home an added Victorian character. Additional significance to the home is its location near Bulloch and Mimosa Halls.

On numerous occasions, the owner of the home has feted her nephew and his wife, President and Mrs. Jimmy Carter, during the time he was Governor of Georgia and President of the United States.

———

DINNER AT DOLVIN HOUSE FOR
PRESIDENT AND MRS. JIMMY CARTER

Chicken Supreme   Wild Rice

Asparagus Casserole
Congealed Pie-Cherry Salad*
Hot Rolls
Ice Cream Pie
Coffee

Pie Cherry Salad

Serves 8

Served at dinner party for Mrs. Dolvin's nephew, President Jimmy Carter.

1 (20 ounce) can pineapple chunks
1 (16 ounce) can pie cherries, NOT pie filling
1 (3 ounce) package cherry Jell-O
1 package Knox gelatin, softened in ½ cup cold water
juice and grated rind of 1 lemon
juice and grated rind of 1 orange
½ cup sugar

Dressing
3 ounces cream cheese
reserved pineapple juice
mayonnaise

Reserve 1 or 2 tablespoons pineapple juice. Combine remaining pineapple juice, juice from cherries and water to make 2 cups. Dissolve Jell-O in combined juices. Mix in remaining ingredients. Pour into mold. Refrigerate to set. Serve topped with dressing.

Dressing: Soften cream cheese with pineapple juice. Add mayonnaise to produce desired consistency.
Emily Dolvin (Mrs. W. J.)
RHS President 1974

Apricot Salad

Serves 12

2 (3 ounce) boxes apricot Jell-O
2 cups boiling water
2 cups cold water
1 cup small marshmallows
1 cup crushed pineapple, drained
1 banana, diced
½ cup pineapple juice
½ cup sugar
1 tablespoon flour
2 tablespoons butter
1 egg
3 ounces cream cheese
½ pint cream, whipped

Dissolve Jell-O in boiling water. Add cold water and marshmallows. Cool. Add drained pineapple and banana. Let jell. Mix pineapple juice, sugar, flour, butter and egg. Cook until thickened. Add cream cheese and chill. Fold whipped cream into thickened sauce and spread over Jell-O. Let set over night.
Frances Hargrove
(Mrs. Lewis L., Jr.)

Darby's Apricot Salad

Serves 12

Best if made day before serving.

1 (6 ounce) peach Jell-O
2 cups boiling water
1 (#2) can apricots
1 (#2) can crushed pineapple
1 can mandarin oranges
1 cup combined apricot,
    pineapple and orange juices
1 cup miniature marshmallows

Topping
1 envelope unflavored gelatin
¼ cup cold water
½ cup sugar
3 tablespoons flour
1 egg, slightly beaten
1 cup combined fruit juices
2 tablespoons butter
1 lemon, juice and rind
1 cup whipped cream
1 cup grated cheese

Dissolve Jell-O in boiling water. Drain fruits and RESERVE ALL JUICES. Add 1 cup combined fruit juices to Jell-O. Chill until thickened. Cut fruits into small pieces. Fold fruits and marshmallows into Jell-O. Pour into 12x8-inch pan and spread with topping.

Topping: Dissolve gelatin in cold water. In double boiler combine sugar, flour, egg and 1 cup juices. Stir in gelatin, butter, lemon juice and rind. Continue cooking, stirring to blend, until thick and smooth. Cool. Fold in whipped cream and spread over salad. Sprinkle with grated cheese.

Darby Butler (Mrs. J. L.)

Congealed Blueberry Salad

Serves 8

2 (3 ounce) packages black cherry
    Jell-O
1½ cups boiling water
2 teaspoons vinegar
1 cup blueberries
1 small can crushed pineapple
8 ounces cream cheese
1 pint sour cream
½ cup sugar
1 teaspoon vanilla
chopped nuts (optional)

Dissolve Jell-O in boiling water. Add vinegar, blueberries and pineapple, including juices. Pour into 2-quart square dish. Refrigerate to set. Soften cream cheese and mix with sour cream, sugar, vanilla and nuts. Spread on top of congealed Jell-O. Refrigerate.

Sylvia Patrick (Mrs. Trummie)

Cranberry Salad

Serves 8

2 cups ground cranberries
1 orange, ground (peeling and all)
2 cups sugar
pinch salt
1 (3 ounce) package lemon Jell-O
1 (3 ounce) package raspberry
    Jell-O
2 cups boiling water
1 cup chopped nuts
1 cup finely chopped celery

Combine cranberries, orange, sugar and salt. Let stand three hours. In separate bowl dissolve Jell-Os in boiling water. Stir in cranberry mixture. As salad begins to congeal add nuts and celery. Pour into greased mold. Refrigerate.

Rose Wing (Mrs. George)

Cranberry Christmas Tree Salad

Serves 6

Excellent with turkey or chicken anyway you mold it!

1 (1 pound) can jellied whole
    cranberry sauce
½ cup hot water
1 envelope gelatin
¼ cup cold water
ground rind and pulp of 1 orange
⅓ cup chopped pecans
⅓ cup diced celery
⅓ cup chopped dates
¼ teaspoon salt
lettuce leaves
cream cheese, tinted green

Crush cranberry sauce and add hot water. Heat well in top of double boiler. Soak envelope of gelatin in cold water for 5 minutes. Add to hot cranberry sauce. Cool. When salad begins to congeal, add next 5 ingredients. Pour into cone-shaped paper cups supported in glasses. When congealed, place on lettuce leaves and peel off cups. Trim with cream cheese, tinted green.

Inez Moss (Mrs. Paul G.)

Frozen Cranberry Salad

Serves 24

8 ounces cream cheese
1 (20 ounce) can crushed
    pineapple, drained and juice
    reserved
2 cans whole cranberry sauce,
    drained
1 (8 ounce) Cool Whip
½ cup finely chopped nuts

Soften cream cheese with pineapple juice. Add cranberries and pineapple. Stir well. Add Cool Whip and pecans. Mix well. Put in bake cups in muffin tins to freeze.

Mary Buford (Mrs. William F.)

Emerald Salad

Serves 10-12

2 tablespoons gelatin
1½ cups cold water
1 cup sugar
½ cup vinegar
dash onion juice
1 medium can crushed pineapple
  with juice
½ cup chopped celery
1 cup thinly sliced sweet midget
  gherkin pickles
1 cup chopped pecans

Dissolve gelatin in ½ cup cold water. Set aside. Cook sugar, vinegar and 1 cup cold water until it forms a light syrup. Add gelatin and stir until dissolved. Add onion juice. When salad begins to congeal, add pineapple, celery, pickles and nuts. Pour into mold. Refrigerate.

Diana Butler (Mrs. Gilbert)

Molded Lime Pineapple Salad

Serves 12

2 cups miniature marshmallows
1 cup milk
1 (3 ounce) package lime flavored
  gelatin
6 ounces cream cheese, softened
⅔ cup mayonnaise
2½ cups (1 pound, 4 ounce can)
  crushed pineapple, undrained
1 cup whipping cream, whipped

Melt marshmallows in milk over low heat. Pour over gelatin, stirring until dissolved. Combine cream cheese and mayonnaise, mixing well. Gradually add gelatin mixture and blend. Stir in pineapple. Chill until slightly thickened. Fold in whipped cream. Pour into 2-quart mold or oblong pyrex dish and chill until firm. Unmold, garnish.

Olive Pratt (Mrs. Palmer C.)

Dorothy's Shamrock Salad

Serves 10-12

Makes a good dessert too!

1 (6 ounce) package lime Jell-O
2 cups hot water
1⅓ cups (11 ounce can)
  evaporated milk
4 tablespoons lemon juice
1 (20 ounce) can crushed
  pineapple, not drained
16 ounces cottage cheese
1 cup chopped celery
1 cup chopped nuts

Mix Jell-O and hot water. Set aside to cool. Do not wait for it to set. In separate bowl mix remaining ingredients. Add cool Jell-O. Refrigerate until set. NOTE: Dieters use unsweetened pineapple; omit milk and nuts. If "taking out", add 1 (3 ounce) package lime Jell-O.

Adrianne Lunsford (Mrs. Emory)

28

Orange Salad
Serves 8

1 (3 ounce) package orange Jell-O
1 (3 ounce) package lemon Jell-O
1 (20 ounce) can crushed pineapple
2 (#2) cans mandarin oranges
2 (6 ounce) cans frozen orange juice, undiluted
½ cup chopped pecans

Dressing
1 cup mayonnaise
2 teaspoons French dressing
3 teaspoons honey
1 teaspoon lemon juice
½ teaspoon celery seed

Place Jell-O in bowl. Drain pineapple and orange sections, reserving liquids. Add liquids to unfrozen orange juice. Add water to make 4 cups liquid in all. Heat and pour over Jell-O. Stir until dissolved. When cool, add pineapple, orange sections and pecans. Refrigerate to set.

Dressing: Mix all ingredients together and blend well.
Bo Buice (Mrs. E. L.)

Congealed Peach Pickle Salad
Serves 15-20

2 (3 ounce) packages peach Jell-O
1 package Knox gelatin
2 cups hot water
1½ cups peach pickle juice
2 jars peach pickles, chopped
¼-½ cup chopped nuts

Mix Jell-O, Knox gelatin, hot water and pickle juice. Add pickles and nuts. Refrigerate until firm. Serve on lettuce topped with mayonnaise.
Mrs. Franklin M. Garrett

Congealed Strawberry Salad
Serves 10

Also good with orange, apricot or mixed fruit Jell-O.

1 (6 ounce) package strawberry Jell-O
1 (20 ounce) can crushed pineapple, undrained
2 cups buttermilk
1 cup chopped pecans or walnuts
1 (9 ounce) Cool Whip

Mix Jell-O with undrained pineapple. Heat and stir until Jell-O is dissolved. Do not boil. Remove from heat; cool slightly. Add buttermilk and chill until thickened. Fold in nuts and Cool Whip. Place in 12x8-inch dish and chill at least four hours.
Etha L. Bearden

Strawberry Jell-O Salad

Serves 12

1 (6 ounce) package strawberry
  Jell-O
2 cups hot water
1 (20 ounce) can crushed
  pineapple, undrained
1 large package frozen sliced
  strawberries
3 or 4 bananas, sliced
8 ounces sour cream

Dissolve Jell-O in hot water. Add pineapple (undrained), strawberries and bananas. Pour half of mixture into 2-quart mold or oblong pyrex dish. Chill until set. Spread sour cream over top and finish with remaining Jell-O mixture.

Pat Tennyson (Mrs. Don)

Strawberry Salad

Serves 8

1 (3 ounce) package strawberry
  Jell-O
1 cup hot water
1 (8 ounce) package cream
  cheese, softened
1 (10 ounce) package frozen
  strawberries or 1 cup sliced,
  slightly sweetened fresh berries
½ cup chopped pecans
1 small can crushed pineapple,
  drained
½ cup cold water
whipped cream
fresh strawberries

Prepare Jell-O as directed on package but use only 1 cup hot water. Add softened cream cheese to Jell-O. Beat with rotary or electric beater a few minutes until smooth. Add strawberries, nuts and well-drained pineapple. Add ½ cup cold water, if needed. Place in mold to congeal. To serve, unmold and top with whipped cream. Garnish with fresh strawberries.

Julia Rucker Crisler

Easy Frozen Salad

Serves 12

1 can cherry pie filling
1 can Eagle Brand milk
1 (number 2) can fruit cocktail
1 can sliced peaches
9 ounces Cool Whip

Mix together all ingredients and freeze.

Mary Alexander Patton

Frozen Fruit Salad

Serves 12

1 (16 ounce) can sliced peaches
1 (8½ ounce) can pear halves
1 (3 ounce) package strawberry
    Jell-O
1 cup boiling water
1 (6 ounce) can frozen lemonade
    concentrate
3 cups Cool Whip, thawed
garnish

Drain and chop fruit. Dissolve Jell-O in boiling water. Add lemonade concentrate and stir until melted. Chill until slightly thickened. Blend in Cool Whip and fold in fruit. Pour into 9x5-inch loaf pan. Freeze until firm (about 4 hours). Unmold and slice. Garnish, if desired.

Marjorie Pless (Mrs. Berlin H.)

Fruit Compote

Serves 8

2 cups strawberries
2 bananas, peeled and sliced
2 apples, chopped in large bite-
    size pieces
1 orange, peeled and sectioned

Mix fruit in large bowl. Pour Shawano Dressing over all.

Shawano Dressing

½ cup salad oil
⅓ cup sugar
⅓ cup catsup
¼ cup vinegar
1 teaspoon salt
1 teaspoon paprika
½ teaspoon dry mustard
2 teaspoons grated onion
1½ teaspoons bottled steak
    sauce

Shawano Dressing: Mix all ingredients in blender. Serve over fruit salad.

Janine Powers (Mrs. W.D.)

Green and Yellow Fruit Salad

Serves 4

Well received as an appetizer too!

1 small honeydew melon
½ large pineapple
4 kiwi fruit (Chinese gooseberries)
juice of 2 limes

Cut melon in half; scoop out seeds and peel off outer rind. Cut flesh into cubes and put into glass bowl. Slice pineapple thickly. Remove center and outer rind from each slice and cut in chunks. Peel kiwi fruit and cut into slices. Add to bowl. Pour in lime juice and mix all together lightly. Chill well before serving.

Ossie Mabry

Nutty Bananas

Serves 12

May also be served for dessert.

6 bananas
2 cups salted blanched peanuts, chopped
1 cup mayonnaise or salad dressing
¼ cup milk
2-3 tablespoons sugar

Slice 2 bananas and place in 2-quart serving dish. Sprinkle with ⅔ cup nuts. Repeat process two more times. Combine mayonnaise, milk and sugar; mix well. Pour over bananas. Chill 2-4 hours. Toss lightly before serving.

Violet Patton (Mrs. V. G.)

Avocado with Tomato Freeze

Serves 8

Beautiful.

1 envelope unflavored gelatin
2 tablespoons water
1 (Number 1) can Progresso tomato paste
½ wedge Roquefort cheese
3 ounces cream cheese
2 heaping tablespoons mayonnaise
1 tablespoon onion, grated
juice of ½ lemon
¼ teaspoon salt
2 teaspoons Worcestershire sauce
4 avocados, halved

Soften gelatin in water. Heat tomato paste and stir in gelatin until dissolved. Set aside to cool. Cream cheeses and add mayonnaise. Blend in gelatin-tomato mixture and remaining ingredients except avocados. Freeze in trays. Scoop out and serve in peeled avocado halves which have been dipped in lemon juice to keep from darkening.

Helen Owens (Mrs. Carl P., Jr.)

Cucumber Salad

Serves 4

Sauce is also delicious on spinach salad.

1 medium cucumber
½ teaspoon salt
1 tablespoon soy sauce
1 teaspoon sesame seed oil
1 tablespoon wine vinegar
1 tablespoon sugar
¼ teaspoon monsodium glutamate

Peel cucumber and slice very thin. Sprinkle with salt and let stand about twenty minutes. Drain. Mix remaining ingredients in small bowl. Pour sauce over cucumbers and mix well. Serve cold.

Mary Ann Meek (Mrs. R. R.)

Refrigerator Cucumber Pickles Salad

Serves 12

7 cups thinly sliced cucumbers
1 cup chopped onion
1 medium green pepper, chopped
1 tablespoon salt
1 tablespoon celery seed
2 cups sugar
1 cup vinegar

Combine cucumbers, onion and pepper in a large bowl. Combine remaining ingredients, mixing until smooth. Pour over vegetable mixture. Cover and refrigerate at least 3 hours. Stir several times. May be stored in refrigerator for several days.

Phyllis Galloway (Mrs. James)

Cottage Cheese Surprise

Serves 6

Family favorite in Rockwood, Tennessee, prepared with homemade mayonnaise and cottage cheese.

24 ounces low fat cottage cheese
1 medium sweet onion, chopped
1 large cucumber, peeled and
    chopped
2 stalks celery, chopped
salt and freshly ground pepper
    to taste
garlic powder to taste
1 tablespoon prepared mustard
2 heaping tablespoons
    mayonnaise
tomato shells

Mix all ingredients except tomatoes in a bowl. Cover and chill. Stuff in tomato shells and serve on bed of lettuce.

Mildred W. Kelley

Broccoli-Cauliflower Salad

Serves 8

1 bunch raw broccoli
1 head raw cauliflower
1 small chopped onion
1 cup mayonnaise
⅓ cup sugar
⅓ cup vinegar
salt to taste

Chop broccoli and cauliflower into small pieces. Mix next 5 ingredients. Toss raw vegetables with dressing. Refrigerate overnight to allow flavors to blend.

Janet W. Russell (Mrs. Gordon A.)
RHS President 1975

Sweet and Sour Carrot Salad

Serves 12

Marinate overnight.

2 pounds fresh carrots
1 onion, chopped
1 can tomato soup
½ cup sugar
½ cup vinegar
½ cup salad oil
1 teaspoon salt
½ teaspoon pepper

Slice carrots; cook and drain. Mix together all other ingredients and pour over cooked carrots. Refrigerate overnight. Serve cold.
Beth St. Jean (Mrs. Robert N.)

"Slick" Salad

Serves 4-6

Easy side dish!

1 (16 ounce) can whole green beans
1 (4 ounce) can mushroom pieces
1 (16 ounce) can tiny carrots
1 (16 ounce) can tomato pieces
¼ teaspoon dill
¼ teaspoon oregano
¼ teaspoon thyme
4 tablespoons grated Parmesan cheese
⅓ cup Italian dressing

Drain beans, mushrooms, carrots and tomatoes. Place in large container with tight fitting cover. Sprinkle dill, oregano, thyme and cheese over vegetables. Pour dressing over all and cover. Invert bowl 4 to 6 times during next 12 hours.
Violet Patton (Mrs. V.W.)

Grace's Tabooley

Serves 8

Wonderful Lebanese salad.

¾ cup cracked wheat
4 stalks celery
1 large onion
1 or 2 tomatoes
½ to 1 head lettuce
1 bunch parsley
handful fresh mint
salt and pepper to taste
juice of 3 lemons
½ cup oil

Wash and then soak cracked wheat in water. Set aside. Chop very fine next six ingredients. Toss together; sprinkle with salt and pepper. Drain well the cracked wheat. Add to salad. Combine lemon juice and oil. Pour over salad just before serving. Toss.
W. D. (Bill) Powers

Oriental Salad

Serves 4-6

Dinner guests love it.

1 bunch spinach
⅓ head lettuce
bean sprouts, fresh or canned,
   drained
1 medium bell pepper, diced
1 can sliced water chestnuts
1 bunch spring onions, diced

Toss all ingredients in salad bowl.

Dressing

¼ cup salad oil
2 tablespoons sugar
2 tablespoons white vinegar
2 tablespoons soy sauce
2 tablespoons catsup
¼ teaspoon ginger
1 teaspoon pepper

Dressing: Blend all ingredients. Chill. Pour over salad just before serving.

Ginia Huff (Mrs. Edward)

Spinach Salad and Dressing

Serves 8-10

4 bunches spinach, stems
   removed
fresh mushrooms, sliced
¾ pound bacon, fried and
   crumbled
3 hard boiled eggs, chopped
3½ tablespoons red wine vinegar
3 tablespoons catsup
3 garlic cloves, pressed
1 tablespoon Worcestershire
   sauce
1 tablespoon steak sauce
1 teaspoon sugar
¾ teaspoon paprika
¼ teaspoon ground pepper
1 cup safflower oil
⅓ cup grated Parmesan cheese
   (or bleu)
½ teaspoon dry mustard
½ teaspoon salt

Assemble spinach, mushrooms, bacon and eggs in bowl and cover. Keep chilled until ready to serve. Combine remaining ingredients in blender. Just before serving, pour dressing over salad makings and toss.

Lee Ann Rousar (Mrs. Derrill J.)

Sandpiper Spinach Salad

Serves 8-10

Always brings raves. Make a day ahead.

1 pound spinach, washed and
    torn in pieces
1 pound can bean sprouts,
    chilled
8 slices bacon, fried, drained
    and crumbled
3 hard cooked eggs, chopped
1 pint fresh mushrooms, sliced

Combine all ingredients in a bowl. Toss with dressing. Salt immediately before serving.

Dressing
1 cup salad oil
½ cup sugar
⅓ cup catsup
¼ cup cider vinegar
1 teaspoon salt
1 teaspoon instant minced
    onions
1 teaspoon Worcestershire sauce

Dressing: Combine all ingredients and chill.

**Janet W. Russell (Mrs. Gordon A.)
RHS President 1975**

Layered Salad

Serves 8-10

Prepare 24 hours ahead.

1 large head lettuce, broken up
1 cup chopped celery
1 cup green onions, chopped
1 can sliced water chestnuts
1 box frozen green peas,
   uncooked
2 cups mayonnaise
2 large tomatoes, chopped
10 slices crisp bacon, crumbled
3 hard boiled eggs, sliced

Layer first five ingredients in order as listed. Spread mayonnaise over top of peas. Cover with Saran wrap and chill 24 hours. Just before serving add chopped tomatoes, crumbled bacon and sliced eggs. Toss and serve.

Grace Smith

Kraut Salad

Serves 8-12

2 cups sugar
1 cup vinegar
1 (1 pound 12 ounce) can
    sauerkraut, drained
2 cups chopped celery
1 cup chopped onion
1 green pepper, sliced
1 small jar pimiento

Bring sugar and vinegar to a boil. Let cool. Combine remaining ingredients. Pour cooled liquid over all. Keep refrigerated until used, stirring often.

Mary Good (Mrs. James O.)

Tossed Chicken Salad

Serves 4-6

2 cups torn fresh spinach
2 cups torn romaine
2 cups torn lettuce
4 tomatoes, cut into wedges
1 avocado, sliced
3 cups chopped, cooked chicken
6 slices cooked bacon, crumbled
3 hard cooked eggs, chopped
3 tablespoons chopped parsley

Toss all ingredients and pour dressing over salad.

Dressing
1 cup mayonnaise
2 tablespoons lemon juice
2 tablespoons chopped, stuffed olives
2 tablespoons chopped onion
2 tablespoons chopped green pepper
1 tablespoon horseradish
¼ teaspoon salt

Dressing: Blend all ingredients and chill.
Lori Adams
Cora Bell Adams

Cranberry Chicken Salad

Serves 8-10

Absolutely divine!

4 cups diced chicken
1 cup chopped celery
2 cups seedless grapes
½ teaspoon salt
½ teaspoon pepper
½ cup mayonnaise
½ cup sour cream
24 salted pecan halves

Mix together all ingredients except pecan halves. Pour dressing over salad. Garnish each serving with 3 to 4 pecan halves.

Dressing
¾ cup salad oil
¼ cup vinegar
1 teaspoon salt
1 teaspoon sugar
½ teaspoon paprika
¼ teaspoon dry mustard
½ cup jellied cranberry sauce

Dressing: Combine oil, vinegar and dry ingredients in jar or blender. Gradually blend in cranberry sauce.
Patsy Turner (Mrs. W. E.)

37

Great Slaw

Serves 12 or more

1 medium head cabbage, shredded
4 stalks celery, sliced thin
2 carrots, grated coarsely
1 medium green pepper, sliced
  thin
1 large white onion, sliced thin
salt and pepper to taste
few drops Tabasco

Mix together all ingredients.

Dressing
¾ cup sugar
¾ cup cider vinegar
¾ cup salad oil
1 tablespoon celery seed

Dressing: Mix ingredients and bring to a boil. Pour over salad ingredients. Chill several hours or overnight. Will keep in refrigerator ten days.

Muriel Grissom (Mrs. W. M.)

Mexican Salad

Serves 12

1 large head lettuce
1 (15 ounce) can Ranch Style
  beans, chilled
2 tomatoes, diced
½ onion, chopped fine
1 pound cheddar cheese, grated
¾ bottle Kraft Catalina dressing,
  chilled
1 large package Fritos, crushed

Prepare lettuce as for any tossed salad. Drain and wash chilled beans and add to lettuce with tomatoes, onion, cheese and dressing. Chill 30 minutes to an hour before serving. Mix in orushed Fritos just before serving.

Dorothy Lyons (Mrs. F. E.)

Grace's Poppy Seed Dressing

Yield: 1½ cups

Recipe over 50 years old. Especially good on avocado-grapefruit salad.

½ cup powdered sugar
1 teaspoon dry mustard
½ teaspoon poppy seed
1 teaspoon salt
½ teaspoon paprika
3 tablespoons white vinegar
¾ cup salad oil

Combine all ingredients except salad oil and mix at high speed for 1 to 2 minutes. Gradually add salad oil while still mixing at high speed. This will be very thick. Keep in refrigerator. Delicious on fresh fruit salad.

Grace Smith

Warehouse Salad Dressing

Yield: 2 cups

1 medium onion, grated
1 teaspoon prepared mustard
⅓ cup white vinegar, or lemon juice
⅔ cup sugar
1 teaspoon celery seed
1 cup salad oil
1 teaspoon salt

Blend all ingredients, adding oil and vinegar small amount at a time, or alternately.

Ruth Anderson

Louise Reid's Salad Dressing

Yield: 3½ cups

This great tasting dressing was a favorite of Mrs. John Reid (mother of architect Neel Reid) and her daughter, Louise, when they entertained at Mimosa Hall.

½ cup Wesson oil
¾ cup vinegar
¾ cup sugar (or to taste)
½ teaspoon salt
½ teaspoon paprika
1 can Campbell's tomato soup
1 teaspoon grated onion
chopped celery to taste
chopped green pepper to taste

Make in blender, or mix and shake in a quart jar.

**Rose Jackson Polatty
(Mrs. George J., Sr.)**

Spicy Red Salad Dressing

Yield: 2 cups

Really super! Keeps indefinitely.

1 cup olive oil
1 cup sugar
½ cup wine vinegar (Spice Island Garlic)
½ cup grated onion
juice of one lemon
¾ cup catsup (Use Brooks. If not available, add some Tabasco)
1 clove garlic

Blend well. Pour into a bottle with a cut clove of garlic in it.

Judy Miller (Mrs. Kent W.)

Lickskillet Salad Oil

Yield: about 4 cups

3 cups salad oil
1 cup vinegar
1 tablespoon lemon juice
4 tablespoons salt
dash of pepper, Accent, garlic salt

Mix and shake well. Serve over crisp salad ingredients of your choice. Do not refrigerate. Will keep 4-6 weeks.

**Lickskillet Farm Restaurant
Old Roswell Road**

Viennese Salad Dressing

Yield: 1½ cups

1 teaspoon sugar
1 teaspoon paprika
½ teaspoon salt
½ teaspoon dry mustard
½ teaspoon crushed celery seed
¼ teaspoon pepper
½ cup tarragon vinegar or white wine vinegar with tarragon
¾ cup olive oil

Combine all ingredients except olive oil and stir until dry ingredients are dissolved. Gradually add the ¾ cup olive oil, stirring constantly or shake in a bottle until well blended.

Marion Tillman

SOUPS
and
CHOWDERS

Mary Lou Carpenter

**THE SMITH PLACE
ALPHARETTA STREET
Circa 1842**

THE SMITH PLACE

Archibald Smith and his wife, Annie Margaret, arrived in Roswell from Savannah on December 30th, 1838, with nineteen servants, and wagons filled with fine furnishings for the home they planned to build. When they first arrived, they lived with friends near the Lebanon Church, later building a cottage of their own on the present Mountain Park Road.

They were in the original group of settlers who organized the Roswell Presbyterian Church, in which Archibald Smith became an elder. Their two-story clapboard farm house was constructed of hand-planed boards joined by wooden pegs and dovetailed at the joints. Underpinnings and chimneys were of brick.

The simple but elegant home and outbuildings were of heart-pine. The kitchen, smoke house, corn crib, carriage house, barn, and servants quarters remain as they were then. Archibald Smith's original 160 acres of land increased to 490 by 1851. He was said to have introduced the first Bermuda grass in the area.

The Smiths sought refuge in Valdosta when Union troops entered Georgia. A son, Archibald, along with other students at Georgia Military Institute in Marietta, served in the Confederate army. A second son, William, lost his life in service. The Smith Place has remained in the family.

———

COMPANY DINNER AT THE SMITH PLACE

Cup of Hot Potato Soup*
Southern Fried Chicken
Rice and Cream Gravy
Snap Beans   Fried Corn
Pineapple Slices on Bed of Garden Lettuce
Topped with Mayonnaise and Grated Cheese
Hot Biscuits
Vanilla Ice Cream and Pound Cake
Iced Tea with Lemon Wedges

Potato Soup

Serves 6

A good warm starter at the Smith Place prepared by the long time family cook.

2 cups diced potatoes
2 cups water
salt and pepper to taste
2 tablespoons butter
2 cups hot milk

Boil potatoes in water until tender. Do not drain. Stir to partially break up potatoes. Do not mash. Small pieces of potato are better. Season with salt and pepper. Add butter and hot milk. Serve hot.

Mamie Grogan Cotton

Artichoke Soup

Serves 6

3 (10 ounce) packages frozen
   artichoke hearts
3 cups chicken stock
2 cups milk
1 tablespoon butter
salt and pepper to taste

Cook artichoke hearts according to package directions. Reserve a few hearts to cut up into soup bowls. Place remaining hearts in blender with stock and blend until smooth. Add milk, butter, salt and pepper. Mix well. Heat, stirring constantly. Be careful not to boil. Place reserved cut up artichoke hearts in bowls. Pour in soup and serve.

Delores Bierworth (Mrs. Clarence)

Famous U.S. Senate Navy Bean Soup

Serves 8

Served everyday since 1907 in U.S. Senate.

2 pounds dry navy beans, rinsed
   in hot water
4 quarts hot water
1½ pounds smoked ham hocks
   or short ribs
2 tablespoons butter
1 onion, chopped
salt and pepper to taste

In large pot, combine rinsed beans with 4 quarts hot water and ham hocks or short ribs. Cover and simmer slowly about 3 hours. In skillet, sauté onion in melted butter. Add onion to soup. Season to taste with salt and pepper.

Marcie Bauman (Mrs. David)

Black Bean Soup

Serves 6

An early 1800 recipe from the Burr family of Philadelphia.

1 pound black beans
4 quarts cold water
dash pepper
1 teaspoon salt
1 teaspoon whole cloves
1 large onion, chopped
beef bone
1 lemon, sliced
2 wine glasses sherry
2 hard cooked eggs, sliced

Soak beans overnight. Drain. Add 4 quarts cold water, pepper, salt, cloves, onion and beef bone. Boil slowly until beans are soft. Let boil ½ hour more. Remove bone and strain. Place lemon slices in tureen. Add sherry and egg slices. Pour in hot soup.

Jo Rudolph (Mrs. Edwin)

Mrs. Chancey's Black Bean Soup

Serves 8

1 pound black beans
½ teaspoon soda
1 cup olive oil
3 onions
3 buttons garlic
½ bell pepper
4 strips breakfast bacon
2 bay leaves
1 tablespoon vinegar
salt to taste
pepper to taste
rice
chopped onion

Add soda to water and soak beans overnight. Wash beans well the next morning. Put beans in 2 quarts cold water and boil slowly. Cut up onions, garlic, bell pepper, bacon and bay leaves and put into frying pan with olive oil. Fry until light brown. Add this mixture, together with vinegar, to beans and cook slowly until done. Season to taste. Beans should set 1-2 hours before eating. Reheat. Serve with side dishes of rice and chopped onions, to be added to the soup to individual taste.

Myrtle M. Mosher (Mrs. L. A.)

Broccoli Soup

Serves 6

1 cup chopped green onion
1 cup sliced fresh mushrooms
3 tablespoons butter
3 tablespoons flour
3 cups chicken broth
1 (10 ounce) package frozen
  chopped broccoli, thawed
1 cup half and half
1 cup shredded Swiss cheese

Sauté onion and mushrooms in butter. Add flour and stir until bubbly. Remove from heat and blend in chicken broth. Return to heat and cook until thick and smooth. Add thawed broccoli and cook until tender. Blend in half and half and cheese. Simmer until heated through.

Mary Holman (Mrs. Penn G.)

Three Bean Chili

Good meatless main dish.

Serves 6

3 tablespoons oil
1 large onion, chopped
1 carrot, shredded
1 clove garlic, mashed, or ¼
   teaspoon garlic powder
1 (16 ounce) can stewed tomatoes,
   cut up and <u>not</u> drained
1 (16 ounce) can red kidney
   beans, drained
1 (16 ounce) can pinto beans,
   drained
1 (16 ounce) can cut green beans,
   drained
½ teaspoon salt
1 or 2 tablespoons chili powder
   (to taste)
Parmesan or cheddar cheese

Heat oil in large skillet; sauté onion, garlic and carrot until tender, but not brown. Add remaining ingredients. Simmer over low heat 30 minutes. Taste and adjust seasonings. Put in serving dish and sprinkle cheese on top. May be prepared in advance. Good served with rice, hot whole wheat rolls or Italian bread.
Kathleen D. Kany

Hearty Beer Soup

Serves 6

1 cup coarsely chopped carrots
1 cup sliced celery
1 cup chopped onion
¼ cup butter
2 cans split pea soup with ham
1 can beer
1 cup beef broth

In large saucepan, sauté carrots, celery and onion in melted butter for 10 minutes. Add soup, beer and broth. Mix well and simmer 10 minutes. Serve hot.
Beth Stark

English Cheese Chowder

Serves 8

½ cup carrots, finely minced
½ cup celery, finely minced
½ medium onion, finely chopped
1 stick butter
¾ cup flour
1 quart milk
1 quart chicken broth
1 (16 ounce) jar Cheez Whiz
salt to taste
cayenne pepper to taste
¼ cup chives, finely minced
   (optional)
1 tablespoon mustard

Boil carrots and celery 5 to 10 minutes in 2 cups water. Sauté onion in butter. Add flour and blend well. Add milk and broth. Stir briskly with whisk. Add cheese, seasonings, carrots and celery (including water in which cooked). Bring to slow boil. Serve.
Vicki DeHart (Mrs. Steve)

Beer and Cheese Soup

Serves 6 to 8

2½ cups (20 ounces) beer
2½ tablespoons chicken stock
　base
1 cup shredded carrot
1 cup thinly sliced celery
⅓ cup thinly sliced onion
3 cups milk
⅓ cup all-purpose flour
1 pound sharp cheddar cheese,
　shredded
salt and freshly ground pepper

Combine beer and stock base in 3-quart saucepan and stir over medium high heat until stock base is dissolved. Add carrot, celery and onion. Cover and simmer until vegetables are tender (about 10 to 12 minutes). Blend 1½ cups milk with flour in medium bowl. Gradually stir into soup, blending well. Add remaining milk and cook, stirring occasionally, until thickened (about 15 minutes). Blend in cheese a little at a time, stirring until melted. Season to taste with salt and pepper. Ladle soup into individual heated bowls and serve immediately.

Betsy Brown Sertich

Cabbage and Ham Soup

Serves 4

¼ cup diced green pepper
½ cup diced celery
½ cup diced onion
2 tablespoons chopped parsley
3 tablespoons butter
2 cups diced cooked ham (little
　less than 1 pound)
1 bay leaf
2 tablespoons flour
1 tablespoon chicken stock
　concentrate
3 cups cold water
2 cups finely shredded cabbage
1 tablespoon water
1 cup sour cream

In wide frying pan, cook green pepper, celery, onion and parsley in 2 tablespoons butter until soft, but not browned. Add ham and bay leaf; cook until ham is heated through. Blend in flour, chicken stock concentrate and 3 cups cold water. Pour into pan with ham. Bring to boil, stirring, and simmer one to two minutes. Pour into tureen or individual bowls and keep in warm place. In same frying pan, melt remaining butter over highest heat. Add cabbage and 1 tablespoon water. Cook, stirring, until cabbage turns brighter in color and softens slightly. Mix into soup. Spoon sour cream into each serving. Dieters omit cream.

Adrianne Lunsford (Mrs. Emory)

New England Fish Chowder

Yield: 3 quarts or 8 large servings

Family recipe from a native New Englander. Roswell's founder, Roswell King, was from Connecticut. It is possible he enjoyed a chowder like this.

2 pounds halibut (raw)
2½ teaspoons salt
3 cups diced potatoes
6 slices bacon
1 cup chopped onion
2 cups milk
2 cups light cream or evaporated milk
¼ teaspoon pepper

Place fish with 2 cups water in large pan; bring to boil. Reduce heat; cover and simmer 15 minutes. Remove fish. To fish broth add 1 teaspoon salt and diced potatoes. Boil covered 8 minutes, or until potatoes are tender. Remove from heat. Sauté bacon until crisp; remove and drain on paper towels. Sauté onions on low heat in bacon fat until tender (about 5 minutes). Flake and bone fish. Add bacon, onion, remaining milk, salt and pepper to potatoes. Slowly bring to boil. DO NOT COVER. Reduce heat; simmer 15 minutes. NOTE: FOLLOW STEPS CAREFULLY. Any inexpensive fresh fish can be used. Serve with coleslaw and crackers. Freezes well.

Betty McKissack (Mrs. W. F.)

East Hampton Clam Chowder

Serves 4-6

¼ pound bacon
1 small onion, finely chopped
1½ cups diced potatoes
2 (16 ounce) cans tomatoes, pureed
⅓ cup chopped celery
few celery leaves
½ teaspoon thyme
salt and pepper to taste
2 (7 ounce) cans clams, minced

Fry bacon; drain and set aside. Sauté onion in bacon drippings. in saucepan combine onion, potatoes, tomatoes, celery and leaves, thyme, salt and pepper. Bring to boil; reduce heat and simmer about ½ hour. Add clams and crumbled bacon; continue cooking a few minutes only to heat clams. Clamato juice or tomato juice may be added to thin broth.

Joan Mars (Mrs. Martin)

47

Crab or Seafood Bisque

Serves 4

Add shrimp or oysters for a seafood bisque.

½ pound fresh crab meat or 1 (6½ ounce) can crab meat
½ cup sherry
1 (10 ounce) can cream of tomato soup
1 (10 ounce) can green pea soup
1 soup can light cream
¼ teaspoon curry powder (optional)
½ teaspoon paprika

Put crab meat in bowl; cover with sherry and let stand 1 hour. Blend together soups, cream, curry and paprika. Heat slowly, but do not boil. Add crab meat. Reheat to boiling point and serve immediately. NOTE: For a seafood bisque, add ½ pound boiled shrimp or ½ pint fresh oysters, or half of each, if adventuresome!

Margaret Smith (Mrs. Charles)

Crab Meat Bisque

Serves 4

To make a shrimp bisque, substitute 1½ cups boiled shrimp.

6 tablespoons butter or margarine
4 tablespoons finely chopped green pepper
4 tablespoons finely chopped onion
1 scallion, chopped
2 tablespoons chopped parsley
1½ cups sliced fresh mushrooms
2 tablespoons flour
1 cup milk
1 teaspoon salt
1/8 teaspoon white pepper
dash Tabasco
1½ cups half and half
1½ cups cooked crab meat
3 tablespoons dry sherry

Heat 4 tablespoons butter in skillet. Add green pepper, onion, scallion, parsley and mushrooms; sauté until soft (about 5 minutes). In saucepan heat remaining 2 tablespoons butter. Stir in flour. Add milk and cook, stirring, until thickened and smooth. Stir in salt, pepper and Tabasco. Add sautéed vegetables and half and half. Bring to boil, stirring. Reduce heat. Add crab meat and simmer uncovered 5 minutes. Just before serving, stir in sherry. NOTE: Frozen king crab is most economical; however, either canned or fresh crab meat may be used.

Gloria Foos (Mrs. Rocky)

Bootsie's Crab Soup

Serves 4

1 can cream of green pea soup
1 can tomato soup
1½ cups half and half
¼ teapsoon curry powder
1 pound crab meat
½ cup sherry
dash Tabasco

Mix together pea soup, tomato soup, half and half and curry powder. Heat to serving temperature. Add crab meat, sherry and Tabasco.

Pamela H. Mundale (Mrs. D. O.)

Crab Bisque

Serves 8

1 can she-crab soup
1 (6½ ounce) can white crab meat
1 (4 ounce) container whipped
   cream cheese with chives
2 cans cream of celery soup
3 soup cans milk
½ soup can dry sherry

Mix and heat all ingredients except sherry in heavy saucepan or double boiler, stirring often. Add sherry just before serving in hot bowls.
Margaret T. Knight

Cream of Cucumber Soup

Serves 10-12

Great cold or hot!

2 quarts white stock (veal or
   chicken)
3-4 cucumbers, peeled and cut
   into ½-inch slices
1 small onion, finely chopped
2 tablespoons butter
1½ tablespoons flour
2 egg yolks
¼ cup (or more) cream or 1
   teaspoon arrowroot
salt and pepper to taste
green coloring
chopped mint
1-2 cucumbers for garnish

Simmer 3-4 cucumbers and onion in stock until soft (15 to 20 minutes). Rub through nylon sieve. Rinse saucepan. Make roux with butter and flour; add sieved liquid. Stir and heat until boiling; simmer 2-3 minutes. Cool. Add egg yolks and cream (or arrowroot). Heat gently until soup has thickened. Do not boil. Color delicately. Correct seasoning by tasting and add a little chopped mint. Serve hot or iced with garnish of cucumber "peas". To make "peas" scoop out peeled cucumbers with pea-sized vegetable scoop. Cook in boiling water; drain and refresh with cold water.
Gloria Conrad (Mrs. Richard)

White Gazpacho

Serves 6

4 medium cucumbers
2½ cups chicken broth (from
   bouillon cubes)
2 cups plain yogurt (not vanilla)
½ teaspoon seasoned salt
3 tablespoons vinegar
2 or 3 tomatoes, chopped
2 or 3 green onions, chopped

Peel and chop cucumbers. Place in blender with half of broth. Blend, leaving some bits of cucumber. Put mixture in bowl and add remaining broth, yogurt, salt and vinegar. Chill. Before serving add tomatoes and green onions. Serve in bowls that have been chilled in freezer.
**Rebecca Waitt Lamar
(Mrs. Shelton B.)**

49

Chilled Norwegian Cucumber Soup
Serves 6-8

3 cups buttermilk
1 cup sour cream
4 medium cucumbers, peeled and grated
1 ounce grated onion
1 teaspoon chopped dill or chives
1 teaspoon minced parsley
salt to taste
Tabasco to taste
½ medium cucumber, sliced thin
2 tablespoons toasted sliced almonds

Combine buttermilk and sour cream. Add grated cucumbers, onion, dill and parsley. Season to taste with salt and Tabasco. (Make it fairly sharp because chilling will mellow flavor.) Refrigerate several hours or overnight. Before serving garnish each bowl with 3-4 thin slices of cucumber and sprinkle of toasted almonds.

Betty Townsend (Mrs. Alto B.)

Hamburger Soup
Serves 6-8

1 pound ground beef
1 medium onion, chopped
1 (16 ounce) can whole tomatoes
4 cups water
2 beef flavored bouillon cubes
1 teaspoon salt
½-1 teaspoon pepper
1 bay leaf
¾ cup sliced celery
1 teaspoon Worcestershire
1 (10 ounce) package frozen mixed vegetables
1 cup medium egg noodles, uncooked
½ teaspoon dried whole thyme

Cook ground beef and onion over medium heat until browned. Drain on paper towels; discard pan drippings. Add tomatoes, water, bouillon cubes, salt, pepper, bay leaf, celery and Worcestershire. Bring to boil; cover and simmer 30 minutes. Add mixed vegetables, noodles and thyme. Bring to a boil; simmer uncovered about 20 minutes, stirring occasionally.

Martha Coursey (Mrs. Bob L.)

Mock Oyster Soup
Serves 4

1 pint sweet milk
2 tablespoons butter or margarine
1 pint canned tomatoes, chopped, with juice
½ teaspoon baking soda
salt and pepper
4 saltines, rolled fine

Heat milk with butter in saucepan. In another pan, bring tomatoes to boil. Add soda and let foam. Add hot milk mixture to tomatoes. Season to taste with salt and pepper. Heat. When mixture simmers, add saltines. Serve very hot.

Frances Boggs (Mrs. Gilbert H.)

Greek Cold Lemon Soup

Serves 6-8

6 cups chicken broth
¼ cup regular rice, uncooked
1 teaspoon salt
4 eggs
½ to ¾ cup lemon juice (to taste, for tartness)
1 lemon, sliced thin

Combine chicken broth, rice and salt in large saucepan. Bring to boil; reduce heat. Cover and simmer until rice is just tender (about 15 minutes). Remove pan from heat. In bowl, beat eggs until fluffy and pale yellow; beat in lemon juice. Slowly stir about 2 cups hot broth into egg-lemon mixture and whisk vigorously. Pour this mixture into rest of soup. Whisk until lightly thickened. Cool to room temperature, then refrigerate until icy cold. Soup will thicken and settle somewhat as it chills. Stir before serving. Garnish with lemon slices.

Ella Zimmerman

Mushroom Soup

Serves 6-8

4 tablespoons butter
1½-2 pounds mushrooms, coarsely chopped
2 cloves garlic, minced
½ cup sliced green onions
salt and freshly ground pepper to taste
½ teaspoon tarragon
5 cups chicken broth (do not use bouillon; use a good canned broth)
½ cup dry Madeira
½ cup heavy cream or half and half

Heat butter in deep, heavy pot. Add mushrooms, garlic and onion. Stir to coat mushrooms with butter. Cook, stirring occasionally, for 15 minutes or until mushrooms have exuded quite a bit of liquid. Add salt, pepper and tarragon. Add broth and bring to boil. Simmer ½ hour. Add Madeira and simmer 5 minutes more. Stir in cream. Taste and adjust seasonings. Serve at once.

Peggy Bartleson (Mrs. Evan R.)

Mushroom and Rice Soup

Yield: 1½ quarts

½ pound mushrooms
2 medium onions
3 tablespoons butter
2 tablespoons flour
5 cups strong chicken stock (do
   not use bouillon)
1 tablespoon rice
bay leaf
chopped parsley

Clean mushrooms. Remove stems and chop fine. Slice caps thin. Chop onions fine. In Dutch oven melt 2 tablespoons butter; sauté onions until soft. Add mushrooms; cover and cook over medium heat 5 minutes. Add rest of butter; melt. Sift in flour. Pour in stock. Season and stir. (Does not need salt.) Add rice and bay leaf. Simmer 15-20 minutes. Remove bay leaf. Adjust seasoning. Add parsley just before serving.

Judy Smith (Mrs. Charles)

Potato Soup

Serves 8-10

2 tablespoons chicken fat
1 onion, diced
1 stalk celery, diced
3 cups diced boiling potatoes
1 cup chicken stock
1 pound mushrooms, cleaned,
   trimmed and sliced
½ pound fresh spinach, chopped
salt to taste
pinch cayenne pepper or curry
   powder
6 tablespoons butter
6 tablespoons flour
3 cups hot chicken stock
1 cup milk (optional)

Heat chicken fat in deep heavy pot. Sauté onion and celery until transparent. Add potatoes and 1 cup stock. Cover and simmer until tender. Stir in mushrooms, spinach, salt and cayenne. Melt 6 table-spoons butter in saucepan. Whisk in flour. Stir and cook over low heat 2-3 minutes. Whisk in 3 cups hot stock. Bring to boil. Stir into potato mix-ture. Add milk. Adjust heat and seasonings. Serve piping hot.

Diana H. Butler (Mrs. Gilbert)

Tomato-Bouillon Soup

Serves 4-6

Try greeting guests at the door with a steaming mug of this soup.

1 (10½ ounce) can beef broth
   (bouillon)
1 (10½ ounce) can tomato soup
1 cup water
¼ teaspoon prepared horseradish
dash Tabasco sauce
sherry (optional)
sour cream (optional)

Simmer first 5 ingredients in medium saucepan until hot. Serve with dash of sherry or float tea-spoon of sour cream on top. This can be served in soup bowls or informal-ly in mugs.

Shirley L. Covington (Mrs. Charles)

Corn Soup

Serves 8

1 medium onion, chopped
1 can creamed corn
1 can cream of chicken soup
1 can cream of mushroom soup
1 can chicken and rice soup
1 large can Carnation milk
4 soup cans milk
1 teaspoon Accent
salt, pepper, garlic salt to taste
1 cup diced celery
paprika
crumbled bacon
slivered toasted almonds

Mix together onion, corn, soups, milks, Accent, salt, pepper and garlic salt. Simmer 10 minutes. (Important to keep heat low or mixture will curdle.) Before serving add diced celery. Sprinkle paprika, crumbled bacon and slivered toasted almonds on top of each serving.

Evelyn Arey (Mrs. Stuart L.)

Plaza III Steak Soup

Serves 10-12

With French bread and a salad, you have a meal!

1 stick margarine
1 cup flour
½ gallon water
2 pounds ground beef
1 cup onions, chopped
1 cup carrots, chopped
1 cup celery, chopped
2 cups frozen mixed vegetables
1 (16 ounce) can tomatoes
1 tablespoon Accent
2 tablespoons beef base
1 teaspoon black pepper
1 teaspoon salt

Melt margarine. Gradually whip in flour to make a smooth paste. Stir in water. Sauté ground beef; drain and add to soup. Parboil onions, carrots and celery until crisply tender. Add to soup mixture with remaining ingredients. Bring to boil. Reduce to simmer and cook until vegetables are tender. Freezes well.

Ellen Bardin (Mrs. Charles N., Jr.)

Vegetable Soup

A meal in itself.

Serves 10-12

1 pound ground chuck
1 large onion, chopped
⅓ cup raw rice
3 cups water
1 (46 ounce) can Sacramento
  tomato juice or V-8 juice
1 (8 ounce) can tomato sauce
1 package frozen vegetables for
  soup
dash Worcestershire sauce

Brown meat and onion. Add rice, water, juice and tomato sauce. Simmer 30 minutes. Add frozen vegetables and Worcestershire sauce. Cook 1-2 hours.

Katherine Singletary (Mrs. P. R.)

Zucchini Soup

Serves 4-6

3 chicken bouillon cubes
1 teaspoon curry powder
2½ cups boiling water
3 small zucchini (one pound),
  grated
1 large onion, sliced thin
½ cup half and half
Parmesan cheese

Dissolve bouillon cubes and curry powder in water. Cook zucchini and onion for five minutes, then puree in blender. Add to broth. Add half and half. Place a little cheese in bowl before serving soup.

**Claudine Washington
(Mrs. James P.)**

MEATS

Anne H. Bishop

**BULLOCH HALL
BULLOCH AVENUE
Circa 1840**

BULLOCH HALL

Soon after their arrival in Roswell from Savannah, Major James Stephens Bulloch and his wife, Martha, began building Bulloch Hall, a columned mansion that would become famous architecturally and historically. Roswell King had offered them a homesite and investment opportunities in his new cotton mill, with the added inducement of a fine climate and abundant land in the north Georgia uplands. They joined the original group of Roswell families who called themselves "The Colony," in 1839.

Bulloch Hall was built in 1840 of heart pine cut from the property and aged for over a year. A large central hallway with a columned arch opens to large, high-ceilinged rooms. Floor-to-ceiling windows open onto a broad portico with four massive Doric columns shadowed by four pilasters. It is one of the few examples in Georgia of the full temple-form Greek Revival houses with pedimented portico. The home was said to have been designed by Connecticut builder Willis Ball, who also designed the Presbyterian Church and the other temple-style mansions of Roswell. The kitchen of Bulloch Hall with the original fireplace and beehive oven is located in the basement.

In December, 1853, the Bulloch's daughter, Mittie, married Theodore Roosevelt, Sr., of New York City, in the dining room of Bulloch Hall. Their son, Teddy, would become the President of the United States. Another son, Elliot, would be father of Anna Eleanor, who married Franklin Delano Roosevelt. Bulloch Hall is listed on the National Register of Historic Places and is owned by the City of Roswell.

BULLOCH HALL ANTIQUES SHOWHOUSE PREVIEW PARTY
September 1978

Fruit Punch	Champagne Fountain	Mint Juleps

Whole Roast Suckling Pig*
Turkey and Chicken Drummettes

Beef Cubes	Sausage and Biscuits
Stuffed Mushrooms	Baked Baby Sweet Potatoes
Fruit and Cheese Trays	Assorted Canapes

Platters of Raw Vegetables with Dip
Large Bowl of Chilled Gulf Shrimp with Seafood Sauce
Pecan, Lemon, Cherry and Pineapple Tarts
Hot Coffee

Whole Roast Suckling Pig

Allow 1 pound per person
325° oven

In the Old South this would have been prepared outside, but at the Bulloch Hall Preview Party we opted for the convenience of the oven.

whole pig
apple
water
watercress
whole cranberries
barbecue sauce or sweet sour
   sauce

Have butcher prepare whole pig for roasting. Stand pig up in roasting pan; spread legs and push pig down gently into pan. Brace mouth open with small piece of wood. Cover pig with cloth and add about 2 inches water. Keep cloth moist during entire baking period by basting every 15-30 minutes with water and juices. Bake 30 minutes per pound at 325°. Uncover last half hour for browning. Pig is done when juices return clear after sticking fork into deepest part. To serve, place pig on display board. Remove wood brace and place apple in mouth. Garnish with watercess and cranberries. Remove crisp dark skin and first layer of fat. Carve meat. Serve with barbecue sauce or favorite sweet sour sauce.

Azar's Party Pantry
Peachtree Street, Atlanta

Hot Ham Casserole

Serves 9-11
375° oven

1 cup elbow macaroni
½ cup celery, chopped
1 (8 ounce) can water chestnuts
2 tablespoons pimiento
1½ pounds ham, cut up
3 tablespoons margarine
1 cup milk
2 eggs
2 cups water
1 cup Rice Krispies

Cook macaroni in water until tender. Drain. Add chopped celery, water chestnuts, pimiento and ham. Mix. Add all remaining ingredients except Rice Krispies and mix well. Place in 2-quart casserole dish and bake 40 minutes at 375°. Remove from oven and sprinkle on Rice Krispies. Return to oven for another 5 to 10 minutes.

Ollie Mae Thomas

57

Ham Baked in Cider

10-12 pound fully cooked, bone-in,
   ham
½ cup sliced onion
1 bay leaf, crumbled
4 cups apple cider, divided
½ cup light brown sugar,
   packed
1 tablespoon lemon juice
¼ cup sliced onion
whole cloves

Wipe ham with damp paper towel and place in shallow roasting pan, without rack. Arrange ½ cup onion slices on ham. Sprinkle with bay leaf. Insert meat thermometer into center of thickest part of ham, not touching bone. Pour two cups cider into pan. Cover pan tightly with foil. Bake 2½-3 hours or until thermometer reads 130°. Remove from oven; drain liquid. In medium saucepan, combine 2 cups cider and remaining ingredients, except cloves, and bring to boil. Boil, uncovered, 5 minutes. Strain. Return ham to roasting pan. With a sharp knife score fat into diamond shapes and stud center of each diamond with whole clove. Pour cider mixture over ham. Bake, uncovered, about 40 minutes, or until meat thermometer reads 140°. (Baste every 15 minutes with pan juices.) Remove ham to serving platter and let stand 20 minutes before carving. Serve with Apple Cider Sauce.

Apple Cider Sauce for Ham
1 quart (4 cups) cider
2 pounds (about 4 cups) McIntosh
   apples, pared and quartered
½ cup sugar

Sauce: In 4-quart saucepan, bring cider to boiling and boil gently until reduced to 1 cup. Add apples and sugar; toss gently to combine. Simmer, uncovered, until apples are soft. Stir once. Serve warm. Makes 3½ cups.

Joan Gaeta (Mrs. Richard)

Mandarin Ham Rolls

Serves 4
350° oven

1 (11 ounce) can mandarin
   orange sections, drained
1½ cups cooked rice
⅓ cup mayonnaise or salad
   dressing
2 tablespoons chopped pecans
2 tablespoons snipped parsley
1 tablespoon sliced green onions
   (with tops)
8 slices boiled ham (8 ounces)
¼ cup orange marmalade
1 tablespoon lemon juice
¼ teaspoon ground ginger

Reserve eight orange sections; chop remainder and combine with cooked rice, mayonnaise, pecans, parsley and onion. Divide mixture among ham slices. Roll up ham and filling. Place seam side down in 10 x 6 x 2-inch baking dish. Combine marmalade, lemon juice and ginger; brush some over ham rolls. Bake, uncovered, at 350° for 25 to 30 minutes, brushing occasionally with remaining sauce. Garnish with reserved orange sections.

**Frances Arrington Elyea
(Mrs. George D.)
RHS President 1981-1982**

Luau Pork Ambrosia

Serves 6-8
375° oven

May be cooked on grill on quilted foil. Marinate overnight.

1 (5 pound) pork roast, chine bone
   removed and tied for roasting
4 jars strained apricots (baby
   food), 1 jar reserved
⅓ cup honey
¼ cup fresh lemon juice
¼ cup soy sauce
½ clove garlic, minced
1 small onion, minced
1 cup gingerale
1/8 teaspoon ginger
1/8 teaspoon pepper
1 can (1 pound 13 ounce) whole,
   unpeeled apricots
1 tablespoon lemon rind, grated
¼ cup coconut (fresh grated or
      frozen)
parsley sprigs

Place roast in marinating dish. Combine next nine ingredients (reserving one jar of strained apricots) and pour over roast. Marinate overnight. Before cooking, pour off and reserve marinade. Roast at 375° for 2½ hours. Baste frequently with marinade. Before serving, heat remaining marinade with reserved jar of strained apricots to serve as sauce over meat. Heat whole apricots and lemon rind together. Remove roast to hot serving platter. Garnish with whole apricots; sprinkle with coconut and parsley sprigs.

Liz Meadow (Mrs. Jack)

59

Cold Ham Loaf

Serves 6

2 envelopes plain gelatin
1 cup cold water, divided
1 can tomato soup
3 ounces cream cheese
2 tablespoons lemon juice
1 tablespoon grated onion
½ cup mayonnaise
2 teaspoons prepared mustard
2 cups ground, cooked ham
salt and pepper to taste
Worcestershire sauce to taste
1 hard boiled egg
a few sliced olives

Dissolve gelatin in ½ cup cold water. Heat tomato soup and remaining ½ cup cold water to boiling point. Add gelatin mixture and cream cheese. Stir until dissolved. Let cool. Add remaining ingredients except egg and olives. Slice egg and place with olives on bottom of chilled loaf pan or comparable mold. Pour in ham mixture and chill until firm. Unmold to serve.

Juanita Mitchell (Mrs. Frank, Jr.)

Pork with Steamed Spiced Sauerkraut

Serves 6
325° oven

½ cup chopped onion
1 tablespoon margarine
1 tablespoon sugar
2 cups cold water
2 pounds sauerkraut, drained, washed and squeezed dry
1 large raw potato, grated
garni (in cheesecloth bag)
  5 whole juniper berries
  6 peppercorns
  2 bay leaves
  ¼ teaspoon caraway seeds
  1 whole allspice
6 pieces pork loin (18 ounces)

Brown onions lightly in margarine; add sugar, water and sauerkraut. Toss with fork until well separated. Add grated potato. Put mixture in 2-quart casserole; burrow hole in sauerkraut and bury garni bag. Brown meat and place on top of sauerkraut. Cover and bake 1½-2 hours. Cover may be removed if meat needs browning.

Sherry Wier (Mrs. T. E.)

Julian's Pork Chop Casserole

Serves 4-6
300° oven

⅔ cup uncooked rice
1 can cream of chicken soup
1 can cream of mushroon soup
½ can onion soup
1½ soup cans water
4-6 pork chops

Place all ingredients in oblong pyrex baking dish with pork chops on top. Bake, uncovered, at 300° to 350° for 1½ hours. Cover to reheat.

Julian Barfield

Savannah Pork and Rice

4-6 lean pork chops (½-¾" thick)
2 cups uncooked rice
2 cans onion soup
½ cup sherry
1 large onion, chopped
1 (8 ounce) can mushrooms,
  drained
2 stalks celery, chopped
salt and pepper to taste

Brown chops slightly. Mix all other ingredients together in oblong baking dish. Place chops on rice mixture. Cover and bake at 350° for 1½ hours. Uncover and bake an additional 30 minutes.

Cathy Robinson (Mrs. David E.)

Spanish Pork Chops

A family favorite!

5 pork chops
1 tablespoon fat
1 onion, sliced
2 cups canned tomatoes
1 teaspoon salt
¼ teaspoon pepper
2 tablespoons flour
¼ cup water
3-4 cups cooked rice

Brown chops slowly on both sides in fat. Remove from pan. In same pan brown onions; add chops, tomatoes, and seasonings. Cover and simmer 30 to 40 minutes. Remove chops and thicken tomato mixture with flour mixed with water. Place cooked rice in center of platter. Arrange chops around rice. Pour tomato sauce over all.

Mary Ann Meek (Mrs. R. R.)

Creole Pork Chops

6 pork chops, dredged in flour,
  salt, pepper and paprika to
  taste
1 (16 ounce) can tomatoes
1 (8 ounce) can tomato sauce
1 small onion, chopped
1 medium green pepper, chopped
½ cup mushrooms, sliced
¼ cup water
cooked rice for 6 servings

Brown chops in small amount of oil after they are dredged in flour and seasonings. Place in 2-quart baking dish. Mix together next six ingredients and add to meat. Bake 1½-2 hours (depending on thickness of chops) at 350°. Serve over rice.

Rena Morris (Mrs. Clyde)

Pork Chops with Amber Rice

Serves 6
350° oven

6 pork chops, ¾ inch thick
salt and pepper
1⅓ cups uncooked quick rice
1 cup orange juice
1 can condensed chicken-rice
  soup

Brown pork chops in heavy skillet. Season with salt and pepper. Place rice in 12 x 10 x 2-inch baking dish. Pour orange juice over rice. Arrange chops on rice. Pour chicken soup over all. Cover and bake at 350° for 45 minutes. Uncover and bake 10 minutes longer.

Wanda Bardin (Mrs. Charles A.)

Marinated Pork Chops

grill or broil

1 cup honey
½ cup soy sauce
2 beef bouillon cubes dissolved
  in 1 cup water
2 tablespoons ginger
1 tablespoon garlic powder

Mix together all ingredients and pour over pork chops. Marinate chops overnight, turning occasionally. Grill over charcoal or broil.

Beverly Shelton (Mrs. C. G.)

Polish Sausage in Sauce

Yield: 2 quarts
325° oven

Serve over rice or use as an hors d'oeuvre. Freezes well.

1 or 2 pounds Polish sausage

Prick sausage and bake slowly (325°) for 45 minutes. While hot, cut in slices and add to sauce.

Sauce
1 bottle hickory smoked barbecue
  sauce
1 (32 ounce) bottle tomato
  ketchup
⅔ cup brown sugar
½ cup apple cider vinegar
1 cup chopped onions
2 cloves garlic, chopped
1 teaspoon salt
1 teaspoon parsley
dash Tabasco

Sauce: Mix all ingredients and cook slowly about one hour. Stir often. Adjust seasonings to taste. As a meal, serves 6. As an hors d'oeuvre, serves about 14.

Dr. J. Herbert West

Sausage Casserole

Serves 12
350° oven

2 pounds bulk sausage
2 large onions, chopped
1 large bell pepper, chopped
1 bunch celery, chopped
2 cups uncooked rice
3 packages dehydrated chicken noodle soup
1½ cups slivered almonds

Brown sausage in chunks. Set aside. Sauté onions, pepper and celery in drippings. Cook rice as directed. Prepare soup as directed, but use only half the water called for. Mix all ingredients together. Bake at 350° for one hour. Freezes well.

Beverly West (Mrs. J. Herbert)

Sausage Brunch

Serves 10
350° oven

May be frozen before final step for later cooking.

2 pounds regular Jimmy Dean sausage
6 green onions, minced
1 (4 ounce) jar pimientos, chopped
½ pound (1 cup) mushrooms, sliced
salt and pepper
pinch dry mustard
16 thin slices white or wheat bread, crusts removed
6 eggs, beaten
3 cups milk
½ teaspoon salt
2 teaspoons Worcestershire sauce
1¼ cups sharp cheddar cheese, grated

Brown, crumble and drain sausage. Sauté onions, pimientos and mushrooms; add salt, pepper and dry mustard. Combine and set aside. In oiled 9 x 13-inch glass baking dish, place 8 slices of bread. Spread sausage mixture evenly on top. Cover with remaining bread slices. Combine all other ingredients except cheese and pour over (at this point casserole may be frozen). Bake at 350° for one hour and 10 minutes, uncovered. Remove from oven; sprinkle with cheese and return to oven until cheese is melted.

Tricia Smith (Mrs. Harry Lee)

Barbecued Hot Dogs

Serves 5-10
350° oven

½ cup brown sugar (firmly packed)
3 medium onions
2 small green peppers
1 (15 ounce) can tomato sauce
1 (pound) package hot dogs
sandwich rolls

Spread brown sugar in 10 x 6-inch baking dish. Grind onions and peppers in blender or processor. Place hot dogs on top of brown sugar. Pour onion and pepper mixture over hot dogs and pour tomato sauce over top. Bake at 350° uncovered approximately 1½ hours. Serve on sandwich rolls.

Carol Banker (Mrs. James N.)

Steak and Bacon Tournedos

Yield: 8 pinwheels
grill

1½ pounds beef flank steak
½ cup dry red wine
meat tenderizer
½ pound bacon
1 teaspoon garlic salt
¼ teaspoon pepper
2 tablespoons parsley
1 container (4 ounce) cream cheese with garlic and herbs
1 jar Bearnaise sauce, or use your own recipe
rice

Four hours before serving, pound flank steak to even thickness (about ½ inch). Sprinkle with meat tenderizer (according to directions). Pour wine over steak and refrigerate until 45 minutes before serving. Meanwhile, fry bacon until almost done (not crisp). Sprinkle steak with garlic salt and pepper. Score diagonally making diamond shaped cuts. Spread cream cheese over steak and place bacon strips lengthwise on top. Sprinkle with parsley. Roll up jellyroll fashion, starting at narrow end. Skewer at 1-inch intervals and cut in 1-inch slices. Grill or broil. Serve on rice with heated Bearnaise sauce.

Mary Hood (Mrs. John K.)

Grilled Beef

grill

1 top round steak, 1½-2 inches thick
½ cup soy sauce
½ cup sweet and sour dressing

Marinate steak over night in soy and sweet-sour mixture. To cook, pour off marinade and reserve to use as a sauce for meat. Grill to your liking.

Henry Wing

Rouladen "Birds"

Serve 2 "birds" per person

sirloin tip or rump roast, sliced
  very thin
salt and pepper
uncooked bacon
chopped onion
pickle relish, drained
flour
cooking oil
1 cup water

Lay all slices of meat on waxed paper. Season with salt and pepper. Layer on bacon (about one slice per), onion and pickle relish. Roll and fold as tightly as possible; secure with toothpicks. Roll each "bird" in flour. Sauté in oil until brown; add water. Cover and simmer 45 minutes.

Janine Powers (Mrs. W.D.)

Mrs. Kerver's Steak

broil or grill

Amounts depend upon personal taste and size of roast. Prepare night before.

1 chuck roast
garlic cloves
meat tenderizer
horseradish mustard

Cut slits in roast and insert garlic cloves. Sprinkle meat tenderizer all over roast and then spread horseradish mustard on both sides. Place in glass dish, cover with plastic wrap and refrigerate overnight. Broil on lowest oven rack 20 to 25 minutes per side, or grill.

Shirley Deuchler (Mrs. Robert)

Teriyaki

Serves 8-10

Oriental dish from Honolulu. Family favorite for years.

3 pounds sirloin strip steaks
  cut into ¼ inch slices
1 cup soy sauce
¼ cup red wine
¼ cup water
2-3 tablespoons sugar
¼ teaspoon MSG (monosodium
  glutamate)
3 cloves garlic, pressed
1 inch piece of ginger root
oil for frying

Combine soy sauce, wine, water, sugar, MSG, garlic and ginger root in large bowl. Add meat slices and let stand 2 hours, turning slices occasionally. To cook, remove meat, drain and fry in hot oil to desired doneness.

John Rittenburg

65

Marinade for London Broil

Yield: 1 cup

Best ever! Use morning of, or night before. May be used more than once.

½ cup soy sauce
½ cup wine vinegar
3 cloves garlic, crushed
pinch oregano
pinch ginger
pinch marjoram
1 large onion, sliced
London broil cut, or flank steak

Mix all ingredients except onion and meat. Layer half the onion on bottom of shallow baking dish. Place meat on top. Layer remaining onion on top of meat. Pour marinade over all. (It should cover half the thickness of meat.) Marinate 3 to 24 hours. Turn meat halfway through time. Grill or broil meat to taste. Refrigerate leftover marinade to use again. Proportions can be altered to taste.

Lizanne Abreu (Mrs. Peter)

Flank Steak Marinade

Yield: 1¾ cups

⅔ cup catsup
⅓ cup lemon juice
½ cup water
1 bay leaf
1 teaspoon celery seed, or celery salt
2 teaspoons Worcestershire sauce
dash pepper
dash Tabasco
flank steak

Mix together all ingredients except meat. Pour over flank steak and marinate overnight. Grill meat about 5 minutes per side.

Shirley Deuchler (Mrs. Robert)

Favorite Casserole

Serves 4-6
300° oven

2 pounds stew beef
salt and pepper to taste
Accent to taste
1 large onion, sliced
6 carrots, cut lengthwise
1 tablespoon sugar
2 tablespoons Minute tapioca (optional)
1 cup V-8 juice

Sprinkle salt, pepper and Accent over meat. Put in 13 x 9-inch pyrex dish. Add remaining ingredients and cover dish loosely with foil. Bake 5 hours at 300°. Freezes well.

Mary W. Long

Daube of Beef Creole

Serves 6
275° oven

An entirely different flavor from the usual because of the rum, tomatoes and salt pork. Wonderful!

3 pounds round of beef
1 dozen pimiento-stuffed olives
1 large onion, sliced
½ pound salt pork, cut in cubes
½ cup rum
4 or 5 tomatoes, roughly chopped
bouquet of herbs (bay leaf, thyme, basil and parsley, tied for easy removal)
2 crushed garlic cloves
freshly milled pepper
noodles

Trim excess fat from meat and make double row of deep incisions on each side. In these stick olives, cut in half lengthwise. Tie meat in oblong shape. In stewing pot cook onion in a little butter until it loses color. Add salt pork. When fat starts to run, add beef and brown on both sides. Heat rum; set light to it and pour, flaming, over meat. Shake and rotate pot until flames die down. Add tomatoes, herbs and garlic and lots of pepper. Cover with sheet of foil and lid. Cook at 275° about 3 hours. Remove herbs. Crush tomatoes into sauce which will be rich and thick. Serve with plain boiled noodles.

Enid McGaughey (Mrs. John E., Jr.)

Burgundy Beef Stew

Serves 6
300° oven

Super company meal. Easy!

2 pounds boneless chuck or stew meat (cut into one-inch cubes)
2 cups sliced carrots
1 cup sliced celery
2 medium onions, sliced
3 tablespoons flour
1 tablespoon sugar
1 tablespoon salt
1 teaspoon basil or marjoram
1 (16 ounce) can tomatoes
1 cup Burgundy wine
1 (6 ounce) can sliced mushrooms, drained
1 (5 ounce) can sliced water chestnuts, drained

In large casserole combine meat, carrots, celery and onion. Mix flour, sugar, salt and basil or marjoram and stir into casserole. Stir in tomatoes and wine. Cover tightly with foil and bake at 300° for 3-3½ hours. Uncover, stir in mushrooms and water chestnuts. Reseal and bake 10 minutes longer.

Betsy Altman (Mrs. Robert E.)

Beef Tips in Wine

Perfect "Open Hearth" recipe! Try it some cold winter Saturday in a black iron pot swung from a cooking crane in an open fireplace. A very successful recipe.

4 pounds sirloin tip, or eye
  of round, cubed
1 teaspoon salt
1 teaspoon coarse-grind black
  pepper
½ cup flour
1 clove garlic, crushed
3 medium onions, sliced thin
2 (4 ounce) cans sliced
  mushrooms, drained
1 cup chopped celery hearts with
  tops
1 teaspoon Worcestershire sauce
2 teaspoons tomato paste
1 (10 ounce) can beef broth
3 tablespoons flour
¼ cup dry red wine
buttered noodles

Toss beef cubes with salt, pepper and ½ cup flour until thoroughly coated. Place in bottom of large slow cooker or iron pot. Add garlic, onions, mushrooms and celery. Stir Worcestershire and tomato paste into beef broth. Pour over meat and vegetables; mix together well. Cover and cook slowly 5 to 6 hours in fireplace, or 7 to 12 hours in slow cooker on low setting. One hour before serving, turn cooker to high, or move pot to hotter place over fire. Make smooth paste of 3 tablespoons flour and wine. Stir into meat and vegetables; cook only until thickened. If using iron pot, empty immediatley into covered soup tureen as wine should not stand in iron. Serve over hot buttered noodles.

Marie DeVane (Mrs. Ernest E.)

Beef and Rice Casserole

1 pound ground beef
⅔ cup chopped onion
⅔ cup chopped celery
1 teaspoon salt
¼ teaspoon black pepper
4 tablespoons margarine
¾ cup raw rice
1 can mushroom soup
1 soup can tomato juice
2 ounces grated cheese

Cook beef until lightly browned. Drain. Add remaining ingredients, except cheese. Bake 60 minutes at 375°. If mixture seems too dry, add water. Sprinkle with cheese and return to oven for 10 minutes.

Ollie Mae Thomas

Poor Boy's Stroganoff

Serves 4

1 pound ground beef
¼ cup onions, chopped
1 clove garlic, chopped
¼ cup margarine
3 tablespoons lemon juice
3 tablespoons red wine
1 can mushroom soup
1 teaspoon salt
1 teaspoon MSG
1 (6 ounce) can mushrooms
1 (8 ounce) carton sour cream
1 (8 ounce) package noodles

Brown meat, onions and garlic in margarine. Add remaining ingredients (except sour cream and noodles). Heat. Cook noodles and add, with sour cream, to heated mixture.

Beth Hamilton (Mrs. Robert A.)

Hamburger Cobbler

Serves 4-6
425° oven

1 pound ground beef
1 clove garlic
1 teaspoon salt
¼ teaspoon pepper
1 small onion, chopped
6 slices yellow cheese
1 (8 ounce) can tomato sauce
3 tablespoons catsup
2 tablespoons Worcestershire sauce
1 (8 ounce) package refrigerated crescent rolls

Brown meat and onion with garlic, salt and pepper. Place in bottom of 1½-quart shallow baking dish. Arrange cheese slices on top of meat. Combine tomato sauce, catsup and Worcestershire sauce and pour over top of cheese. Make crust for top from rolls. Bake at 425° for 20-25 minutes, or as directed on roll package.

Dottie Picquet (Mrs. Paul)

Quick Hamburger Casserole

Serves 4-6
400° oven

1 pound ground beef
1 onion, chopped
1 clove garlic, minced
1 cup celery, diced
1 cup frozen or canned peas
1 cup carrots, thinly sliced
1 (8 ounce) can tomato sauce
1 teaspoon salt
1 teaspoon Worcestershire sauce
1 (8 ounce) can tomato sauce
½ cup cheddar cheese, shredded

Brown beef in skillet and drain. Sauté onion and garlic in same skillet. Add celery, peas, carrots, one can tomato sauce, salt and Worcestershire sauce. Simmer all for 10 minutes. Place in casserole. Pour second can of tomato sauce over meat mixture and sprinkle cheese on top. Bake at 400° for 8-10 minutes.

Joan Soldavini (Mrs. Alfred C.)

69

Sour Cream Noodle Bake

Serves 6
350° oven

1 (5 ounce) package medium noodles
1 pound ground beef
1 tablespoon butter
1 teaspoon salt
½ teaspoon pepper
¼ teaspoon garlic salt
1 cup (8 ounce can) tomato sauce
1 cup creamed cottage cheese
1 cup sour cream
1 cup chopped green onions
1 cup sharp cheddar cheese, grated

Cook noodles according to package directions; rinse and drain. Brown meat in butter. Add salt, pepper, garlic salt and tomato sauce; simmer 3-5 minutes. Combine cottage cheese, sour cream, onions and noodles, mixing well. In 2-quart casserole, alternate layers of noodle mixture and meat mixture. Begin with noodles and end with meat mixture. Top with grated cheese. Cover and bake at 350° for 20-30 minutes or until cheese is melted and brown.

Florence Tolbert

Chili-Kidney Beans

Serves 6

Good served over spaghetti.

1 pound ground beef
2 medium onions, chopped
½ green bell pepper, chopped
2 tablespoons fat
2 teaspoons salt
1/8 teaspoon pepper
2 tablespoons chili powder
1 (1 pound) can tomatoes
1 (1 pound) can red kidney beans

Cook beef, onion and bell pepper in fat until lightly browned, stirring often. Add seasonings and tomatoes. Simmer gently 1 hour. Add kidney beans and simmer 5 minutes.

Mary Wright Hawkins (Mrs. Aubrey)

Spicy Beef Brisket

250° oven

1 beef brisket
1 teaspoon celery salt
1 teaspoon garlic salt
1 teaspoon onion salt
2 tablespoons liquid smoke
3 tablespoons Worcestershire sauce
½ teaspoon black pepper

Rub first four ingredients into beef brisket. Wrap in foil and refrigerate overnight. Next day, sprinkle with Worcestershire sauce and pepper. Reseal foil and bake at 250° for 5 hours. Cool slightly before cutting across grain. Can be reheated.

Jo Ann M. King

Lasagna

Serves 8
375° oven

For improved flavor prepare meat sauce the day before.

1½ pounds ground beef
1 pound ground pork
1 teaspoon oil
1 clove garlic, minced
1 tablespoon fresh parsley, chopped
1 tablespoon basil
2 teaspoons salt
2½ cups tomatoes (No. 2 can)
1 (6 ounce) can tomato paste
1 package lasagna noodles
2 (12 ounce) cartons cottage cheese
2 eggs, beaten
½ teaspoon pepper
2 tablespoons fresh parsley
½ cup Parmesan cheese
2 teaspoons salt
1 pound mozzarella or American cheese, grated or sliced

Brown meats in hot oil. Add next six ingredients. Simmer, uncovered, until thick (about one hour), stirring occasionally. Cook noodles in boiling, salted water until tender. Drain and rinse in cold water. Combine cottage cheese with next five ingredients. Place layer of noodles in large baking dish. Spread half the cottage cheese over noodles. Add half the mozzarella or American cheese and half the meat mixture. Repeat layers. Bake at 375° for 30 minutes.

Sara Newton (Mrs. Charles)

Green Chili Enchilada Casserole

Serves 6
375° oven

1 pound ground chuck
1 can cream of chicken soup
1 medium onion, finely diced
1 small can diced green chilies (not hot)
1 (6-8 ounce) can diced tomatoes with jalapeño peppers or chilies (hot)
½ cup water
12 ounces Longhorn Colby cheese
12 ounces Monterey Jack cheese
12 ounces mozzarella cheese
10-12 corn tortillas

Brown meat and drain. Mix next five ingredients together and simmer 10-15 minutes. Grate all cheeses. Fry tortillas on low heat until edges are slightly crisp. Layer tortillas, beef, sauce and mixed cheeses. Reserve half of sauce to cover whole casserole. Bake at 375° for 45 minutes.

Marianne Miller

Taco Hot Dish

Serves 6-8
350° oven

2 pounds ground chuck
1 large onion, chopped
1 package taco seasoning mix
8-12 ounces small tortilla chips
½ head lettuce, shredded
4-6 tomatoes, sliced
5-8 ounces mozzarella cheese, grated
5 ounces cheddar cheese, grated

Brown meat and onion. Drain off fat. Add taco seasoning mix, mixed with water as directed on package. Simmer ½ hour. Spread tortilla chips on bottom of deep 9 x 13-inch pan. Break up a little. Layer meat mixture, shredded lettuce, tomato and cheeses. Bake at 350° for 25 minutes, or until cheese is melted.

Norma Harris (Mrs. Lyndon A.)

Special Rump Roast

325° oven

rump roast, over 5 pounds
garlic powder or garlic salt
water

Place roast fat side up in shallow roasting pan. Sprinkle with garlic salt or powder. Allowing one hour per pound, roast at 325°, uncovered, for half the total cooking time. Add enough water to have about one inch in roasting pan. Cover roast and pan with heavy foil and cook at 300° for remaining time. Slice roast and put on meat platter. Heat juice (do not thicken) and season to taste. Pour as much juice over slices as platter will hold.

Caroline Dillman

(Mrs. Frederick E., Jr.)

Lamp Chops a la Sylvain

Serves 4

8 lamb chops
1 teaspoon chopped onion
2 tablespoons butter
8 chicken livers
4 ounces port wine
½ cup consommé
salt and pepper

Broil lamb chops. While they are cooking, sauté onions in butter. Add chicken livers. Pour in wine and consommé. Salt and pepper to taste. Simmer 15 minutes. Serve broiled lamb chops on bed of chicken liver preparation.

Eileen Harbrecht (Mrs. John W.)

Beef Short Ribs

Serves 6
300° oven

4 pounds short ribs, cut in 1 inch
pieces
1 pound (2 cups) onions, sliced
thin
¾ cup ketchup
6 tablespoons sugar
1 cup water
5 tablespoons soy sauce
2 tablespoons Worcestershire
sauce
2 tablespoons vinegar
1 teaspoon paprika
1 teaspoon salt

Flour, salt and pepper meat and place in Dutch oven. Place sliced onions on top of meat. Mix remaining ingredients and pour over all. Cover. Bake in 300° oven for 3 hours. Serve ribs over rice.

Sondra Cooley (Mrs. James H., Jr.)

Lamb on Skewers

Serves 4-6
broil

Marinate overnight. Cook in or out.

2½ pounds boned leg of lamb,
cut in ½ inch cubes
½ teaspoon salt
½ teaspoon freshly ground
pepper
1½ tablespoons finely snipped
parsley
¼ teaspoon each thyme, oregano
and rosemary
1 clove garlic, minced
½ cup salad oil
1 cup Burgundy wine
whole fresh mushrooms
green peppers, cut in pieces
onions, quartered

Place lamb cubes in large bowl. Combine next seven ingredients and pour over lamb. Cover and refrigerate overnight. Reserve marinade. Thread mushrooms, lamb, green peppers and onion on skewers. Broil on grill 6 inches above medium hot coals 15 minutes, turning skewers frequently and brushing with marinade, or broil 4 inches from heat in oven, turning and basting until done.

Mary Jane Klein

Veal Veronique

Serves 4-6

Subtle combination of grapes with wine to enhance the delicate flavor of veal.

6 veal chops (rib, loin or shoulder)
1 tablespoon salad oil
1 tablespoon butter
½ cup chicken broth
½ cup dry white wine or sauterne
1 tablespoon cornstarch
¼ cup water
snipped parsley
1 tablespoon chopped green
  onion or chives
1 cup halved green grapes
1 tablespoon lemon juice

Brown chops in oil and butter. Add broth and wine; cover and simmer over low heat 30 minutes or until meat is tender. Remove chops to warm platter. Combine cornstarch and water; stir into pan juices along with parsley and onion. Cook and stir until mixture thickens and bubbles. Stir in grapes and lemon juice. Pour sauce over chops and serve. May be garnished with lemon slices and clusters of parsley.

Mary Jane Klein

Vitello All 'Uccelletto Con Carciofi

Serves 6

Wonderful Italian way to do veal.

18 round veal scallops, cut ¼
  inch thick
flour
salt and freshly ground pepper
½ cup butter
2 cans (10 count) artichoke hearts
juice of 2 lemons
2 lemons cut into wheels
¼ cup Marsala wine
2 tablespoons chopped parsley
1 cup chicken stock

Place veal scallops between sheets of waxed paper and pound with flat side of meat cleaver to make as flat as possible without breaking through them. Season with salt and pepper and dust with flour. Heat 5 tablespoons butter until golden in large frying pan over fairly high heat. Quickly brown veal slices, a few at a time, about 2 minutes on each side. Transfer to hot serving platter to keep warm. Drain artichoke hearts and sauté in remaining butter. When hot add lemon juice, lemon wheels, parsley, wine and chicken stock. Simmer 5 minutes or until sauce has thickened. Pour over scallops and serve.

**Gene & Gabe's Lodge Restaurant
Canton Street**

Sesame Parmesan Veal

Serves 8
350° oven

1½ pounds veal cutlets
¼ cup enriched flour
1 teaspoon salt
1 teaspoon paprika
½ teaspoon poultry seasoning
¼ teaspoon pepper
2 tablespoons shortening
2 tablespoons butter or margarine, melted
1 cup bread crumbs
½ cup grated Parmesan cheese
¼ cup sesame seeds, toasted
½ cup hot water
1 can cream of chicken soup
1 cup sour cream

Combine flour and seasonings. Dredge meat in mixture and brown slowly in hot fat. Reserve drippings. Arrange meat in two 8 x 11-inch baking dishes. Combine butter, bread crumbs, cheese and sesame seeds and spoon over meat. Stir water into pan drippings and pour around meat. Bake at 350° for 30 minutes. Blend chicken soup and sour cream. Heat in saucepan and serve with meat.

Mary Ann Johnson (Mrs. James)

Liver in Gravy

Serves 4

1-1½ pounds liver, sliced in strips, shake in flour to coat
1 medium onion, diced
8 (or more) strips bacon, cut up
1 package mushroom soup mix
1½ cups water

Soft fry onions and bacon. Remove from pan. Quick brown liver in bacon drippings. Return onions and bacon to pan. Mix mushroom soup mix with water and add to pan. Cover and cook over low heat 15-20 minutes. Remove cover and continue cooking for another 10-15 minutes. Stir often. Add more water, if necessary.

Ginia Huff (Mrs. Edward S.)

GRAIN, GREENS AND INGENUITY

Carved out of the wilderness before Atlanta was no more than an idea on an engineer's drawing board, Roswell had always been surrounded by a large rural area. The founding families who lived in the big houses in town were as dependent upon their own gardens, vineyards, cows and chickens for food as were the farmers who lived in the outlying areas. One of Roswell King's first deeds for his new Colony was to plant lots of fruit trees that would bear profusely for the pioneer families and generations to follow. Regular trips to the flour and corn mills were essential.

Destruction of grounds, crops and mills during the Civil War caused hard times in Roswell. Miss Katharine Simpson recalled her grandmother, Barrington King's daughter, telling of boiling grains for coffee and sifting through the soil under the smokehouse at Barrington Hall to obtain salt. Irene Howell's grandmother recounted tales of Billy Seldoms and Johnny Constants. Billy Seldoms were biscuits made with white flour which was very hard to get during the war, so they were served on Sunday only! Johnny Constants were the corn bread or corn meal biscuits that families ate everyday.

Hard times challenged the imagination and resulted in many money-saving, mouth-watering dishes that remain a part of the charm of Southern cooking. Any edible green could be transformed into delicious, satisfying fare. The delectable "poke sallet" crop still comes every spring, growing wild along the roadsides and around garden borders. Nellie McDowell's recipe, passed down from generation to generation, reminds us to wash the poke at least three times before cooking like turnip greens in a boiler. Then strain and wash once more! Put a good bit of grease into a pan, break in a few eggs, and scramble with some onion. Add the poke and enjoy!

Preserving the fresh crops for enjoyment all year long brought back vivid memories. Taylor Williams always remembered his grandmother's "leather britches", string beans which were dried out and had to be soaked overnight before cooking. Tater hills in the backyard were stored up sweet potatoes piled with a protective covering of dirt and hay. Sara Mabry had no difficulty visualizing the peanuts spread out to dry in the sun on the tin roof of her father's barn!

The catch of the day has always meant dinner to someone. "Turkles" were considered a delicacy by a certain group of neighbors. They loved this superior blend of chicken and fish flavored meat fried up like chicken. So on a Saturday night, with the help of a little corn whiskey, the gay young blades would steal down to the creek and grapple for turtles, pulling them out of holes along the banks of the creek. The corn whiskey was just in case they happened upon a snake instead of a "turkle"!

POULTRY

Scarlett Rickenbaker

HOLLY HILL
MIMOSA BOULEVARD
Circa 1842

HOLLY HILL

Holly Hill was built in 1842 for Robert Adams Lewis and his wife, Catharine Anna Barrington Cooke, niece of Roswell King. Barrington King supervised construction of the "summer home" for the Lewis family before they arrived in Roswell. The raised-cottage style, so prevalent on the coast, was unique in the upcountry.

The family was so pleased with the home, the mild climate, and the village, they remained to make Roswell their permanent home. Robert Lewis was a leading merchant and one of the most prominent men of Savannah, where he served as justice of the inferior court, member of the city council, and acting mayor.

Holly Hill was situated on two wooded acres with nine servants to care for the place. The handsomely detailed portico sets the tone and character of the house. Slender Doric columns grace the front and back piazzas, and a dentil trim at the cornice encircles the house.

The first floor, partly below ground level in front, held the original kitchen and larders. Broad front steps lead to the main floor with its large entrance hall. Meticulous craftsmanship is evident in the superb moldings, mantels, and trim. The staircase is lined with slender, lathe-turned balusters and newel post. Black Italian marble fireplaces add to the elegance of the home.

Holly Hill is listed on the National Register of Historic Places.

———

SUNDAY DINNER AT HOLLY HILL

Tossed Green Salad with Italian Dressing
Breast of Chicken with Cream*

Carrot Souffle   Rice Timbales

Broccoli with Hollandaise Sauce
Green Seedless Grapes in Sour Cream
Sprinkled Lightly with Brown Sugar
Demitasse

Breast of Chicken with Cream

Serves 4
400° oven

Small groups of intimate friends enjoyed this dinner dish at Holly Hill.

4 supremes (boned breast of
chicken from 2 fryers)
½ teaspoon lemon juice
¼ teaspoon salt
large pinch white pepper
4 tablespoons butter

Rub supremes with drops of lemon juice and sprinkle lightly with salt and pepper. In heavy 10-inch casserole heat butter until foaming. Quickly roll supremes in butter. Lay buttered round of waxed paper over them; cover casserole and place in hot oven. After 6 minutes press top of supremes with finger. If still soft, return to oven a few moments. When meat is springy to the touch, it is done. Place on warm platter. Pour Cream Sauce over supremes.

Cream Sauce
3 cubes chicken bouillon
(¼ cup liquid)
¼ cup Madeira wine or dry
white vermouth
1 cup whipping cream
salt and white pepper to taste
2 tablespoons Kitchen Bouquet
¼ cup lemon juice
2 tablespoons minced fresh
parsley

Sauce: Pour bouillon and wine in casserole with cooking butter and boil down quickly over high heat until syrupy. Add cream, stirring constantly, and simmer until thickened slightly. Remove from heat. Season to taste with salt, pepper and Kitchen Bouquet. Add drops of lemon juice to taste. Pour sauce over supremes. Sprinkle with parsley.
Evelyn Hannah Sommerville

Bacon Wrapped Chicken Breasts

Serves 6
350° oven

6 chicken breast halves, skinned
and boned
6 slices cooked ham
6 slices mozzarella cheese
6-12 strips bacon

Pound chicken until ¼ inch thick. Top each piece with ham and cheese. Fold over with chicken. Wrap each bundle in 1-2 strips of bacon, depending on size of breasts. Place bundles side by side in shallow baking dish. Bake at 350° for 40-45 minutes or until chicken is cooked. Turn to 400° for about 15 minutes to brown bacon.
Irene Irvin (Mrs. W. A.)

Chicken Supreme

Serves 4-8
350°-375° oven

Entrée at dinner party for President and Mrs. Jimmy Carter at Dolvin House.

4 whole (8 halves) chicken breasts
2 eggs
½ cup milk
dash cardamon
dash chervil
fresh bread crumbs
butter or margarine
4 ounces brandy
2 ounces Burgundy
1 cup chicken broth (not bouillon)

Bone chicken breasts. Salt lightly. Beat eggs with milk. Sprinkle spices over chicken. Dip chicken into egg mixture and coat with bread crumbs. Sauté chicken in butter until brown. Transfer to oblong baking dish. Combine brandy, Burgundy and chicken broth. Pour over chicken. Bake at 350°-375° for 30-40 minutes, or until chicken is well done.

Emily Dolvin (Mrs. W. J.)
RHS President 1974

Chicken Breasts Supreme

Serves 6
350° oven

¼ cup flour
2½ teaspoons salt
1 teaspoon paprika
6 whole chicken breasts, split
¼ cup butter
¼ cup water
2 teaspoons cornstarch
1½ cups half and half
¼ cup sherry
1 tablespoon lemon juice
1 teaspoon lemon peel
1 cup grated Swiss cheese

Combine flour, salt and paprika. Coat chicken. Brown in butter. Add water and simmer, covered, 30 minutes. Arrange in 12x7x2-inch baking dish. Mix cornstarch with ¼ cup half and half. Stir into pan drippings. Over low heat stir in remaining half and half, sherry, lemon juice and peel. Cook until thickened. Pour over chicken. Cover and bake for 35 minutes at 350°. Sprinkle with cheese and return to oven until cheese is melted.

Nan Warren (Mrs. James P., Jr.)

Chicken and Shrimp Supreme

Serves 12
350° oven

Prepare and let season several hours or overnight before baking.

5 chicken breasts
1 onion, cut in half
few celery tops
1 stick margarine
8 tablespoons flour
2 cups milk
2 cups chicken broth
2 cups grated medium sharp
   cheddar cheese
½ cup dry white wine
1 (8 ounce) can mushrooms,
   drained
1 can cream of chicken soup
2 egg yolks, beaten
salt and pepper to taste
2 pounds cooked, cleaned and
   deveined shrimp

Place chicken in pot with onion and celery tops. Add water to cover and salt to taste. Cook until chicken is tender. Cool and remove from bones, leaving meat in fairly large pieces. Strain broth and reserve 2 cups. Melt margarine in saucepan over low heat and blend in flour. Cook a few minutes, stirring constantly, but do not brown. Remove from heat; add milk and chicken broth, stirring until smooth. If sauce becomes lumpy, strain through a sieve. Add cheese and cook, stirring until cheese melts. Add wine and mushrooms. Blend in chicken soup. Add some of hot mixture to egg yolks and then blend into sauce. Salt and pepper to taste. Fold chicken into sauce and pour into buttered 9x13-inch casserole. Refrigerate several hours or overnight. Let come to room temperature and bake at 350° for 30-40 minutes. During last 15 minutes add shrimp, pushing them into chicken mixture.

Charlotte Hollingsworth (Mrs. L. C.)

Chicken Seafood Supreme

Serves 6
350° oven

Try this with Stuffed Shells, salad and Italian bread!

3 large chicken breasts, boned, cut in half, then in thirds (18 pieces)
½ cup flour
1 onion, diced
½ green pepper, diced
1 clove garlic
1 (8 ounce) can tomato sauce
1 teaspoon salt
½ teaspoon pepper
1 teaspoon basil
2 teaspoons parsley, chopped
1 teaspoon paprika
1 (6½ ounce) can minced clams with juice
¼ cup sherry
½ pound fresh mushrooms
1½ pounds raw shrimp, shelled and deveined

Shake chicken parts in bag containing flour. Brown lightly in oil. Place in casserole. Sauté onion and green pepper lightly in pan in which chicken was cooked. Add remaining ingredients except mushrooms and shrimp. Simmer 10 minutes. Trim, clean and slice mushrooms. Cover with water in saucepan. Bring to boil and cook 2 minutes. Add drained mushrooms to sauce. Pour sauce over chicken. Cover and bake at 350° for 1 hour. Uncover. Add shrimp, pushing into sauce. Bake 10 minutes more. Can be kept warm one hour without drying out. May be prepared early to let chicken season.

Mary Jane Zaccheo (Mrs. John)

Orange Chicken

Serves 6
350° oven

6-8 chicken breasts
salt and pepper
butter
4 onions, sliced
1 (6 ounce) can frozen orange juice concentrate
¼ teaspoon ginger
1 (4½ ounce) can pitted black olives, drained and cut in rings
1 (11 ounce) can mandarin oranges, drained

Salt and pepper chicken. Brown in frying pan with small amount of butter. Place chicken in greased 9x13-inch pan and set aside. Sauté onions in same pan used for chicken, adding more butter. Add orange juice, ginger; heat. Pour mixture over chicken and top with olives. Bake at 350° for 1 hour. Top with mandarin oranges. Broil lightly. Serve hot. Sauce in bottom of pan is good served over rice.

Lee Spence

Sesame Chicken in Cumberland Sauce

Serves 10
425° oven

2 cups bread crumbs
¾ cup sesame seeds
½ cup freshly grated Parmesan cheese
¼ cup chopped fresh parsley
1 teaspoon freshly ground white pepper
6 chicken breasts, skinned, split, boned and pounded to ¼ inch thick
2 tablespoons butter, melted

Combine first five ingredients in bowl and blend well. Dip breasts in butter and coat with sesame breading. Place on baking sheet and bake 20 minutes. Serve with warm Cumberland Sauce.

Cumberland Sauce

3 large oranges
3 large lemons
1 cup red currant jelly
2 tablespoons port wine
2 teaspoons Dijon mustard
¼ teaspoon ground ginger
dash red pepper

Sauce: Grate peel and squeeze juice from oranges and lemons. Cover peel with cold water in large saucepan. Bring to boil and drain. Repeat twice and set aside. Combine juice and remaining ingredients in small saucepan and heat. Stir in grated peel to taste. Sauce may be poured over chicken, but is best if served as a dip in individual bowls.

Helen Owens (Mrs. Carl P., Jr.)

Buttermilk Pecan Chicken

Serves 8
350° oven

1 cup buttermilk
1 egg, slightly beaten
1 cup flour
1 cup ground pecans
¼ cup sesame seeds
1 tablespoon salt
1 tablespoon paprika
1/8 teaspoon pepper
2 (2½-3½ pound) fryers, cut up
½ cup margarine or shortening, melted
pecan halves

Mix buttermilk with egg. Stir together flour, ground pecans, sesame seeds, salt, paprika and pepper. Dip chicken in buttermilk mixture, then in flour mixture. Place margarine or shortening in large shallow roasting pan. Add chicken, skin side down, then turn pieces skin side up to coat with oil. Place pecan halves on each piece of chicken. Bake at 350⁰ for 1¼ hours or until tender and golden brown.

Carol Bentley (Mrs. Howard)

Viennese Chicken

Serves 8

lemon juice for marinade
4 chicken breasts, boned and
    skinned
1 cup flour
½-1 teaspoon poultry seasoning
½-1 teaspoon Italian Herb
    Seasoning
3 eggs, beaten
2 tablespoons cognac (optional)
1½ cups seasoned bread crumbs
    (packaged)
olive oil

Submerge chicken in lemon juice for 2-3 hours. Lightly dust with flour mixed with poultry seasoning and Italian Herb Seasoning. Dip in eggs and cognac. Dust in seasoned bread crumbs and place in refrigerator for 30-45 minutes. Fry in olive oil until golden brown. These ingredients are approximate. Adjust to your taste.

Marion Tillman (Mrs. William P.)

Lickskillet Farm Chicken in Wine

Serves 2

Makes a nice sauce to serve over the chicken and rice.

2 split chicken breasts (4 pieces)
butter
1 cup white wine
8 ounces mushrooms, sliced
2 tablespoons flour
2 tablespoons lemon juice
water

Brown chicken in butter. Add wine and mushrooms. Cover; let simmer until tender. Remove chicken; set aside. Make sauce by adding to the wine and mushrooms: flour, lemon juice and water to bring to desired consistency. Simmer, uncovered, 5 -10 minutes, stirring constantly. Serve sauce over chicken and rice.

**Lickskillet Farm Restaurant
Old Roswell Road**

Barbecued Chicken

Serves 6
325° oven

6 chicken breast halves
1 cup brown sugar
1 cup catsup
4 tablespoons white vinegar

Remove skin from chicken and place in baking dish. Make sauce with next 3 ingredients and pour over chicken. Cover and bake at 325° for 1½ hours. Remove cover for final 15 minutes. The sauce is good over pork chops or ribs.

Dot Beebe (Mrs. Philip)

Chicken California

Serves 4
350° oven

2½-3 pounds chicken pieces, skinned, boned
flour
2-3 large cloves garlic, sliced
olive and/or Wesson oil
dash chili powder
1 large onion, coarsley chopped
1 large green pepper, cut in strips
1 (3 ounce) can chopped green chilies (not jalapeño)
1 chicken bouillon cube
2 cups fresh tomatoes, skinned and coarsely chopped or 1 can tomatoes, chopped (use juice)

Dredge chicken lightly in flour. Shake off excess. Season with salt and pepper. (Lawry's Salt is good.) Sauté garlic slices in oil until dark golden brown. Remove and discard. Sauté chicken in this oil until golden. Place in large deep casserole dish. Dust lightly with chili powder. Sauté onion until golden; spread over chicken. Add more oil to pan, if needed, and sauté green pepper. Place over chicken and onion. Sprinkle green chilies over casserole. Add 1½ cups water to pan; dissolve bouillon cube and pour over chicken. Spread tomatoes over all and distribute down through chicken. Cover and bake at 350º for 1 hour or until tender. Add more liquid if necessary.

Dolores Lotze (Mrs. Carl R.)

Chicken Over Rice

Serves 4

Served at luncheon for Senator and Mrs. George McGovern when he was campaigning for the Presidency.

1 frying chicken, 3-3½ pounds
flour
oil for browning
3 ounces frozen pineapple or orange juice concentrate
½ cup water
1 cup white wine
½ teaspoon curry powder
¼ teaspoon turmeric
½ teaspoon salt
½ teaspoon white pepper
½ cup grated onion
1 apple, grated
½ to 1 cup heavy cream
2 cups seedless grapes
rice

Cut raw chicken into bite-size pieces. Dredge in seasoned flour. Brown in oil. Combine fruit juice, water, wine, seasonings, onion and apple. Pour over chicken; cover and simmer for 35-45 minutes until tender. Skim off fat. Add half the cream; continue cooking another 10 minutes. Sauce should thicken slightly. Taste and correct seasonings, if necessary. Add remaining cream. Add grapes. Cook 10 minutes longer. Serve chicken over rice.

Peggy Loughman (Mrs. Ralph D.)

85

Lee's Favorite Chicken Casserole

Serves 6-8
350° oven

6 chicken breasts
4 chicken thighs
1 package frozen chopped
   broccoli
2 cans cream of chicken soup
1 cup chicken stock
¾ cup mayonnaise
1½ teaspoons lemon juice
¾-1 teaspoon curry powder
¾ package Pepperidge Farm
   Seasoned Cornbread Dressing
⅓ pound butter

Cook chicken and cut into bite-size pieces. Reserve stock. Place chicken in greased 8x12-inch casserole dish. Cook broccoli according to package directions and place over chicken. Mix soup with chicken stock, mayonnaise, lemon juice and curry powder. Pour over chicken and broccoli. Sprinkle dressing over all. Melt butter and drizzle over top. Bake at 350° for 20 minutes or at 300° for 30 minutes.

Evelyn W. Callaway (Mrs. Lee)

Country Casserole

Serves 6-8
350° oven

2 cups cooked cubed chicken
2 cups cooked cubed ham
3 celery ribs, chopped and cooked
1 cup peas (or carrots, zucchini)
   cooked
1 cup cut green beans, cooked
8 ounces noodles, cooked

Combine ingredients and set aside.

Sauce
⅓ cup butter
⅓ cup flour
2 cups half and half
1½ cups milk
⅓ cup chicken broth
⅔ cup shredded sharp cheese
⅓ cup grated Parmesan cheese
juice of one lemon
1 clove garlic, minced
1 medium onion, diced
1 tablespoon prepared mustard
1 tablespoon parsley, chopped
1½ teaspoons salt and pepper
pinch rosemary
⅔ cup mayonnaise

Sauce: Combine first five ingredients. Add cheeses, lemon juice and seasonings. Cook until melted. Take from heat and stir in mayonnaise. Add sauce to above ingredients and transfer to casserole. Bake uncovered at 350° for 30 minutes or until bubbly.

Evelyn Baker Arey (Mrs. Stuart L.)

Country Captain Chicken

Serves 8
350° oven

3 pound hen
1 tablespoon butter
1 medium onion, thinly sliced
1 large bell pepper, chopped
1 garlic bud, sliced
1 teaspoon salt
1 teaspoon white pepper
1 teaspoon curry
1 teaspoon thyme
1 teaspoon chopped parsley
2 teaspoons sugar
2 teaspoons Worcestershire sauce
2 tablespoons chicken fat
¼ pound blanched and browned
   non-salted almonds (optional)
2 tablespoons dry currants,
   washed (optional)
cooked rice

Bake and season hen. Cut in small pieces and place in 9x13-inch covered dish. Combine butter, onion, bell pepper and garlic in saucepan. Simmer 10 minutes. Add spices, sugar and Worcestershire. Simmer 5 more minutes. Stir in chicken fat. Simmer to blend and pour over chicken. Cover dish and bake at 350° for 45 minutes. To serve: border serving platter with cooked rice and pour chicken mixture in middle. Sprinkle almonds and currants on top, if desired.
Jackie Buttram

Ginger Chicken

Wonderful camping dish.

Serves 4

2 whole chicken breasts, boned
   and skinned
2 tablespoons butter
1 large onion, sliced
¼ pound fresh mushrooms, sliced
2 carrots, cut in julienne strips
1 (14 ounce) can undiluted
   chicken broth
2 tablespoons soy sauce
½ cup sherry, divided
½ teaspoon salt
½ teaspoon ground ginger
1 teaspoon chopped ginger root
dash pepper
½ pound fresh spinach
1 (16 ounce) can bean sprouts,
   drained
2 tablespoons cornstarch
2 cups cooked rice
¼ cup slivered almonds

Slice chicken breasts in ½ inch thick julienne strips. Heat butter in skillet and sauté chicken until golden. Add onion and mushrooms; sauté until golden. Add carrots, broth, soy sauce, ¼ cup sherry, salt, ginger, ginger root and pepper to mixture. Cover and simmer 15 minutes. Wash spinach and remove stems. Add spinach and sprouts to chicken mixture. Cover and simmer 5 minutes. Make paste of ¼ cup sherry and cornstarch. Add to chicken. Cook, stirring, until thickened. Combine almonds with cooked rice. Serve with chicken. Add soy sauce, if desired.
Jackie Winecoff (Mrs. A. F., Jr.)

Chicken Breasts With Wine and Rice

Serves 6-8
275° oven

8-10 boneless chicken breasts
1 can cream of chicken soup
1 can cream of celery soup
1 can cream of mushroom soup
1½ soup cans milk
½ soup can white wine
½ cup melted butter
1-1½ cups uncooked rice
1 full cup grated Parmesan
  cheese
parsley flakes

Combine soups, milk, wine and butter. Spread rice in bottom of roasting pan. Pour half the mixture over rice. Place chicken over rice. Pour remaining mixture over chicken. Sprinkle with cheese and parsley. Bake at 275° for three hours.

Dolores G. Miller

Chicken Dumplings Barrington

An old recipe still enjoyed today at Barrington Hall.

1½ cups sifted plain flour
1 teaspoon salt
freshly ground pepper
2 tablespoons double-acting
  baking powder
3 tablespoons shortening
2 tablespoons chopped fresh
  chives
¾ cup milk
broth of stewed chicken

Sift flour, salt, pepper and baking powder. Cut in shortening. Stir in chives and milk. Drop by big tablespoons into boiling chicken broth. Cover and cook about 15 minutes.

Miss Katharine Baker Simpson

Chicken Loaf

Serves 6
350° oven

3 cups cooked, chopped chicken
1 cup stale bread crumbs
2 cups chicken broth or milk
1½ cups chopped celery
3 eggs, beaten slightly
½ cup mushrooms (optional)

Mix all together and pour into loaf pan. Bake at 350° about 40 minutes or until firm. Serve with cream sauce or chicken gravy made from broth of chicken.

Helene Moorman (Mrs. J. W., Sr.)

Pete's Sunday Supper Chicken Salad

Serves 4

Special sandwiches or hors d'oeuvres.

3 fried chicken breasts, preferably
  Kentucky Fried
3 slices bacon
½ onion, chopped
chutney, preferably Major Grey's
mayonnaise
toasted bread or crackers

Remove meat from chicken bones. Remove crispy part of skin and save. Chop chicken and skin finely in blender or food processor. Cook bacon until crispy; remove. Cook onions in bacon fat until soft and lightly browned. Drain on paper towel. Put chopped chicken, bacon and onion in bowl. Add chutney to desired sweetness (a few spoonsful) and mayonnaise to desired spread. Put on toasted bread, with lettuce, if desired. Spread on toast rounds or crackers for hors d'oeuvres. Proportions can be altered to taste. Whole mixture can be heated slightly.

Pete Abreu

Hot Chicken Salad

Serves 6
450° oven

2 cups cubed cooked chicken
2 cups diced celery
½ cup chopped toasted almonds
½ teaspoon Accent
2 tablespoons lemon juice
½ cup grated sharp cheddar
  cheese
½ teaspoon salt
2 teaspoons grated onion
1 cup mayonnaise
1 cup crushed potato chips

Mix all ingredients except potato chips. Sprinkle chips over the top. Bake at 450° for 20 minutes.

Ann Ledsinger (Mrs. Lewis, Jr.)

Glazed Cornish Game Hens
with Avocado and Orange Slices

Serves 6
325° oven

6 Cornish game hens, thawed
salt
lemon juice
2 cups tomato puree
1 tablespoon grated onion
¼ cup soy sauce
¼ cup vinegar
¼ teaspoon Tabasco
1 teaspoon dry mustard
2 avocados
2 navel oranges

Wash game hens and pat dry. Rub inside and out with salt and lemon juice. Roast 30 minutes on rack in shallow pan. Combine tomato puree, onion, soy sauce, vinegar, Tabasco and mustard. Roast game hens additional 30 minutes, brushing with spice mixture every 10 minutes. Hens are done when legs can be easily moved. Peel avocado and cut into lengthwise slices. Brush with lemon juice. Peel oranges and separate into segments. Place game hens on warmed platter. Garnish with alternating slices of avocado and orange.

Chris Spielmann (Mrs. Robert J.)

SEAFOOD and FISH

Marge Bubeck

**CANTON STREET STORES
CANTON STREET
Circa 1920**

CANTON STREET STORES

The Canton Street Stores in uptown, or north, Roswell were developed several decades later than downtown Roswell, location of the Roswell Stores and Square. An early resident recalls, "in the olden days, uptown and downtown Roswell seemed as far apart as Roswell is from Alpharetta."

One of the town's four public water wells was located near the park and intersection of Canton Street, Elizabeth Way, and Alpharetta Street. Other wells were located at the river and Roswell Road, near the bandstand on the square, and at the school adjacent to the Roswell Presbyterian Church.

A harness shop where buggies, wagons, and caskets were made, was on Alpharetta Road at Norcross Street. Original stores on Elizabeth Way, dating from the 1880's, are discernible from early photographs, although the facades have been altered. The most significant is the Perry Building, a two-story brick structure with a columned Victorian veranda built in the 1890's by Charles Jefferson Perry. It was a general store selling hats, shoes, dry goods, and notions.

Charles Perry was instrumental in organizing the Citizens Bank of Roswell on Elizabeth Way, no longer in operation. He also built a substantial two-story home on land acquired from Hugh W. Proudfoot, at Canton Road and Martin's Ferry, now Woodstock Road. The home has been restored and adapted for offices.

Uptown Roswell stores all have interesting architectural details and are historically significant to Roswell's heritage.

BEST FISHING IN ROSWELL

The backwaters of the Chattahoochee River which actually form lakes or oxbows, Oxbow Dam on Vickery Creek and private ponds.

Bass, crappie, chain pickerel, red breast, channel catfish, and since the building of Lake Lanier, rainbow trout and yellow perch.

Typical fish fry might include filleted catfish, slaw, French fries, fried onion rings, hush puppies and ice cold beer.

Shrimp and Crab Okra Gumbo

Serves 6

Gumbo crabs are the hard shell crabs used for cooking. Any hard shell crab available in your area can be used. Whether you eat the cooked crab served in the gumbo is a matter of taste....some of us do and some of us don't. A delightful and slightly extravagant variation is to use lump crab meat or crab claws in addition to or as a substitute for hard shell crabs. The sausage in this gumbo adds a fine smokey flavor. Reserve half the shrimp and, if you use it, half the lump crab meat. Add them just a few minutes before the end of the cooking time. Your gumbo will have both the cooked-in taste of shrimp and also good firm shrimp for eating. Be sure to have everything else ready before you start the roux because you can't do all the chopping and tend the roux at the same time! The more seafood the better!

Roux

½ **cup vegetable oil**
½ **cup flour**

Roux: Heat oil in heavy 6 to 8-quart pot over medium heat. Gradually add flour, stirring constantly. Cook over low heat, always stirring, until roux is a medium brown color (20-30 minutes).

Gumbo Base

1 **cup chopped onion**
½ **cup chopped green pepper**
¼ **cup thinly sliced scallion**
   tops
1 **tablespoon minced fresh**
   parsley
1 **tablespoon minced garlic**
1 **cup coarsely chopped creole**
   (beefsteak) tomatoes
1 **creole (Polish, French garlic)**
   smoked sausage, chopped fine
1 **pound fresh raw shrimp, peeled**
   and deveined
½ **to 1 pound gumbo crabs,**
   broken in half-crab claws
½ **pound okra, sliced 3/8"**
   thick

Gumbo Base: To the roux immediately add onion, green pepper, scallion tops, parsley and garlic. Cook about 10 minutes, stirring constantly. Vegetables should be lightly browned. Add tomatoes and sausage and mix thoroughly. Add ½ pound shrimp, half the crabs, and the okra.

(continued on next page)

Liquid and Seasonings

(continued from previous page)
1¼ quarts cold water
1½ bay leaves, crushed
¾ teaspoon thyme
2½ teaspoons salt
¾ teaspoon freshly ground black
   pepper
1/8 teaspoon cayenne
2 teaspoons lemon juice
5 whole allspice
¼ teaspoon mace
4 whole cloves

Liquid and Seasonings: To base add 1 quart water and seasonings. Bring mixture to a boil; lower heat and simmer 1 hour. Stir occasionally, scraping down sides and bottom to prevent scorching. At end of hour add remaining ¼ quart cold water and stir. Remove pot from heat and let stand at room temperature about 15 minutes. Before serving bring gumbo to a boil; add remaining shrimp and crab. Simmer until shrimp turn pink (10-12 minutes). Stir well, turn off heat and cover pot. Let sit about 15 minutes. Serve over mounds of rice in gumbo or deep soup bowls.

Lee David

Steamed Clams Bordelaise

Serves 6

Serve in soup bowls with crusty French bread.

4 pounds clams
½ cup chopped scallions
2 garlic cloves, minced
1 stick butter
2 cups dry white wine
salt and pepper to taste
2 tablespoons chopped parsley
   (Italian is best)

Scrub clams under running cold water; set aside. In large kettle saute scallions and garlic in butter until tender but not browned. Add wine, salt and pepper. Bring to rapid boil; add clams. Cover and cook 5 to 7 minutes or until shells are open. Shake pan frequently. Stir in parsley and serve.

Billie Boyles (Mrs. T.W.)

Crab Fondue

Yield: 2 cups

8 ounces cream cheese
½ cup mayonnaise
2 tablespoons grated onion
½ teaspoon horseradish
1 teaspoon confectioners' sugar
6-8 ounces crab meat
sherry or white wine
French bread cubes

Combine all ingredients except wine and bread; heat slightly. Add crab meat. Add sherry or white wine to proper consistency for fondue. Salt and pepper to taste. French bread cubes are great for dipping.

Joan Mars (Mrs. Martin)

94

Crab Quiche Casserole

Serves 10-12
350° oven

3 cups grated zucchini or
  yellow squash
1 cup crab meat (tuna or shrimp)
1 small onion, chopped
8 ounces fresh mushrooms,
  chopped
1 cup Bisquick
4 large eggs, beaten
½ cup oil
½ cup Parmesan cheese
1 teaspoon chopped parsley

Mix all ingredients. Place in greased 9 x 12-inch pan. Bake at 350° for 30 minutes.

Laurie Engel (Mrs. Herbert)

Crab Meat Casserole

Serves 6
350° oven

1 (6½ ounce) can crab meat,
  drained and flaked
1 (5 ounce) can shrimp, drained
1 cup chopped celery
¼ cup chopped green pepper
2 tablespoons chopped onion
¾ cup mayonnaise
1 teaspoon Worcestershire sauce
½ teaspoon salt
dash pepper
1 cup soft bread crumbs
1 tablespoon butter, melted

Mix together all ingredients except bread crumbs and butter. Pour into 1½-quart buttered casserole. Mix bread crumbs and butter and sprinkle over top. Bake at 350° for 35 minutes.

Lucile Wing Hockenhull

Crab-Shrimp Bake

Serves 8
350° oven

1 medium green pepper, chopped
1 medium onion, chopped
1 cup chopped celery
1 (6½ or 7½ ounce) can crab
  meat
1 cup cleaned, cooked shrimp
½ teaspoon salt
dash of pepper
1 teaspoon Worcestershire sauce
1 cup mayonnaise
1 cup buttered crumbs

Combine all ingredients except crumbs. Place in individual seashells or greased 2-quart casserole dish. Sprinkle with crumbs. Bake at 350° for 30 minutes.

Rena Morris (Mrs. Clyde)

Crab Cristo Sandwich

Serves 6

Sandwich

1 cup chopped green onion
6 large mushrooms, sliced
6½ tablespoons margarine
1 pound Alaskan King Crab meat
12 slices sour dough bread
18 ounces Swiss cheese
6 ounces Crab Cristo Sauce

Egg Wash

6 eggs
¾ cup milk

Crab Cristo Sauce

4 ounces sour cream
4 tablespoons horseradish
1 tablespoon chives
dash white pepper
dash paprika

Sauté onions and mushrooms in margarine 10 minutes. Add crab meat and sauté 5 minutes more. Remove from stove and cool. On each slice of bread place 1½ ounces shredded Swiss cheese. On each of 6 slices put 3 ounces of crab mixture. Place other 6 slices on top. Dip in egg wash and grill. Serve with one ounce Crab Cristo Sauce per sandwich.

Sauce: Mix all ingredients with a wire whip until well mixed.

Public House Restaurant
Roswell Square

Crab Meat au Gratin

Serves 6
325° oven

4 tablespoons butter
4 tablespoons flour
1 cup heavy cream
1 cup milk
¾ cup freshly grated Parmesan
  cheese
salt and pepper to taste
1 pound lump crab meat
¼ cup freshly grated Parmesan
  cheese

Melt butter; add flour, stirring constantly, to make smooth roux. Slowly stir in heated cream and milk. When sauce is smooth, add ¾ cup cheese. Add desired salt and pepper after tasting. Fold in crab meat. Pour into baking dish. Sprinkle remaining cheese on top. Bake at 325° about 45-50 minutes until brown.

Paul Moss, RHS President 1980

Shrimp and Rice

Serves 6-8

1 (10 ounce) box yellow rice
1 stick butter
1 pound medium shrimp, peeled
  and deveined
salt
pepper

Cook rice slowly until almost tender. Add butter and shrimp. Cook 25 minutes more. Add salt and pepper to taste.

Marion Melton (Mrs. Bruce)

Seafood Casserole

Serves 12
350° oven

1½ cups cooked brown rice
  (a little over 1 cup raw)
2 cans mushroom soup
⅔ cup mayonnaise
1½ pounds shrimp (10 ounce
  package frozen)
1 can white crab meat
1 can sliced water chestnuts
½ cup chopped spring onions
⅔ cup celery (put through
  blender)
¼ teaspoon cayenne pepper
¼ teaspoon nutmeg
salt and pepper to taste

Mix together all ingredients. If it seems dry, add a little milk. May top with grated cheddar cheese. Bake in 9 x 12-inch greased casserole for 1 hour at 350°.

Dorcas David (Mrs. John H., Sr.)

Shrimp a La Palmer

Serves 8

Makes a very nice entrée served over rice or Chinese noodles.

½ pound mushrooms, sliced
1 pound shrimp, cooked and
  cleaned
½ pound scallops (bay, if
  possible)
1 pound crab meat
1 large green pepper, minced
1 (8 ounce) can water chestnuts,
  quartered
3 tablespoons butter
4 tablespoons flour
¼ teaspoon salt
¼ cup dry sherry
¾ cup light cream
2 cans shrimp soup (frozen is
  best)

Sauté mushrooms. Mix with next five ingredients. Set aside. Make white sauce by melting butter, stirring in flour and salt. Gradually add sherry and cream, stirring briskly and constantly. Stir in soup. Combine with mixture that was set aside.

Peggy Swenson

Shrimp Curry with Sauce

Serves 4-6

Shrimp and sauce may be prepared and refrigerated (separately) a day ahead.

Shrimp

1½ pounds medium large shrimp
  (40 count to pound)
3 tablespoons vinegar
¾ teaspoon salt
1 bay leaf
parsley sprigs
1 celery stalk, with leaves
1 carrot, cut in half

Shrimp: Cook shrimp by boiling 3 minutes in water to cover with the next 6 ingredients. Peel and clean shrimp. Set aside.

Sauce

3 beef bouillon cubes
2 cups boiling water
3 teaspoons curry powder
¾ teaspoon ginger
3 strips bacon
1 medium onion, minced
½ sour apple, minced
½ cup medium white sauce made
  by using 1 tablespoon fat, 1
  tablespoon flour, ½ cup milk
  and pinch salt
rice to serve 4-6

Sauce: Dissolve bouillon cubes in water. Add curry and ginger and cook 5 minutes. Fry bacon, remove and crumble. Fry onion and apple. Make white sauce as directed and mix with bouillon liquid, bacon, onion, apple and cook over low heat for 10 minutes. Add shrimp and let stand several hours.

Condiments

Chopped hard cooked egg mixed with crumbled bacon, shredded moistened coconut, chopped ginger mixed with chopped walnuts, chutney sauce made with mangoes, raisins, etc.

To serve: Reheat. Serve with rice and condiments.

Gerald B. Warthen

Shrimp Soufflé

Serves 6
350° oven

Draws raves! Best if made the night before.

6 slices white bread
½ pound Old English cheese slices
1 pound (or more) shrimp, cooked
   and cleaned
4 tablespoons melted butter
3 eggs
½ teaspoon dry mustard
salt to taste
cayenne pepper to taste
2 cups milk

Break bread and cheese into bite size pieces. Arrange bread, cheese and shrimp in several layers (starting with bread on bottom) in buttered 8-inch square casserole. Pour melted butter on top. Beat eggs with mustard, salt and cayenne. Add milk. Mix and pour over all. Let stand at least 3 hours (better overnight) covered and refrigerated. Bake covered at 350° for one hour. Uncover and brown the last few minutes. NOTE: If doubling recipe, use 3 pounds shrimp.

Tillie Wood (Mrs. Roy)

Shrimp Casserole

Serves 8

May be prepared ahead of time.

6 slices bread, cubed
salt and pepper
dry mustard
2 (4¼ ounce) cans shrimp, drained
2 cups grated cheddar cheese
4 eggs
2 cups milk

Place cubed bread in bottom of a buttered 14 x 10 x 2-inch baking dish and sprinkle with seasonings. Add shrimp and cheese. Beat eggs with milk and pour over all. Bake in shallow pan containing about an inch of water for 1 hour at 350°.

Jean Sentinella (Mrs. Alan)

Perfect Boiled Shrimp

Serves 2

The S & W Seafood Company people recommended preparing shrimp like this and it's perfect every time! Excellent peeling and eating!

1 pound shrimp, unpeeled
2 tablespoons Old Bay Seasoning, or 1 bag Zatarains Shrimp
   and Crab Boil

In large pot place 3 quarts water and seasoning. Bring to full boil. Add unpeeled shrimp. Bring to boil again. Boil exactly 1½ minutes. Remove pot from heat. Keep shrimp in water exactly 30 minutes. Drain and chill. Peel and eat or proceed with favorite recipe.

Denny and Darlene Walsh

99

Scalloped Oysters

Serves 6
350° oven

2 cups bread or cracker crumbs
½ cup butter
1 pint oysters
1 teaspoon salt
1/8 teaspoon pepper
1 cup milk

Roll crumbs fine. Melt butter, mix with crumbs and set aside. Mix oysters, salt, pepper and milk. Spread ⅓ of the crumbs in bottom of 1½-quart baking dish. Cover with half the oysters, then another ⅓ of the crumbs, remaining oysters and top with remaining crumbs. Bake 20-30 minutes at 350°.

Eva Clement (Mrs. P. E.)

Very Simple Scallops

Serves 4
500° oven

1½ pounds scallops, cut into
    small pieces
3 tablespoons finely chopped
    onions
1 small clove garlic, minced
6 tablespoons butter
¼ cup dry white wine
1 tablespoon chopped parsley
½ cup fine dry bread crumbs

Preheat oven to 500°. Combine scallops with onion and garlic. Melt 4 tablespoons butter and add scallop mixture. Cook over brisk heat, stirring, 2 or 3 minutes. Add wine and parsley. Mix in all but 3 tablespoons of the bread crumbs and simmer gently 2 minutes. Divide among 4 scallop shells. Mix remaining crumbs and butter; sprinkle on top. Cook 3 minutes at 500° (until lightly browned).

Connie Lindstrom (Mrs. Kelsey C.)

Grilled Catfish Fillets

Serves 2
grill

2 pounds catfish fillets
1 stick butter, melted
chopped fresh onion
1-2 ounces dry vermouth
parsley

Place fillets in aluminum foil tray. Spread with melted butter and chopped onion. Splash with vermouth. Place on grill over hot coals. Cook 8 minutes per side. When turning baste with butter and replace onions to top side. Garnish with parsley.

Denny and Darlene Walsh

100

Flounder Foldovers

Serves 4-6
350° oven

2 pounds flounder fillets
1 teaspoon salt
¼ teaspoon pepper
1 cup shredded mozzarella cheese
oregano
1 (8 ounce) can tomato sauce
  with onions
1 tablespoon butter
1 tablespoon dry bread crumbs

Soak fish in heavily salted water at least 2 hours. Then sprinkle both sides with salt and pepper. Put some cheese and oregano at one end of each fillet. Fold over. Place in greased 10 x 10 x 2-inch baking dish. Pour tomato sauce on top. Dot with butter and sprinkle with bread crumbs. Bake at 350° for 25-30 minutes (until fish flakes).

Lucy Yankee (Mrs. Paul)

Alaska Salmon with Dill Sauce

Serves 4
broiler

Can be made on the charcoal grill also.

½ stick margarine
1 small onion, sliced
juice of one lemon
1 pound salmon fillets
  or steaks
2 tablespoons snipped dill
½ cup sour cream
2 tablespoons snipped dill

In small saucepan combine margarine, onion and lemon juice. Cook until onion is transparent. Arrange salmon in oiled broiler pan. Cover with half the onion mixture. Broil 5 minutes. Turn over. Spread remaining onion mixture on second side and add 2 tablespoons dill. Broil 5 minutes. Remove fish to platter and top with warmed mixture of sour ceam and dill.

Marie Mitchler (Mrs. H. G.)

Salmon Mousse

Serves 8

1 (15 ounce) can pink salmon
2 packages plain gelatin
5 teaspoons lemon juice
½ cup boiling water
1 cup chopped celery
2 teaspoons dehydrated onion
  flakes
1 teaspoon chopped parsley
1 (12 ounce) container cream
  cheese
1 teaspoon salt
¼ teaspoon pepper
chopped olives

Drain salmon and remove bones. Soften gelatin with lemon juice and add boiling water. Blend well. Add remaining ingredients; blend. Chill overnight in mold or 10 x 6 x 2-inch baking dish.

Dorothy S. Speir

101

Salmon Loaf with Olive Sauce

Serves 4
350° oven

1 (15½ ounce) can pink salmon
½ can cream of celery soup
1 cup cracker or bread crumbs
2 eggs
1 small onion, finely minced
1 stalk celery, finely minced
black pepper
4 tablespoons mayonnaise
salt

Drain salmon and reserve juice. Mix celery soup with reserved juice and pour over crumbs; mix. Add eggs, onion, celery, pepper and mayonnaise; mix well. Remove bones and skin from salmon, flake and add to previous mixture. Salt to taste. Place in a loaf pan or casserole. Bake at 350° about 45 minutes.

Olive Sauce

½ can cream of celery soup
½ cup milk
2 teaspoons cornstarch
3 tablespoons mayonnaise
1 (3 ounce) jar olives, sliced
½ juice from jar of olives

Sauce: Blend soup and milk. Cook until smooth. Add remaining ingredients. Turn out salmon loaf, slice and pour sauce over it.

Pamela H. Mundale (Mrs. D. O.)

Salmon Mousse

Serves 12-16

Perfect pièce de résistance for a buffet style luncheon! Prepare the day before.

8 ounces cream cheese, softened
1 can tomato soup
2 packages unflavored gelatin,
    softened in ¼ cup cold water
½ teaspoon salt
¼ teaspoon white pepper
1 tablespoon Worcestershire
    sauce
1 cup bland mayonnaise
1 medium green pepper, minced
    fine
1 cup celery, minced fine
1 medium onion, grated
1 pound can salmon, drained,
    boned and flaked
olive slices
parsley

Grease 5-quart fish mold with cooking oil. Dissolve cream cheese in tomato soup over low heat, stirring constantly. Add softened gelatin to soup mix and stir well. Add salt, pepper, Worcestershire sauce and mayonnaise. Mix well. Stir in green pepper, celery and onion. Mix well. Remove from heat. Add salmon and pour into fish mold. Cool on cake rack one hour. Cover and refrigerate overnight. To serve, chill serving platter at least one hour. Unmold. Use olive slices for "eyes" and surround with a "sea" of parsley.

Marie B. DeVane (Mrs. Ernest E.)

Tuna Casserole

Serves 12-16
325° oven

Freezes well.

2 (6½ ounce) cans tuna
2 (10¾ ounce) cans mushroom
  soup
1 can water chestnuts, chopped
2 cups diced celery
1 cup chopped onions
1 cup chopped parsley
¼ pound cashew nuts, chopped
¾ cup water or liquid from water
  chestnuts
1 can slivered almonds
2 (10¾ ounce) cans dry Chinese
  noodles

Mix together all ingredients, adding noodles last. Bake in 325° oven about 45 minutes (until heated through). May be easily reduced by half for a small group.

Martha W. Stovall

Tuna Fish Soufflé

Serves 4
325° oven

Green salad and potato chips go well with this soufflé.

3 tablespoons butter or margarine
3 tablespoons flour
dash salt
pepper to taste
1 cup chicken broth
3 eggs, separated
1 tablespoon sherry (optional)
1 (7 ounce) can tuna

Melt butter in saucepan. Stir in flour, salt and pepper. Slowly add chicken broth, stirring and cooking until it thickens. Remove from stove. Add egg yolks, sherry and tuna. Whip egg whites until stiff and fold into tuna mixture. Pile into 4 small casseroles or 1 large casserole. Bake at 325° until brown and springy to touch (20-30 minutes).

Grace E. Berger

Quick Tuna Dinner

Serves 4

Delicious over rice.

¾ stick butter
1 clove garlic, minced
1 onion, chopped
1 tablespoon curry powder
1 (8 ounce) can tomato sauce
salt and pepper to taste
¼ cup white wine
¼ cup water
1 (7 ounce) can tuna

Melt butter in skillet and sauté garlic and onion. Add all other ingredients except tuna. Cook until a little thickened (about 5-10 minutes). Mix in tuna. Serve over cooked rice.

Joan Soldavini (Mrs. Alfred)

Tuna Stuffed Zucchini

Serves 4
375⁰ oven

4 zucchini (1½ pounds)
½ cup chopped onion
½ cup chopped celery
3 tablespoons melted butter
½ cup soft bread crumbs
1 (3½ ounce) can tuna,
　drained and flaked
½ teaspoon salt
1 teaspoon fresh lemon juice
1/8 teaspoon pepper

Parboil zucchini in boiling water 5 minutes; drain. Cut zucchini in half lengthwise. Scoop out pulp leaving a ¼-inch shell. Chop pulp; saute with onion and celery in butter until tender. Mix in bread crumbs, tuna, salt, lemon juice, and pepper. Place zucchini shells on greased baking sheet. Fill shells with tuna mixture. Bake at 375⁰ for 25 minutes.

Judi Doud Morris (Mrs. David)

EGGS, CHEESE, PASTA and RICE

Janet Rothberg

BARRINGTON HALL
MARIETTA STREET
Circa 1842

BARRINGTON HALL

Barrington Hall, typifying the beauty and grace of the true Southern mansion, commands a view of the Roswell Square and Mill Village, as it has since 1842. Fourteen fluted Doric columns tower above a massive portico on three sides of the home, an example of Greek Revival architecture in its most classic form.

The balustraded captain's walk, with its breathtaking view of the surrounding countryside, links the home to its New England heritage. The home was built for Barrington King, co-founder of the town with his father, Roswell King.

Doric columns support an archway dividing front and rear halls opening to large rooms on either side. Upstairs bedrooms to the East view the original boxwood gardens laid out by Francis Minhinnet, a stone mason from Plymouth, England.

The cottage in which the King family first lived, later became the kitchen. Barrington Hall originally had forty acres of land, with gardens, fruit trees, and arbors. On the property were barns, servants' quarters, smoke house, ice house, and wells.

An inside kitchen was added in the late 1870's, and cooking was done on a wood stove. Fond memories still linger of thin, crisp wafers baked on long-handled irons, of peeling them off while still hot and rolling them into wafers.

Barrington Hall is listed on the National Register of Historic places.

OLD SOUTH SUMMER BREAKFAST AT BARRINGTON HALL

Chilled Scuppernong Juice
Smoked Country Ham, Sliced and Fried
Eggs Cooked, Sunny Side Up, in Fresh Churned Butter
Fried Hominy Grits* Served with a Choice of
Wild Strawberry Jam, Fig Preserves, Clabber, Honey
or Syrup
Bowl of Fresh Figs Sprinkled with Sugar
Hot Biscuits

Coffee   Milk

Fried Hominy Grits

Serves 6-12

Old South breakfast favorite enjoyed at Barrington Hall. Grits can be eaten plain, but more commonly topped with choice of clabber, wild strawberry jam, fig or scuppernong preserves, syrup or honey.

**1-2 cups hominy grits
egg batter (1 egg to 1 tablespoon
    milk or water)
flour
butter**

Prepare grits according to instructions on package. Pour into pan to ½-inch thickness. Let stand overnight. Next morning grits will be firm. Cut into 3 x 2-inch strips. Dip in egg batter and flour lightly. Fry in butter on both sides until slightly brown.

**Miss Katharine Simpson
Miss Lois Simpson**

Omelette

Serves 1

**2-3 eggs
salt and white pepper
1-2 tablespoons butter
2 tablespoons Gruyere or
    Parmesan cheese
sprinkling of thyme, freshly
    chopped (optional)
sprinkling of parsley, freshly
    chopped (optional)**

Beat eggs with salt and pepper. Heat omelet pan or small skillet. When hot, add butter and coat bottom and sides of pan completely. When butter has sizzled, but before it browns, quickly add eggs and stir with one hand while shaking pan with other hand. When eggs are no longer runny, spread cheese and herbs over them and fold one third of omelet toward the center. Turn it out on plate folding over other third.

John David III

Bachelor's Brunch

Serves 8
350° oven

**1 pound sausage (extra hot)
bread slices, cubed
1 cup grated cheddar cheese
    (extra sharp)
6 eggs, slightly beaten
2 cups milk
1 teaspoon salt
1 teaspoon dry mustard
pepper to taste**

Brown sausage. Pour off grease. Make layer of bread cubes to cover bottom of 9 x 13-inch casserole dish. Make one layer sausage, one layer cheese. Beat eggs slightly. Add milk. Add salt, dry mustard and pepper. Mix well. Pour over layers. Cover and refrigerate 12 hours. Bake, covered, at 350° for one hour.

Martha Mansell

Huevos Rancheros

Serves 4

Eggs, Ranch Style!

1 tablespoon onion, minced
2 tablespoons oil
1 small clove garlic, peeled
½ teaspoon oregano
2 small piquant green chilies
   or 2 tablespoons bell pepper,
   chopped, with 2 drops Tabasco
   sauce or 2 tablespoons
   salsa jalapeño
1 (8 ounce) can tomato sauce
salt
4 eggs

Sauté onion in oil. Add remaining ingredients except eggs. Simmer a few minutes. Poach eggs in sauce or fry sunny side up separately and pour sauce over them. NOTE: You may fry four tortillas until hard and crisp. Put a fried egg on each tortilla and pour tomato sauce over top. Garnish with slices of avocado.

Bobbie Pridmore

Eggs in Spice Cheese Sauce

Serves 10-12
350° oven

18 eggs, hard cooked
½ pound bacon
¼ cup butter
¼ cup flour
1 cup light cream
1 cup milk
1 pound grated sharp cheddar
   cheese
1 small garlic clove, crushed
¼ teaspoon thyme
¼ teaspoon marjoram
¼ teaspoon basil
¼ cup chopped parsley
buttered bread crumbs

Peel cooled eggs and slice thinly. Sauté bacon until crisp. Drain and crumble. Make cream sauce by melting butter; add flour; then add light cream and milk slowly. Cook until thickened. Add cheese, stirring until cheese is melted. Season with spices. Pour some of sauce into greased 9 x 13-inch baking dish. Add layer of egg slices, then layer of bacon. Alternate until all is used. Sprinkle with buttered bread crumbs. Bake at 350° for about 20 minutes until bubbly and browned.

Mamie Burleigh

Eggs Supreme

Serves 6

Makes a great brunch with biscuits, fruit and champagne!

½ pound bacon, cut in small
    pieces
½ green pepper, chopped
1 onion, chopped
2 medium potatoes, cooked and
    sliced
10 eggs, beaten
6 ounces Monterey Jack cheese,
    shredded

Brown bacon in skillet; drain and RESERVE 3 tablespoons bacon drippings. Sauté green pepper and onion in 1 tablespoon drippings. Remove from skillet. Brown potatoes in 2 tablespoons drippings. Add bacon, green pepper, onion and eggs to potatoes. Mix and scramble over low heat. When eggs are almost set, sprinkle with cheese. Cover until cheese melts. Serve immediately.

Gloria Foos (Mrs. Rocky)

Brunch Egg Casserole

Serves 6
325° oven

2 cups croutons
1 cup shredded cheddar cheese
4 eggs
2 cups milk
½ teaspoon salt
½ teaspoon prepared mustard
1/8 teaspoon onion powder
dash pepper
4 slices cooked bacon, crumbled

Combine croutons and cheese in greased 10 x 6 x 2-inch baking dish. Beat eggs; add milk and seasonings. Pour over crouton mixture in casserole. Sprinkle bacon over top. Bake in 325° oven for one hour or until eggs are set. Garnish with bacon curls, if desired.

Jean McFarland (Mrs. Charles)

Quiche

Serves 6-8
350° oven

½ pound bacon, cooked and
    crumbled
2 cups chopped onions
1 medium green pepper, chopped
1½ cups milk, scalded
½ pound cheddar cheese, grated
3 eggs, beaten
1 teaspoon salt
¼ teaspoon pepper
1 teaspoon Worcestershire sauce
pastry crust, uncooked

Mix all ingredients and pour into uncooked pastry crust. Bake at 350° for 50 minutes.

Susan Finley (Mrs. Allen R.)

Ham and Spinach Quiche

Serves 6
350° oven

9-inch unbaked pie shell
2 slices Swiss cheese
  (7 x 4 inches)
½ cup chopped spinach
½ cup sliced mushrooms
3 eggs, beaten
1 cup half and half
½ teaspoon salt
2 teaspoons flour
1 (6¾ ounce) can Hormel chunk
  ham, flaked
¼ cup shredded cheddar cheese

Place Swiss cheese slices in un-baked pie shell. Sprinkle with spinach and mushrooms. Mix eggs, half and half, salt and flour. Pour in-to pie shell. Sprinkle evenly with ham, then cheddar cheese. Bake in 350° oven for 45 minutes.

Jane Carter (Mrs. S. J.)

Crab Quiche

Serves 6-8
375° oven

8 ounces crab meat
3 tablespoons butter
3 large green onions, minced
1 teaspoon salt
¼ teaspoon pepper
2 tablespoons dry vermouth
3 eggs
1 cup half and half
1 tablespoon tomato paste
½ cup grated Swiss cheese
10-inch baked pie shell

Melt butter in skillet. Add onions and ½ cup water. Boil until all the water is gone and onions are soft. Add salt, pepper, crab, vermouth and bring to boil. Beat eggs, half and half, tomato paste to mix. Stir in crab mixture. Pour into baked shell. Add cheese on top. Bake at 375°, 25 to 30 minutes or until inserted knife comes out clean. This may be made and frozen to bake later.

Martha Knight (Mrs. J. T.)

Baked Eggs Fondue

Serves 6
325° oven

6 slices day old bread
butter
2 cups milk
1 cup grated cheddar cheese
¼ teaspoon salt
½ teaspoon dry mustard
3 eggs, slightly beaten
3 slices bacon, cooked crisp and
  crumbled

Lightly butter bread slices. Cut into cubes and line a buttered 10 x 6-inch baking dish. Mix remaining ingre-dients, except bacon, and pour over bread. Bake at 325° for one hour. Sprinkle bacon over top.

Susan Finley (Mrs. Allen R.)

Greek Cheese Pie

**Serves 8
425° oven, crust
350° oven, filling**

Food processor recipe that may be made early in day and reheated.

9-inch unbaked pie shell
¾ pound feta cheese, cut into
    small pieces
1 cup light cream
3 eggs
½ teaspoon dried thyme leaves
1 teaspoon cornstarch
1 small clove garlic, crushed
9 large pitted ripe olives
9 large pitted green olives
1 pimiento, cut into strips

Preheat oven to 425°. Bake shell 10 minutes; cool. Blend cheese with cream and eggs in bowl of processor with steel blade. Process 30 seconds. Add thyme, cornstarch; pulse to blend. Add garlic; pulse. Pour into shell. Bake pie 10 minutes. Arrange olives on top. Bake 25 minutes longer or until filling is set. Decorate with pimiento; serve warm. NOTE: Goes great with a green salad and Chablis.

Peggy Cottam

Main Course Cheese Cobbler

**Serves 6
400° oven**

1 cup sifted flour
2 teaspoons baking powder
½ teaspoon soda
¼ cup sugar
¾ teaspoon salt
1 cup yellow cornmeal
1 tablespoon dehydrated or
    minced onion
2 eggs
1 cup buttermilk
¼ cup soft shortening
1½ cups shredded sharp
    processed cheese
1 cup sour cream

Combine in medium bowl flour, baking powder, soda, sugar and salt. Stir in cornmeal and onions. Add eggs, buttermilk and shortening, beating with egg beater about one minute. DO NOT OVERBEAT. Pour into well-buttered 9 x 9 x 2-inch pan or casserole. In small mixing bowl, combine shredded cheese with sour cream, mixing well. Drop by tablespoons over top of cornbread batter. Bake at 400° for 25 minutes or until firm.

**Colleen Briesemeister
(Mrs. Edward)**

Cheese Soufflé

Serves 6-8
350° oven

Must be prepared the night before.

½ pound butter
8 slices bread, cut in cubes
5 eggs
2 cups milk
small (2½-4 ounce) can or jar of mushrooms
10 ounces grated sharp cheese
1 can cream of mushroom soup
¾ can evaporated milk

Melt butter in 9 x 13-inch casserole dish. Add bread cubes. Mix eggs and 2 cups milk. Add drained mushrooms. Pour mixture over bread cubes. Sprinkle cheese over top. Refrigerate overnight. Mix together soup and ¾ can milk. Pour over casserole. Bake at 350° for 45 minutes.

Judy Miller (Mrs. Kent W.)

Baked Cheese Sandwiches

Serves 2
325° oven

Must prepare the day before.

4 slices bread
butter
mustard
1 cup grated cheese
1 cup milk
2 eggs
1 tablespoon minced onion
1 tablespoon parsley
1 tablespoon Worcestershire sauce

Spread 2 slices of bread with butter and other 2 slices with mustard. Put grated cheese between slices, making 2 sandwiches. Place in baking dish. Mix remaining ingredients and pour over sandwiches. Cover and refrigerate overnight. Bake approximately 1 hour in preheated 325° oven.

Jo Rudolph (Mrs. Edwin L.)

Emory's 1939 Vienna-Honeymoon-Cheese Snack

Yield: 3 snacks
broiler

1 cored apple, sliced round
butter or margarine
3 slices bread
1 can Vienna sausages
3 slices American cheese

Fry apple slices in butter until slightly brown and limp. Toast and butter bread. Place an apple slice on each piece of toast. Stack 2 Vienna sausages on apple and warm slightly under broiler. Cover with slice of cheese and broil until cheese melts. Serve garnished with leftover apple slices. One for the bride, two for the groom!

Emory Lunsford

English Muffin Cheese Broils

Serves 4

Super lunch or late evening snack.

- 4 ounces cheddar cheese, grated
- 10 slices bacon, fried and
  crumbled
- 1 tablespoon grated onion
- mayonnaise
- 1 package English muffins

Moisten cheese, bacon and onion with mayonnaise. Broil split muffins lightly on both sides. Spread cheese mixture on muffin halves. Broil until bubbly. Mixture may be prepared in advance.

Betsy Altman (Mrs. Robert E.)

Stuffed Shells

Serves 6
350° oven

Serve with Chicken Supreme, salad and Italian bread. Can be prepared the night before.

- 1 (16 ounce) package pasta shells
- 2 pounds ricotta cheese
- ½ pound mozzarella cheese,
  shredded
- 2 large eggs
- ½ cup grated Parmesan cheese
- 1 tablespoon chopped parsley
- 1 teaspoon salt
- ½ teaspoon pepper
- ½ teaspoon nutmeg (optional)
- ¼ cup melted butter or
  marinara sauce

Parboil shells 9 minutes in salted water. Drain in colander. Mix all remaining ingredients until well blended and fill parboiled shells with knife or spoon. Arrange shells side by side in single layer in baking dish. Cover with melted butter or marinara sauce and bake at 350° for 30 minutes.

Mary Jane Zaccheo (Mrs. John N.)

Noodles Alfredo (Fettucini)

Serves 6-8

- ½ cup butter
- ½ cup cream
- salt and pepper
- 1 (8 ounce) package medium
  noodles, cooked
- ½ cup Parmesan cheese
- ¼ cup shredded Swiss cheese

Melt butter in small pan. Add cream, salt and pepper. Heat thoroughly. Pour over hot cooked noodles. Add cheeses and mix lightly. Serve at once.

Betty Bell (Mrs. William J.)

Macaroni and Cheese

Serves 6-8
300° oven

Custard-like texture.

2 cups macaroni
2 cups milk
8-10 ounces Velveeta cheese
3 beaten eggs
grated cheddar or Swiss cheese

Cook macaroni according to package directions. Place in 2-quart casserole. Heat milk and Velveeta cheese slowly. Add eggs after cheese melts. Pour mixture over macaroni. Bake at 300° until done. Top with cheddar or Swiss cheese and brown.

Lee Spence

Fried Rice

Serves 8
375° oven

1½ cups rice
½ stick butter or margarine
3 cups bouillon (use 4 cubes
    to 3 cups water)
¾ cup grated carrots
¾ cup diced celery
¾ cup chopped parsley
    (or 2 teaspoons dehydrated)
½ cup slivered almonds

Brown rice in butter. Add bouillon. Bake in covered 1½-quart casserole 30 minutes. Stir in vegetables and nuts. Cover and bake 10 minutes more. NOTE: When vegetables are added, if rice looks dry, add about ½ cup water.

Burma Denny (Mrs. J. B.)

Green Rice That Waits

Serves 6

If rice must wait on dinner, turn into casserole with tight fitting lid and place in warm oven until time to serve.

4 tablespoons butter or margarine
4-5 green onions, tops and all,
    finely chopped
½ green pepper, finely chopped
⅓ cup minced fresh parsley
3 cups chicken broth or bouillon
    cubes and hot water
1½ cups long grain rice
¼ teaspoon salt
1/8 teaspoon pepper

Heat butter in saucepan. Add onions and green pepper; saute until tender (5 to 10 minutes). Stir in remaining ingredients; bring to a boil. Reduce heat; check seasonings for taste. Cover and simmer 20 minutes or until done. Rice may be served as soon as tender. NOTE: To serve 10, increase chicken broth to 5 cups and rice to 2½ cups.

Charlotte Hollingsworth (Mrs. L. C.)

Curried Fruit and Rice Mold

Serves 8

Individual molds that go well with any meat or poultry.

½ cup raisins
½ cup dried apricots, snipped
1 tablespoon sugar
½ cup sherry
1 teaspoon curry powder
½ teaspoon salt
2 tablespoons melted butter
3 cups hot rice cooked in chicken broth
¼ cup toasted slivered almonds

Combine raisins, apricots, sugar and sherry. Bring to a boil. Remove from heat and allow to stand about ten minutes. Blend curry powder and salt into butter. Combine fruits, rice, butter mixture and almonds. Toss lightly to blend flavors. Press into individual molds. Let stand over hot water about 5 minutes. Invert on serving plate.

Enid McGaughey (Mrs. John)

Layered Wild Rice-Broccoli Casserole

Serves 6-8
350° oven

1 (5 ounce) Uncle Ben's brown and wild rice with onions and mushrooms
½ cup white rice
2 tablespoons butter
2 tablespoons finely chopped onion
2 tablespoons flour
½ teaspoon salt
1 cup milk
½ cup sour cream
2 (10 ounce) packages frozen broccoli spears
1 cup shredded cheddar cheese
6 slices bacon, fried, drained and crumbled

Prepare rice and set aside. In frying pan, melt butter and sauté onion until soft. Sprinkle in flour and salt; cook over low heat until smooth. Gradually stir in milk until sauce thickens slightly. Fold in sour cream and set aside. Steam broccoli until barely tender; drain well. Mix rices. Layer half of rice in greased 9 x 13-inch casserole. Slice broccoli spears lengthwise and place cut side down over rice, alternating stems and flower heads to left and right. Spoon remaining rice down center of broccoli. Pour white sauce over rice and top with cheese and bacon. (At this point it can be covered and refrigerated to be baked later.) Bake covered, 20 minutes at 350°. Uncover and bake 10 minutes more until cheese is bubbly.

Norma Harris

BISCUITS, CLABBER AND GRITS

Southern breakfasts are legendary and folks here in Roswell enjoy a fine tradition of leisurely morning gatherings with good conversation and good food. Perhaps the most noteworthy invitation to breakfast was extended by Mrs. Evelyn King Baker of Barrington Hall to President Theodore Roosevelt in 1905 when he visited the girlhood home of his mother, Mittie Bulloch. Mrs. Baker had been a dear friend of Mittie and a bridesmaid at her wedding. It was unprecedented at the time for the President to accept an invitation to a private home and word was sent that Mrs. Baker could see the President at a reception at the church. "I sent word that if President Roosevelt did not care enough to come see his mother's old friend, I certainly would not go to see him. That very day I had a lovely visit from the President and his wife.", Mrs. Baker was quoted in the "Atlanta Journal Magazine".

Mrs. Baker, who was the daughter of Barrington King, did serve wonderful hearty breakfasts according to the recollections of her granddaughter, Miss Katharine Baker Simpson. Miss Katharine fondly recalled Grandmother Baker's care and preparation to bring clabber to the breakfast table. They would milk the cows in the evening and set out the milk in a pan to let the cream rise. The next morning Grandmother Baker would dip off the cream to be used at breakfast and let Miss Katharine lick the spoon! Due to lack of refrigeration, the remaining milk would become sour and gelatin-like, resembling a smooth cottage cheese. This then was the clabber. Grandmother Baker would spoon whole pieces into small dishes and serve it with sugar, cream and nutmeg. The leavings in the pan were put into a curd press which had little holes around the edges to allow the whey to squirt out the sides. The whey was fed to the chickens. The curd, which came out in the lovely diamond shape of the press, was transferred to a platter and taken to the table. Grandmother Baker always did the serving and was very generous with the sugar, cream and nutmeg! Fresh fruit, hominy grits and hot biscuits, scrambled eggs on toast, fried potatoes or tomatoes, bacon and sometimes little channel catfish from the river filled hungry tummies of the young children gathered around the dining room table at Barrington Hall. As soon as the children finished their breakfast, they all lined up on a small sofa in the dining room and waited quietly for the grown-ups to finish their meal. Then Grandfather Baker would turn to the family Bible which was kept on a little table nearby and read prayers. Sometimes one of the older children would play hymns on the piano. A gracious beginning to a new day!

VEGETABLES

Dolores Lotze

**ALLENBROOK
ATLANTA STREET
Circa 1840**

ALLENBROOK

From a bluff overlooking Vickery Creek, or Big Creek, Allenbrook served as an office for the Ivy Woolen Mills, located downstream on the banks of the Chattahoochee River. It also served as the home for Theophile Roche, a Frenchman who managed the mills. The simple, two-storied structure, built of heart pine, with solid brick walls eighteen inches thick, stands as structurally sound today as when it was built in the early 1840's.

The brickwork, laid in Flemish bond, testifies to the craftsmanship of the early masons. Cornice and window trim is similar to that of the Roswell Stores, the Old Bricks, and the Old Mill building. The salt-box style of Allenbrook reflects the new England background of Roswell King, the town's founder.

Square pillars and the portico were later additions. Random width heart-pine floors are original, as are the golden pine mantels and brick fireplaces. A narrow free-standing stairway leads to two upstairs bedrooms.

Theophile Roche ran up the French flag in an attempt to save the home and mills from destruction during the Union occupation of Roswell. The home was spared, but the mills were destroyed and Roche was arrested for treason.

Allenbrook was included in the United States Parks Service Chattahoochee River National Recreation Area approved by Congress in 1978.

ALFRESCO LUNCH ON THE TERRACE AT ALLENBROOK

Platter of Thin Sliced Baked Ham
Surrounded by Pickled Peaches
Hot Mustard Sauce
Potato Salad
Asparagus Vinaigrette*
Hot Rolls
Lime Sherbert with a Sprig of Fresh Mint
Hot or Iced Tea with Lemon Slices

Asparagus Vinaigrette
Serves 4

Favorite warm weather vegetable dish. Perfect for patio lunch or supper and very pretty!

1 pound fresh asparagus
Bibb lettuce
1 hard cooked egg, chopped fine
3 slices cooked bacon, crumbled

Boil or steam asparagus until done, but crisp (about 10 minutes). Cool and arrange on bed of Bibb lettuce. Sprinkle with egg and bacon. Just before serving, pour vinaigrette dressing over all.

Vinaigrette Dressing
½ cup olive oil or Wesson oil
3 tablespoons vinegar
1 teaspoon salt
½ teaspoon freshly ground
   pepper
dash cayenne pepper
¼ teaspoon paprika
1 tablespoon pimiento, chopped
   fine
1 tablespoon cucumber pickle,
   chopped fine
¾ tablespoon chopped green
   pepper
½ teaspoon chopped parsley
½ tablespoon chopped olives

Combine oil, vinegar, salt, pepper, cayenne and paprika. Heat thoroughly. Add chopped pimiento, pickle, green pepper, parsley and olives.
Agnes Bell (Mrs. Barnett A., Sr.)
by Laura Bell (Mrs. Barnett A., Jr.)

Artichoke Casserole
Serves 8
425° oven

2 (14 ounce) cans artichoke hearts
4 tablespoons melted butter
⅔ cup mayonnaise
2 tablespoons lemon juice
½ teaspoon celery salt
¼ cup Parmesan cheese
¼ cup sliced almonds

Drain artichoke hearts and place in shallow baking dish. Set aside. In saucepan combine butter, mayonnaise, lemon juice and salt. Whip until smooth. Cook over low heat, stirring constantly, until heated thoroughly. Do not let mixture boil. Pour over artichokes. Sprinkle with almonds and cheese. Bake about 10 minutes.
Peggy Bartleson (Mrs. Evan)

Gratin of Asparagus

Serves 4-6
425° oven

1 to 2 pounds asparagus,
  trimmed, peeled and tied in a
  bundle
4 tablespoons butter
2 tablespoons flour
1 cup milk, heated
¼ cup heavy cream
2 slices cooked ham, chopped
  (optional)
salt and pepper
grated nutmeg
4 to 6 eggs, hard boiled and
  sliced
¼ cup freshly grated cheese
  (preferably Gruyère)
1 tablespoon fresh bread crumbs

Cook asparagus, uncovered, in boiling salted water about 10 minutes (until tender). Drain on kitchen towel and remove tie. Reserve 1 cup asparagus water. In heavy pan melt half the butter. Stir in flour and let bubble a moment or two. Gradually add milk and reserved asparagus water to make a smooth sauce. Simmer 15 minutes or more until sauce is thick. Add cream and ham. Season with salt, pepper and nutmeg. Arrange asparagus in oval gratin dish with sliced eggs on top. Pour sauce over leaving ¼ inch at top of dish so sauce does not boil over. Mix cheese and bread crumbs; scatter over sauce. Melt remaining butter and dribble evenly over top. Bake at 425° about 20 minutes (until dish is bubbling and brown).
Leta Carter-Beck

Bean Bundles

Serves 4

Marinated beans in lemon ring.

1 (16 ounce) can whole green
  beans
1 teaspoon dill seed
¾ cup warm water
juice of one lemon
2 tablespoons vinegar
2 teaspoons salt
lemon peel rings

Soften dill seed in warm water about 10 minutes. Add juice of lemon, vinegar, salt and bring to a boil. Pour mixture over beans and let marinate for several hours. Serve cold about 10 beans inserted through a ring of lemon peel.
John E. McGaughey, Jr.

Green Beans in Wine Sauce

Serves 8

4 cups cooked green beans
3 slices bacon, diced
1 medium onion, chopped
3 tablespoons sugar
2 teaspoons cornstarch
3 tablespoons tarragon vinegar
½ cup sherry

Sauté bacon and onion. Add sugar, cornstarch, vinegar and sherry. Cook until thickened, stirring constantly. Pour over hot beans and serve.

Tera G. Morris (Mrs. Aubrey R.)

Sweet and Sour Beans

Serves 4

3 slices bacon
1 (20 ounce) can green beans, drained
1 medium onion, sliced and separated
½ cup white vinegar
½ cup sugar
½ cup slivered almonds

Fry, drain and crumble bacon. Set aside. To bacon drippings add beans, onions, vinegar, sugar and almonds. Mix gently. Cover and simmer 25 minutes. Place in serving dish and top with bacon.

Kathie Wing (Mrs. Henry C., Jr.)

Braised Beet Slices

Serves 2-3

2 tablespoons butter or lard
2 onions, thickly sliced
1 garlic clove, thinly sliced
3 large fresh beets, peeled and sliced
2 teaspoons flour
1 tablespoon wine vinegar
¾ cup chicken or veal stock
salt and pepper

Melt fat in skillet; brown onions and garlic over low heat. Add beet slices; cook until golden brown. Sprinkle flour on both sides of beet slices. Stir with wooden spoon until flour browns. Add vinegar and stock. Season with salt and pepper. Cover and simmer gently about 25 minutes until beets are cooked thoroughly.

Leta Carter-Beck

Cheese Broccoli Bake

Serves 4
400° oven

1 box frozen chopped broccoli
½ can cream of mushroom soup
1 cup extra sharp grated cheddar cheese, divided
½ cup mayonnaise
1 tablespoon grated onion
1 beaten egg

Thaw and drain broccoli. Combine soup, ½ cup cheese, mayonnaise, onion and egg. Blend with broccoli. Pour into buttered casserole (1-quart size). Sprinkle top with remaining ½ cup cheese. Bake at 400⁰ for 20 minutes.

Blanche Lantz (Mrs. W. E.)

Broccoli Casserole

Serves 6
350° oven

2 (10 ounce) packages frozen
broccoli, cooked and chopped
1 stick margarine
2 cups chopped celery
1 cup chopped bell pepper
1 cup chopped onions
2 cans mushroom soup, undiluted
1 (16 ounce) jar Cheez Whiz
1 cup cooked rice
bread crumbs or grated cheese
for topping

Sauté celery, pepper and onion in margarine and set aside. Prepare rice and add Cheese Whiz while rice is still hot. Mix well. Combine sautéed vegetables, broccoli, rice and soup and place in buttered 1½-quart casserole. Top with crumbs or cheese and bake at 350° for 20-30 minutes.

Frances Garrett (Mrs. Franklin M.)

Broccoli-Corn Bake

Serves 6
350° oven

1 (16 ounce) can cream style corn
1 (10 ounce) package frozen
chopped broccoli, thawed
1 egg, beaten
½ cup Ritz cracker crumbs
1 tablespoon instant minced
onion (never fresh)
2 tablespoons margarine, melted
½ teaspoon salt
dash pepper
½ cup Ritz cracker crumbs
4 tablespoons margarine, melted

In a mixing bowl combine corn, broccoli, egg, ½ cup crumbs, onion, margarine, salt and pepper. Pour into buttered one-quart casserole. Combine remaining ½ cup crumbs and margarine. Sprinkle over vegetable mixture. Bake, uncovered, at 350° for 35-40 minutes.

Martha C. Dew (Mrs. J. Harris)

Brussels Sprouts and Artichokes

Serves 6
425° oven

1 (10 ounce) package frozen
brussels sprouts
½ cup water
1 (14 ounce) can artichoke hearts,
drained
⅔ cup mayonnaise
½ teaspoon celery salt
¼ cup grated Parmesan cheese
¼ cup margarine, melted
2 teaspoons lemon juice
¼ cup sliced almonds

Cook brussels sprouts in ½ cup water until just tender; drain. Arrange brussels sprouts and artichokes in a greased one-quart casserole. Combine remaining ingredients and spoon over vegetables. Bake, uncovered, at 425° for 8-10 minutes.

Mary Louise Phipps (Mrs. J. M.)

122

Red and Green Cabbage

A very pretty dish.

Serves 6-8
350° oven

- 1 medium head cabbage
- 2 tablespoons margarine
- 1 tablespoon sugar
- 1 medium onion, thinly sliced
- 1 green pepper, thinly sliced into rings
- 1 (28 ounce) can tomatoes, drained and cut into quarters
- ½ teaspoon salt
- ¼ teaspoon pepper
- 2 ounces Parmesan cheese, grated

Cut cabbage into 6 wedges, removing core. Cover and cook 10 minutes in small amount of salted boiling water. Drain well and carefully place wedges in a greased 2-quart shallow baking dish. Melt margarine in saucepan. Add sugar, onions and green pepper; cook over medium heat, stirring occasionally, until vegetables are tender. Stir in tomatoes, salt and pepper. Pour tomato mixture over cabbage, sprinkle with cheese and bake at 350° for 25-30 minutes.

Hazel McDaniel (Mrs. Harry)

Orange Glazed Carrots

Serves 4-6

- 1 pound carrots, washed and peeled
- ½ stick butter
- ½ (6 ounce) can orange juice, frozen concentrate

Boil carrots until barely tender (don't overcook). Drain; place in skillet over high heat. Stir in pats of butter and orange juice. Cook few minutes until very hot.

Lois Bourne (Mrs. David)

Marinated Carrots

Refrigerate 24 hours before serving.

Serves 8-10

- 5 cups carrots
- 1 cup tomato soup
- 1 onion, chopped
- 1 green pepper, chopped
- ½ cup salad oil
- ¾ cup vinegar
- ½ cup sugar
- 1 teaspoon (heaping) prepared mustard
- ½ teaspoon black pepper
- 1 teaspoon salt
- 1 teaspoon Worcestershire sauce

Slice carrots and cook until tender. Mix remaining ingredients well and pour over drained carrots. Cover and refrigerate for 24 hours.

Irene Irvin (Mrs. W. A.)

Stir Fry Carrots and Bananas

Serves 4-6

3 tablespoons butter or margarine
3 carrots, thinly sliced
2 tablespoons lemon juice
2 tablespoons brown sugar
¼ teaspoon ginger
3 bananas, cut in ½-inch slices
½ cup raisins

Melt butter in large skillet. Add carrots and cook over medium heat until tender. Combine lemon juice, brown sugar and ginger; pour over carrots. Add bananas and raisins and cook until heated through.

Beth St. Jean (Mrs. Robert N.)

Cauliflower Deluxe

Serves 6-8

1 large head cauliflower
1 egg white
¼ cup mayonnaise
½ teaspoon salt
1/8 teaspoon pepper
1 teaspoon lemon juice
Parmesan cheese

Prepare cauliflower for steaming (whole or buds). Cook until tender, but firm. Drain and place in baking dish. Beat egg white until stiff. Combine mayonnaise, salt, pepper and lemon juice. Fold into egg white. Cover cauliflower with mixture. Sprinkle with Parmesan cheese. Broil six inches from heat until lightly browned.

Betty Bell

Company Cauliflower

Serves 6
350° oven

1 medium head cauliflower
½ pound mushrooms, sliced
¼ cup diced green pepper
⅓ cup butter
¼ cup flour
2 cups milk
1 teaspoon salt
6 slices pimiento cheese
paprika

Separate cauliflower into bite-size pieces and cook in boiling salted water 10-15 minutes. Drain. Sauté mushrooms and pepper in butter. Stir in flour. Stir in milk slowly and cook until thickened. Add salt. Put half cauliflower in casserole, cover with half cheese, top with half of sauce. Repeat and sprinkle with paprika. Bake uncovered 15 minutes (until golden).

Suzie Schutt

Celery Casserole

Serves 6
350° oven

4 cups celery (½-inch pieces sliced diagonally)
1 cup sliced water chestnuts
1 can cream of chicken soup
½ jar pimiento pieces
½ cup bread crumbs
paprika to taste

Cook celery 2 or 3 minutes in one inch boiling water. Drain. Combine celery with water chestnuts, soup and pimiento. Pour into 1-quart casserole. Sprinkle bread crumbs over celery and paprika to taste. Bake 350° for 30 minutes.

Beverly West (Mrs. J. Herbert)

Corn Pudding

Serves 4-6
325° oven

Traditional Southern fare!

6 ears sweet white corn, grated fine
3 tablespoons melted butter
1 teaspoon cornstarch
1 teaspoon sugar
1 teaspoon salt
3 eggs, separated
1 pint milk

Mix corn, butter, cornstarch, sugar and salt. Add beaten egg yolks and milk. Beat egg whites until stiff and fold into corn mixture. Bake in ungreased casserole at 325° for 45 to 60 minutes until fairly firm (as a baked custard).

Juanita Mitchell (Mrs. Frank, Jr.)

Stewed Corn

Serves 6-12

This can be made ahead of time and reheated.

6-12 ears of corn
bacon fat, about 1 tablespoon per ear
1 cup milk (approximately)
salt and pepper to taste

Cut corn from cob onto large platter or shallow pan, making sure not to cut all the way to the cob. After removing corn, scrape "milk" from cob onto same dish or pan. Heat some fat in large skillet; add corn and scrapings. Cook, stirring occasionally, for just a few minutes. Add fat as necessary to keep corn from sticking or scorching. Do not brown corn. Pour enough milk into skillet to almost cover corn. Season to taste. Cook on low heat a few minutes, stirring occasionally.

**Caroline Dillman
(Mrs. Frederick E., Jr.)**

Swiss Corn Bake

Serves 4
350° oven

2 cups kernel corn
1 cup cream style corn
1 small can evaporated milk
1 egg, beaten
2 teaspoons finely chopped onion
½ teaspoon salt
1/8 teaspoon pepper
4 ounces Swiss cheese, grated
½ cup bread crumbs
1 tablespoon butter, melted

Combine corn, milk, egg, onion, salt, pepper and ¾ of the Swiss cheese. Pour into a 1-quart, greased casserole. Combine bread crumbs, butter and remaining cheese and spread over top. Bake at 350º for 30 minutes. NOTE: If doubling recipe, bake 40 to 45 minutes.
Marianne Miller

French Onion Casserole

Serves 6
broiler

4 medium onions, sliced
3 tablespoons butter
2 tablespoons flour
dash ground pepper
¾ cup beef bouillon
¼ cup dry sherry
1½ cups plain croutons
2 tablespoons butter
2 ounces grated Swiss cheese
3 tablespoons Parmesan cheese

Cook onion in butter until just tender. Blend in flour and pepper; add bouillon and sherry. Cook and stir until thickened. Place in casserole. Toss croutons with 2 tablespoons butter and place on top of onions. Put Swiss cheese on top of croutons. Sprinkle with Parmesan cheese. Put under broiler until cheese melts.
Rick Willix

Hot Mushrooms Gabriel

Serves 4

1 clove garlic
2 tablespoons olive oil
2 tablespoons butter
1 pound fresh mushrooms
¼ cup dry Marsala wine, or
    dry sherry
salt and pepper
large pinch oregano
Parmesan cheese, shredded
4 slices mozzarella cheese

Sauté garlic in olive oil and butter. When garlic is brown, remove from skillet. Sauté mushrooms in same pan until just hot. Add Marsala, salt and pepper to taste, and oregano. Place mushrooms in small individual baking dishes. Sprinkle with Parmesan cheese and top with mozzarella. Place under broiler until cheese is melted. Do not overcook mushrooms. Serve immediately.
Gene & Gabe's Lodge Restaurant
Canton Street

Stuffed Mushrooms Elegante

Serves 6-8
350° oven

1 pound medium mushrooms
1 cup finely chopped pecans
3 tablespoons chopped parsley
¼ cup softened butter or
   margarine
1 clove garlic, crushed
¼ teaspoon thyme
½ teaspoon salt
pepper to taste
½ cup heavy cream

Remove stems from mushrooms and wipe caps with damp cloth. Arrange caps hollow side up in shallow baking dish. Chop stems (about one cup) and mix with all other ingredients except cream. Heap into mushroom umbrellas. Pour cream over all and bake at 350° for 20 minutes, basting once or twice with cream in the dish.

Elizabeth S. Mills (Mrs. George)

Eggplant and Mushroom Casserole

Serves 6-8
microwave

1 medium eggplant
6 tablespoons butter, divided
1 cup finely chopped onion
1 cup finely chopped fresh
   mushrooms
4 eggs, beaten
1 cup mayonnaise
3 ounces cream cheese
¼ cup finely chopped parsley
1/8 teaspoon thyme
½ cup grated Swiss cheese
¼ cup fine white bread crumbs,
   toasted
½ teaspoon salt
1/8 teaspoon pepper

Peel eggplant and cut into 1-inch cubes (about 6 cups). Place in 8-inch square glass dish with 2 tablespoons water. Cover tightly with plastic wrap and cook 5-7 minutes on full power. Allow to carry over cook 2-3 minutes; drain water and press eggplant to remove moisture. In glass measuring cup melt 4 tablespoons butter 30-40 seconds on full power. Stir in onion and mushrooms. Cook 3-4 minutes on full power, stirring after 2 minutes. Allow to carry over cook 2-3 minutes; drain away liquid. Thoroughly mix eggs and mayonnaise; pour into 8½x11-inch glass dish. Stir in onions and mushrooms; add eggplant, mixing evenly. In food processor mix cream cheese, parsley, thyme, Swiss cheese, bread crumbs, salt and pepper. (Makes a paste.) Crumble paste over top of casserole. Pour 2 tablespoons melted butter evenly over casserole. Cook 10-12 minutes on 70% power.

Carol Jean Wheeler (Mrs. Bob)

127

Eggplant Soufflé

Serves 4-5
350° oven

1 medium eggplant
2 tablespoons butter
2 tablespoons flour
1 cup milk
2 eggs, separated
1 cup grated cheddar cheese
¾ cup fine light bread crumbs
2 teaspoons grated onion
1 tablespoon catsup
salt and freshly grated pepper

Peel eggplant; cut in small pieces and cook in boiling salted water until barely tender. Drain thoroughly and mash. Make a cream sauce of butter, flour and milk. When thick and smooth, add mashed eggplant, cheese, crumbs, onion, catsup and egg yolks. Beat egg whites until stiff. Fold eggplant mixture into egg whites. Pour into buttered 2-quart casserole or soufflé dish and bake at 350⁰ for 45 minutes.

Louise Barksdale

Eggplant Casserole

Serves 6
450°, 350° oven

May be assembled early in day and baked at dinnertime.

1 eggplant (about 1¼ pounds)
about ⅓ cup salad oil
6 slices bacon
1 large onion, chopped
1 green pepper, chopped
½ pound mushrooms, sliced
1 clove garlic, minced
1 pound fresh or canned
    tomatoes, cut in chunks
2 tablespoons brown sugar
salt and freshly ground pepper
    to taste
1½-2 cups shredded mozzarella
    cheese

Wash (and peel if desired) eggplant. Cut into ½-inch slices and brush all sides with oil. Arrange in single layer on baking sheet; bake uncovered at 450⁰ about 20 minutes (until soft). Cook bacon in large frying pan until crisp; drain and crumble. Discard all but 2 tablespoons drippings. Add onion, green pepper, mushrooms and garlic. Sauté until limp. Stir in tomatoes and their liquid, sugar, salt and pepper. Cook over medium-high heat, uncovered, until most of the liquid has evaporated. Layer eggplant, bacon and sauce in shallow 2-quart casserole. Top with cheese and bake, uncovered, at 350⁰ until bubbly (about 15 minutes).

Marian David (Mrs. John H., Jr.)

Sautéed Snow Peas

Serves 4

Goes well with grilled lamb chops or mackerel.

½ pound snow peas
1 clove garlic
3-4 tablespoons olive oil
salt and pepper
soy sauce

Trim snow peas by breaking stem and pulling off the string. Wash and dry. Rub heavy skillet with garlic and discard garlic. Heat oil in skillet and add peas. Season with bit of salt, generous amount of pepper and a few splashes of soy sauce. Sauté briskly, shaking pan often, for 3-4 minutes.

Peggy Black (Mrs. Richard)

Good Eating Potato Casserole

Serves 10-12
350° oven

1 (32 ounce) package frozen
  Southern hash brown potatoes
½ cup chopped onion
1 can cream of chicken soup
2 cups sour cream with chives
10 ounces Velveeta cheese,
  cubed
1 teaspoon salt
¼ teaspoon pepper
½ cup margarine, melted
2 cups corn flakes

Defrost potatoes; mix together with all ingredients except ¼ cup butter and corn flakes. Place in 9x13-inch pan. Mix corn flakes with ¼ cup butter and sprinkle over top of casserole. Bake 1 hour at 350° (325° for glass dish).

William (Bill) Harris

Potato Casserole

Serves 8
325° oven

8 potatoes cooked, peeled and
  cubed
¾ cup mayonnaise
¾ pound Velveeta cheese, cubed
6 slices bacon
stuffed olives

Mix potatoes, mayonnaise and cheese in greased casserole (13½x7½). Dice 6 slices uncooked bacon and desired amount sliced stuffed olives; arrange on top. Bake one hour, first half hour covered, last half hour uncovered. May make ahead and refrigerate. Serve hot.

Betty Jane Sandell

Patrician Potatoes

Serves 8
350° oven

4 cups cooked mashed potatoes (about six medium potatoes cooked with two teaspoons salt)
3 cups cream style cottage cheese
¾ cup sour cream
1½ tablespoons finely grated onion
2½ teaspoons salt
1/8 teaspoon white pepper
melted butter
½ cup chopped toasted almonds

Mash potatoes thoroughly (add no milk or butter). Press cottage cheese through a sieve, or buzz in blender. Mix together warm mashed potatoes and cheese. Add sour cream, onion, salt and pepper. Mix well. Spoon into shallow, buttered 2-quart casserole. Brush surface with melted butter. Bake at 350°, for ½ hour. Place under broiler a few minutes to brown surface lightly. Sprinkle with almonds.

Fran Buttolph (Mrs. Robert)

Hot Swiss Scalloped Potatoes

Serves 4-6
350° oven

Add a layer of ham to make an excellent main dish.

1 cup (4 ounces) shredded Swiss cheese
½ cup sliced green onions (with tops
1 tablespoon dill weed
2 tablespoons butter
2 tablespoons regular all-purpose flour
1 teaspoon salt
1 cup milk
1 cup dairy sour cream
6-7 cups cooked, peeled, thinly sliced potatoes (4 large)
½ cup shredded Swiss cheese
¼ cup fine dry bread crumbs
¼ cup butter, melted

In small bowl toss together Swiss cheese, onion and dill weed; set aside. Melt butter in saucepan; stir in flour and salt. Remove from heat; gradually stir in milk. Cook over medium heat, stirring constantly, until thickened. Cook 2 more minutes, remove from heat and stir in sour cream. In 3-quart buttered shallow baking dish, layer ⅓ potatoes, ½ Swiss cheese mixture and ½ sour cream mixture. Repeat, making top layer with last ⅓ of the potatoes. Combine ½ cup Swiss cheese, bread crumbs and melted butter. Sprinkle over top of casserole. Bake at 350° 30-35 minutes. Serve immediately. NOTE: If adding layer of ham, use 3 cups (1 pound) diced cooked ham, cut in ¼-inch pieces.

Jackie Winecoff (Mrs. A. F., Jr.)

Cheese and Potato Pie

Serves 6
425° oven

9-inch unbaked pastry shell
8 slices bacon
2 cups diced raw potatoes
2 tablespoons finely chopped
  onion
½ pound sharp cheddar cheese,
  shredded
1 tablespoon flour
3 eggs
1 cup evaporated milk
½ teaspoon salt
½ teaspoon pepper
tomato wedges (optional)

Cook bacon in fry pan until crisp; drain on paper towel. Reserve ¼ cup drippings; add potatoes and onions, stirring to coat well. Cover and cook over low heat 10 minutes. Crumble 6 slices bacon into potatoes and mix well. Remove from heat. Mix cheese and flour with fork. Place ⅓ of the cheese in bottom of pastry shell and top with half the potato mixture. Repeat layers. Place remaining cheese on top. Crumble two slices bacon over cheese. Beat eggs well; blend in evaporated milk and seasonings. Pour egg mixture over ingredients in pastry shell. Bake 15 minutes at 425°. Reduce heat to 325°; cover pie lightly with aluminum foil and bake 30 minutes or until knife inserted in center comes out clean. Serve hot. Garnish with tomato wedges, if desired.

Fran Eubanks

Candied Shredded Sweet Potato

Serves 6-8
350° oven

3 medium sweet potatoes
¼ stick butter
1 cup sugar
¼ cup white Karo syrup
½ cup water
1 small can crushed pineapple
butter

Shred sweet potatoes into small strips. Drop immediately into cold salted water. Make a syrup of butter, sugar, syrup and water. Squeeze all water out of potatoes and place in greased casserole with crushed pineapple. Pour syrup mixture over all. Put a few small pats of butter on top. Bake in 350° oven for 35 minutes.

Laura Roberts Wing (Mrs. Henry C.)

131

Sweet Potato Soufflé

Serves 6-8
350° oven

Choice of options allows for several variations.

Soufflé
3-4 medium sweet potatoes
½-¾ cup sugar (white or brown)
½ teaspoon salt
1 stick butter or margarine
1 cup coconut (optional)
chopped pecans (optional)
marshmallows (optional)

Peel and slice potatoes thinly across the grain. Cook in hot water to cover until done. Drain and reserve liquid. Add butter, salt and sugar. Mash with pastry blender. Beat with electric beater, adding potato liquid a little at a time until mixture is fairly soft. Add coconut or pecans. Place in buttered 1-quart casserole and bake 30 minutes at 350⁰. Top with marshmallows, if desired, during last few minutes, or top with Orange Sauce.

Orange Sauce
⅓ cup sugar
1 tablespoon cornstarch
1/8 teaspoon salt
1 teaspoon grated orange peel
1 cup orange juice
1 tablespoon fresh lemon juice
2 tablespoons butter or margarine
1 tablespoon Grand Marnier
3 dashes Angostura Bitters

Orange Sauce: Blend first six ingredients in saucepan, slowly bring to boil, stirring constantly until sauce is thickened. Remove from heat; stir in butter, Grand Marnier and bitters. Makes 1 cup.
Julia Rucker Crisler

Sweet Potato Casserole

Serves 10
350° oven

8 sweet potatoes (about 4 pounds)
3 eggs, separated
½ can Eagle Brand condensed milk
butter
marshmallows

Peel potatoes and cook until tender; drain and mash. Beat in egg yolks. Add milk and mix well. Fold in stiffly beaten egg whites. Put in 3-quart casserole, forming peaks. Dot with butter. Bake 45 minutes at 350⁰. Top with marshmallows last 5 minutes.
Donna Bingham (Mrs. Norm)

132

Sweet Potato Pone

Serves 8-10
350° oven

Served at Magnolia Hall during the Roswell Historical Society's Natchez Pilgrimage. Recipe provided by our tour guide, Jane Kimbrell.

2 tablespoons flour
1¼ cups sugar
3 eggs, beaten
1 teaspoon cinnamon
1 teaspoon allspice
1 teaspoon nutmeg
2½ cups milk
¾ cup whiskey or orange juice
3 cups finely grated sweet potato
1 cup pecans, cut up
1 cup melted butter
pinch of salt

Mix flour and sugar together, add beaten eggs, spices, milk and whiskey. Add grated potatoes, nuts, butter and salt. Stir well. Bake at 350°, uncovered, for two hours.
George D. Elyea

Spinach Casserole

Serves 4
350° oven

1 (10 ounce) frozen chopped
  spinach
1 cup chopped onions
1 can cream of mushroom soup
½ cup grated sharp cheese
1 cup Pepperidge Farm Herb
  Seasoned Stuffing
½ cup melted margarine

Thaw spinach, squeeze out water. Combine with onion, soup and cheese. Place in 1-quart casserole. Combine stuffing with margarine; spread on top of spinach mixture. Bake at 350° for 45 minutes.
Mary Buford (Mrs. William F.)

Spinach Graziosa

Serves 2-4

Favorite brunch dish at Aida's Acres.

1 (10 ounce) frozen cut leaf
  spinach
½ cup boiling water
1 lime, sliced
cheddar finger slices, or Cheez
  Whiz

Place frozen spinach in 7-inch cook and serve dish with ½ cup boiling water. Bring to a boil and separate with fork. Reduce heat to low. Place lime slices on top of spinach; cook gently about 3 minutes. Turn off heat. Remove lime slices. Arrange cheese over spinach. Cover again. When cheese has melted, decorate with lime slices and serve.
Aida de Bray (Mrs. Fred)

133

Spinach-Artichoke Casserole

Serves 6-8
350° oven

2 packages frozen spinach
1 large onion, chopped
3 tablespoons butter
6 ounces cream cheese
1 can or jar artichokes, drained
salt and pepper
1 cup bread crumbs

Cook spinach by directions on package; drain well. Sauté onion in butter until clear. Add cream cheese and mix well. Add to spinach and mix well. Line bottom of 8x8-inch casserole with artichokes (cut in half). Spoon spinach mixture over this. Add salt and pepper. Sprinkle with bread crumbs. Cook at 350º for 30 minutes.

Wynelle G. Hosea

Squash Soufflé

Serves 6-8
325° oven

3 tablespoons butter
1 cup milk (more or less)
1 cup dry bread crumbs or 4
    slices bread, crumbled
2 cups cooked, mashed, yellow
    squash or zucchini
1 small onion, grated
salt and pepper to taste
2 eggs, beaten
1 cup grated sharp cheese
buttered cracker crumbs

Melt butter in hot milk. Pour over bread crumbs. Mix well and add to squash. Add onion. Season with salt and pepper. Stir in beaten eggs and pour into 9 x 13-inch baking dish. Cover with cheese; poke down a little. Cover with buttered cracker crumbs. Bake at 325º for 25-30 minutes.

Frances Coleman Rucker

Squash Casserole

Serves 8-10
350° oven

4 cups cooked yellow squash
2 medium carrots, shredded
1 medium onion, chopped
1 (4 ounce) jar pimiento strips
½ can cream of chicken soup
½ cup sour cream
3 eggs, beaten
salt and pepper to taste
1 stick margarine
¾ package Pepperidge Farm
    Corn Bread Stuffing

Drain and mash squash. Mix all ingredients except margarine and stuffing. Melt margarine and pour over stuffing. Line bottom of 9x11-inch casserole dish with half the stuffing mix. Spoon in squash mixture and top with remaining stuffing. Bake, uncovered, at 350º for 30 minutes. Can be frozen and cooked later.

Wynelle G. Hosea

Squash and Egg Casserole

Serves 8
350° oven

2 pounds yellow squash, thinly
  sliced
2 medium onions, thinly sliced
¼ cup plus 2 tablespoons butter
½ cup flour
2 cups milk
½ teaspoon salt
6 hard cooked eggs, finely
  chopped
½ cup soft bread crumbs
2 tablespoons melted butter
parsley

Cook squash and onion in small amount of boiling water until tender (8-10 minutes). Drain well. Make thick white sauce: Melt butter in saucepan over low heat. Add flour and cook one minute. Stir constantly. Gradually add milk. Cook over medium heat, stirring constantly, until thickened. Stir in salt. Combine squash, onion, thick white sauce and eggs. Stir well. Spoon into greased 2½-quart casserole. Combine bread crumbs and butter. Sprinkle over casserole. Bake at 350° for 20-25 minutes until hot and bubbly. Garnish with parsley.
**Colleen Briesemeister
(Mrs. Edward)**

Stuffed Butternut Squash

Serves 6
350° oven

3 large butternut squash
2 cups Pepperidge Farm Stuffing
1 bell pepper, finely chopped
1 onion, finely chopped
1 stick butter
1 cup grated sharp cheese
6 pieces bacon, cooked crispy

Split squash; bake turned cut side down in water for 20 minutes or until barely tender. Very carefully remove inside of squash to leave a pretty shell. Mix squash with all ingredients leaving a little cheese to place on top. Stuff shell and bake at 325° for 30 minutes. May be made ahead and baked when needed.
Inez McMurtray

Zucchini Casserole

Serves 6-8
350° oven

1 cup sliced celery
1 cup sliced onion
½ green pepper, cut in strips
4 tablespoons butter
2 pounds unpeeled zucchini,
   scrubbed and sliced
1 teaspoon salt
1 cup grated aged cheddar
   cheese
dash cayenne pepper
dash nutmeg
½ to 1 cup Pepperidge Farm
   Herb Seasoned Stuffing
butter

Sauté celery, onions and green pepper in butter until wilted, but not brown. Remove from skillet. Cook zucchini in small amount salted water for 5 minutes; drain well and sauté a few minutes to evaporate moisture. In buttered 2½-quart casserole alternate layers of zucchini, vegetables and cheese, reserving 2 tablespoons cheese. Sprinkle each cheese layer with just a dash of cayenne pepper and nutmeg. Top with herb stuffing, remaining cheese and bits of butter. Bake at 350° until browned (about 25 minutes).
Suzie Schutt

Zucchini a' la Richard

Serves 6
350° oven

3 small zucchini
salt
flour
4 tablespoons olive oil
4 medium tomatoes
1 small clove garlic, crushed
2 tablespoons chopped parsley
¼ teaspoon sugar
1/8 teaspoon ground black pepper
½ teaspoon dried oregano
1 cup soft bread crumbs
⅓ cup Parmesan cheese, grated

Wash and cut zucchini in lengthwise quarters. Sprinkle with salt and let stand 15 minutes. Wipe off salt, dredge in flour, and fry in shallow hot oil, turning to brown all sides. Place zucchini side by side in rows in baking dish. Peel, seed and dice tomatoes; cook 5 minutes in 2 tablespoons hot oil, adding salt to taste, garlic, parsley, sugar, pepper and oregano. Spread over zucchini. Mix bread crumbs with 2 tablespoons oil and Parmesan; sprinkle over tomatoes. Cook in preheated oven 30 minutes (until crumbs are brown).
Richard Jones
Richard's Restaurant
Market Place

Zucchini Casserole

Serves 4
375° oven

6 small or 3 large zucchini
2 tablespoons butter or margarine
1 cup sour cream
6 tablespoons grated cheddar
  cheese
½ teaspoon seasoned salt
2 slices white bread, buttered on
  both sides

Slice zucchini in ½-inch slices. Boil in salted water 5 minutes. Drain well. Melt butter in saucepan. Add sour cream, cheese and seasoned salt; blend. Place drained squash in 9-inch square greased casserole. Pour sour cream mixture on top. Tear buttered bread in tidbits and put on top. Bake at 375⁰ for 15 minutes (until bread is golden).

Joan L. Hancock (Mrs. John C.)

Fire and See Tomatoes

Serves 6

6 large tomatoes
1 large green pepper
1 large red onion
1 cucumber, sliced

Sauce
¾ cup vinegar
1½ teaspoons celery salt
1½ teaspoons mustard seed
½ teaspoon salt
4½ teaspoons sugar
1/8 teaspoon red pepper
1/8 teaspoon black pepper
¼ cup cold water

Skin and quarter tomatoes. Cut pepper into strips. Slice onion and separate into rings. Place above in a bowl. Set aside cucumber.

Sauce: Combine all ingredients in saucepan. Bring to boil and boil 1 minute. Pour over tomato mixture immediately. Cool. Just before serving add cucumber.

Mary Ann Johnson (Mrs. Jim)

Herbed Tomato Slices

Serves 5
350° oven

3 tomatoes
salt
⅔ cup soft bread crumbs
2 tablespoons butter or margarine
¼ teaspoon dried basil, crushed

Cut tomatoes in slices about ¾-inch thick. Arrange in 10x6x1½-inch baking dish. Sprinkle with salt. Toss crumbs with melted butter or margarine and basil. Sprinkle on tomatoes. Bake uncovered for 20-25 minutes.

Ginny Riley

Vegetable Casserole

Serves 8
350° oven

1 (1 pound) can white shoe peg
  corn, drained
1 can cream of celery soup
1 cup grated sharp cheese
1 onion, chopped
1 (1 pound) can French style
  green beans, drained
½ cup sour cream
1 (2 ounce) jar pimiento (optional)

Mix together all ingredients and place in tightly covered dish. Store in refrigerator overnight.

<u>Topping</u>
1 stick margarine, melted
1 cup chopped nuts
1½ cups crushed cheese crackers
  (Cheez-Its)

Topping: Mix together all ingredients and spread over casserole just before baking. Bake at 350° for 45 minutes.

Marjorie Pless (Mrs. Berlin)

Carolyn Price's Vegetable Casserole

Serves 8-10
350° oven

1 (10 ounce) package frozen
  cauliflower
1 (10 ounce) package frozen
  brussels sprouts, or chopped
  broccoli
1 (10 ounce) package frozen peas
1 (10 ounce) package frozen
  carrots
2 tablespoons cornstarch
1 (8 ounce) jar Cheez Whiz
1 (10 ounce) can celery soup
dash salt
1 tablespoon butter

Arrange vegetables in large casserole. Dissolve cornstarch in small amount of water. Combine with Cheez Whiz and soup. Pour mixture over vegetables. Sprinkle with salt and dot with butter. Bake at 350° for 1½ hours.

Carolyn Pratt

SAUCES
and
ACCOMPANIMENTS

Phyllis Gottschalk

**THE ROSWELL STORES AND SQUARE
ATLANTA STREET
Circa 1839**

THE ROSWELL STORES AND SQUARE

The unique character of Roswell is preserved within a single block of ancient stores facing the town square with its lovely fountain and bandstand. A glimpse of the history from early mill days in the 1840's to the present is revealed through the old buildings, each joined to the other and each distinctive to its time and place in Roswell's heritage.

The original building, a two-storied structure constructed in 1839 of hand-molded brick and ax-hewn timbers, was a commissary for the mill workers. The building is a study in detail. The pedimented roof, decorative brick work, and ornamental pilasters on the facade, reveal a classic design similar to that of the early homes. The building later served the community as a general store where one could purchase an unlimited assortment of goods and equipment.

Later stores in the group are different in design, simpler and less imaginative, the workmanship less precise, though unique. Specialty shops and a restaurant occupy the buildings. As additional structures have taken their place in the complex, each has contributed its individual design and character to the history of Roswell.

The Roswell Stores and Square are listed on the National Register of Historic Places.

———

1909 SHOPPING LIST

100 pound sack of salt	$ .50
48 pounds of flour	$1.60
12 pounds whole wheat flour	$ .65
2 pounds nuts	$ .40
ketchup	$ .20
olives	$ .10
vinegar	$ .10
1250 pounds coal	$3.43

C. B. K. Tomato Catsup
AD 1800 "C. B. K."

This recipe belonged to Catherine Barrington King, wife of the town's founder, Roswell King. Mrs. King passed it on to her daughter, Catherine Barrington King Pratt, who was the wife of Nathaniel Pratt, first minister of the Roswell Presbyterian Church. Mrs. Pratt's son, Charles Pratt, wrote the recipe in a letter to a friend in 1918. This letter was in the possession of Mr. Pratt's grandson and his wife, Palmer and Olive Pratt. We reprint the recipe here as it appeared in that letter.

> 12 lbs. cut up ripe tomatoes
> 3 gills best vinegar
> 6 oz. salt
> 12 oz. Brown sugar
> 12 oz. onions cut up
> 2 oz. blk. pepper
> ½ oz. cayene pepper
> ¾ oz. cloves
> 1¼ oz. all spice
> 1 oz. cinnamon
> ¾ oz. nutmeg

Boil tomatoes, salt, vinegar, and onion, cut small, on a slow fire for 1½ hours. Strain thru cheese cloth and then add pepper, spices & vinegar & boil slowly for 3 to 4 hours. The pepper, spices, etc. should be ground fine, wrapped in muslin and squeezed or hand pressed after boiling to give flavor and not much color to the fin. product.

Bottle but do not cap until cool. Properly made this catsup will --------(?) without being sealed.

> Yours truly,
> Chas. Pratt
> C. B. K. Tomato Catsup   AD 1800

Billie's Bar-B-Q Sauce

Yield: 2 pints

Excellent on pork or beef.

2 cups vinegar
1 cup ketchup
4 garlic cloves, pressed
2 sticks butter
1 cup Worcestershire sauce
juice of 2 lemons
¾ cup brown sugar
salt to taste
pepper to taste
1½ teaspoons celery salt

Combine all ingredients. Mix well. Bring to a boil. Reduce heat and simmer 2-3 hours. Will keep in Mason jars in the refrigerator for several months.

Gloria Barkley Bond (Mrs. Robert)

Sauce for Meat

Yield: 1½ cups

Especially good with beef.

4 tablespoons honey
4 tablespoons catsup
4 tablespoons soy sauce
1 bouillon cube
½ cup water
1 teaspoon ginger
½ teaspoon pepper
salt to taste

Mix together all ingredients in a small saucepan. Simmer for 10 minutes.

June Lindgren (Mrs. Gray M.)

Raisin Sauce for Ham

Yield: 2½ cups

1 cup raisins
1 cup water
5 whole cloves
¾ cup brown sugar
1 teaspoon corn starch
¼ teaspoon salt
pinch of pepper
1 tablespoon butter
1 tablespoon vinegar
¼ teaspoon Worcestershire

Cover raisins with water. Add cloves and simmer ten minutes. Mix together sugar, cornstarch, salt and pepper. Add this mixture to raisins. Stir until slightly thickened. Add remaining ingredients.

Louise DeLong (Mrs. R. Luke)

Apricot Chutney

Yield: about 4 cups

1 pound dried apricots
4 cups boiling water
8 cloves garlic, peeled and
  coarsley chopped
1½-inch cube fresh ginger, peeled
  and coarsely chopped
1¼ cups red wine vinegar
2 cups sugar
¼ teaspoon salt
1/8-½ teaspoon cayenne pepper
¾ cup golden raisins

Put apricots in bowl. Pour boiling water over and soak two hours. Put garlic, ginger and ¼ cup vinegar into container of electric blender or food processor. Blend until smooth. Empty apricots and soaking liquid into heavy pot. (Do not use aluminum.) Add garlic-ginger mixture, remaining 1 cup vinegar, sugar, salt and cayenne. Bring to boil. Simmer 45 minutes, stirring often. Do not let chutney stick to bottom of pot. Lower heat, if necessary. Add raisins and cook, stirring, another half hour or until chutney takes on thick, glazed look. Cool and store, refrigerated, in glass jars.
Lorrie Berry (Mrs. Roger W.)

Spaghetti Sauce

Serves 6

Best made ahead and reheated to serve.

2 onions
¼ pound prosciutto (or bacon
  or extra thin ham)
2 tablespoons olive oil
2 tablespoons butter
2 carrots
2 sticks celery
1 pound ground chuck
½ cup chopped mushrooms
4 cups plum tomatoes
1 (6 ounce) can tomato paste
1 bay leaf
fresh parsley
¼ teaspoon oregano
salt and pepper
Parmesan cheese, fresh grated

Sauté chopped onions and prosciutto in butter and olive oil until onions are golden. Add finely chopped carrots and celery and cook until vegetables are slightly browned and softened. Add meat and mushrooms. Continue cooking, stirring occasionally, until meat is browned. Add tomatoes, tomato paste, bay leaf, parsley, oregano, salt and pepper. Cover and simmer two hours. Serve over spaghetti topped with grated cheese.
Merijoy Rucker (Mrs. Rodney)

Shrimp Sauce

Serves 6-8

Excellent over spaghetti.

1 stick butter
6 cloves garlic, finely chopped
3 pounds shrimp, shelled,
  coarsely chopped
⅓ cup butter
⅓ cup plain flour
1⅔ cups chicken stock
1 can evaporated milk
3 ounces grated Romano cheese
1 teaspoon oregano

Melt stick of butter in skillet. Add garlic and shrimp; cook until shrimp is pink. Set aside. Melt ⅓ cup butter in saucepan; add flour. Whisk in stock and evaporated milk. Cook, stirring with whisk, until sauce thickens. Add cheese and stir until melted. Whisk in shrimp and oregano. Cook over low heat until hot. Season to taste.

Martha Stevenson (Mrs. J. B., Jr.)

Clam Sauce for Spaghetti

Yield: 2-3 servings

4 tablespoons olive oil
4 tablespoons butter or margarine
1 clove garlic, finely chopped
3 tablespoons shallots, finely
  chopped
1 (10 ounce) can whole baby
  clams, drain and reserve ½ cup
  juice
½ cup fresh parsley, finely
  chopped, or 2 tablespoons
  parsley flakes

Heat oil and butter. Add garlic and shallots. Sauté until lightly colored. Add clam juice and simmer 5 minutes. Stir in clams and parsley; bring to a boil. Use over 2-3 servings of spaghetti. Can be doubled.

Mark and Nancy Collis

Marinara Sauce

Serves 1 pound pasta

3 tablespoons olive oil
½ stalk celery, chopped
1 small onion, chopped
1 clove garlic, minced
1 large can Italian plum
  tomatoes
1 medium can tomato puree
salt and pepper
¼ cup fresh parsely
½ teaspoon basil
½ teaspoon oregano
1 bay leaf

Place oil, celery, onion and garlic in small saucepan; brown lightly. Add tomatoes, tomato puree, salt and pepper. Simmer 45 minutes. Add remaining herbs and cook 15 minutes longer. NOTE: Make day ahead to season through and add ¼ cup red wine for zest.

John Zaccheo

Meat Sauce for Spaghetti

Yield: 3½ quarts

May be frozen to be used as needed.

- 1 (3 pound) roast (round, chuck, rump)
- 3 teaspoons salt
- ¼ cup flour
- ¼ cup olive oil
- 2 cups hot water
- 1 pound Italian sausage, skinned and cut into chunks
- ¼ teaspoon garlic powder
- 1 teaspoon onion powder
- 2 bay leaves
- 1 teaspoon celery salt
- 1 teaspoon black pepper
- 2 teaspoons sugar
- ½ teaspoon crushed red pepper
- 1 tablespoon Season-all
- ¼ teaspoon MSG
- ½ teaspoon each: oregano leaves, basil leaves, parsley flakes, rosemary leaves - all crushed
- ¼ teaspoon nutmeg
- 4 (6 ounce) cans tomato paste
- 1 quart (4 cups) water
- 1 cup red wine (optional)
- ½ cup sliced ripe olives
- 2 (4 ounce) cans mushrooms

Season roast with salt and dredge with flour. In Dutch oven, brown slowly on all sides in hot olive oil. Add hot water. Cover and cook slowly about 3 hours or until meat is tender and almost falls apart. Tear into small pieces with a fork. Add remaining ingredients. Cover and continue cooking until sauce thickens to desired consistency.

Mark and Nancy Collis

Mock Hollandaise Sauce

Yield: 1¼ cups

Good served over broccoli, asparagus and other green vegetables.

- ¾ cup mayonnaise
- ⅓ cup milk
- ¼ teaspoon salt
- ⅛ teaspoon pepper
- 1 tablespoon lemon juice
- 1 teaspoon grated lemon rind

Combine mayonnaise, milk, salt and pepper. Cook over low heat (or over hot water) 5 minutes, stirring constantly. Add lemon juice and grated lemon rind just before serving.

Louise DeLong (Mrs. R. Luke)

Peanut Butter Chantilly Sauce

Yield: 1¼ cups

Very good with broccoli, green beans, carrots or asparagus.

¼ cup smooth or crunchy peanut butter
½ pint sour cream
1½ tablespoons horseradish (drained)
1 teaspoon salt
dash pepper
1½ tablespoons lemon juice

Put peanut butter in small bowl. Gradually mix in sour cream until blended. Fold in remaining ingredients.

Ella Zimmerman

Red Sauce for Blackeyed Peas

Yield: 1½ cups

A New Year's tradition at our house for good luck!

1 (16 ounce) can tomatoes or equal amount of fresh tomatoes, chopped
1 medium green pepper, chopped
½ cup vinegar
½ cup sugar
1 teaspoon black pepper, or to taste
1½ teaspoons salt

Combine all ingredients. Simmer over low heat, stirring occasionally, until mixture reaches consistency of chili sauce. Serve piping hot over blackeyed peas. Recipe may be doubled. May be reheated as needed.

"Sam" and Harry Doud

Hot Fudge Sauce

Yield: 3 cups

3 squares (3 ounces) unsweetened chocolate
1½ cups sugar
dash salt
dash cream of tartar
1 cup evaporated milk
1 teaspoon vanilla
¼ cup butter

Melt chocolate over low heat. Add sugar, salt and cream of tartar. Gradually stir in evaporated milk. Heat until mixture comes to rolling boil. Remove from heat; stir in vanilla and butter. Serve hot over ice cream. Can be reheated in top of double boiler.

Beth Benson (Mrs. Kenneth)

Zucchini Jam

Yield: 5 pints

6 cups peeled and grated zucchini
6 cups sugar
½ cup lemon juice
1 cup pineapple juice
1 (6 ounce) package apricot Jell-O

Mix together all ingredients except Jell-O. Boil 6 minutes. Remove from heat and add Jell-O. Put in jars with covers. Keep refrigerated or freeze for future use.

Jeanne Bump (Mrs. Gerald J.)

Herb Butters

Yield: ¼ pound

Delicious on freshly baked bread and steamed vegetables. Nice to baste meat when broiling. Freezes well.

½ cup (1 stick) butter, room
   temperature
1 tablespoon lemon juice
3 tablespoons finely chopped
   fresh herb (chervil, basil,
   rosemary, thyme, parsley or
   marjoram)
salt to taste
freshly ground pepper to taste

Cream butter and beat in lemon juice a little at a time. Beat in herb. Season with salt and pepper. Chill. May freeze in small individual crocks or butter jars and thaw as needed.

Jackie Williams (Mrs. Walton S.)

Homemade Mustard

Yield: 4-6 small jars

Makes a nice Christmas gift.

3 egg yolks
½ cup vinegar
1 tablespoon Lea and Perrin's
   Worcestershire sauce
½ cup Coleman's dry mustard
½ cup sugar
1 tablespoon flour
½ cup hot water
¾ cup butter

Beat egg yolks; stir in vinegar, Worcestershire, mustard, sugar and flour. Cook in double boiler until mixture begins to thicken. Add water and last of all butter. Cool and place in small jars. Mustard must be refrigerated.

June Lindgren (Mrs. Gray M.)

Mustard Sauce

Yield: about 3 cups

An old family recipe. Will keep indefinitely in refrigerator.

1 pint (2 cups) half and half
½ teaspoon salt
1 tablespoon sugar
4 tablespoons Coleman's dry
   mustard
1 egg, well beaten
1 cup vinegar

Bring cream to a boil. Add salt, sugar and mustard which has been softened with some cream and the egg. Stir constantly for 2 minutes. Gradually add vinegar and stir while boiling 6 to 10 minutes more.

Mildred Holland

147

Onion Pie au Gratin

Serves 8
350° oven

Meat accompaniment or substitute.

Pie crust
30 square saltines
⅓ cup butter or margarine, melted

Filling
3 cups thinly sliced onions
2 tablespoons butter
½ pound sharp cheddar cheese, grated
1½ cups scalded milk
3 eggs, beaten
½ teaspoon salt
½ teaspoon pepper

Crust: Crush saltines and mix with butter. Pat into deep pie pan, quiche dish or baking pan.

Filling: Sauté onions in butter. Arrange on cracker crust. Sprinkle cheese on top. This much may be prepared quite ahead of dinner. When time to put in oven, mix scalded milk, eggs, salt and pepper. Pour over onions and cheese. Bake at 350° about ½ hour until custard sets.
Eva Corder (Mrs. J. B.)

Pineapple Cheese

Serves 8
350° oven

Excellent with ham.

2 (20 ounce) cans pineapple chunks
1 stick butter
1 cup flour
½ pound cheddar cheese, shredded

Place pineapple and juice in 6x10-inch or 8x8-inch baking dish. Cut butter into flour and mix into pineapple. Top with cheese. Bake at 350° for 30-45 minutes. Top should be golden.
Marge Bubeck (Mrs. Herbert)

Williamsburg House Aroma

Yield: 1 pint

Makes your house smell wonderful for holiday entertaining! Delightful gift from your kitchen. **(Not for consumption.)**

¾ teaspoon ground cloves
¾ teaspoon ground cinnamon
heaping teaspoon instant orange peel
1 teaspoon whole cloves
3 twists fresh orange peel
2 cups cold water

Mix together all ingredients. Simmer on stove in small saucepan. Let steam for aroma. Add water as necessary. If using for holiday gift, pour into pint Mason jar and seal. Decorate with calico and ribbon.
Anne Tierney Walsh

PICKLES
and
RELISHES

Dot Beebe

GREAT OAKS
MIMOSA BOULEVARD
Circa 1842

GREAT OAKS

The impressive three-storied home standing on a gentle rise amid towering oaks, was completed in the early spring of 1842 for the Reverend Nathaniel Alpheus Pratt and his wife, Catherine King, daughter of Roswell King. Dr. Pratt served as the first minister of the Roswell Presbyterian Church, where he occupied the pulpit for 39 years.

Great Oaks was made of hand-formed brick laid in Flemish bond. Identical fireplaces with reeded pilasters in the double parlors attest to the proficiency of the early woodcarvers. Walls of solid brick and mortar are 18 inches thick. The small columned portico was added in later years. A large country kitchen with massive fireplace was built onto the rear of the house, with a summer kitchen in the yard, attached to the house by a breezeway.

During the War, Union General Kenner Garrard maintained his headquarters in the house. The Reverend Pratt and his wife chose to remain in their home during the occupation. In a letter written to his nephew in December 1864, Dr. Pratt told of the destruction done to the town and to his property, writing that "there were 1000 wagons and 6000 mules packed on my premises." The crops of corn, wheat, and sorghum were destroyed, fences torn down, and outbuildings stripped of doors and shutters. He wrote, "But my dwelling was not disturbed. God permitting us to live in safety. On the whole we were treated with respect."

Great Oaks is listed on the National Register of Historic Places.

BICENTENNIAL COCKTAIL PARTY AT GREAT OAKS

Whiskey Punch · Wine · Fruit Punch

Onion, Watercress, and Cucumber Finger Sandwiches

Pineapple Boats Filled with Fresh Fruit

Hot Cheese and Sausage Balls · Biscuits with Ham

Tray of Raw Vegetables with Clam Dip

Wheels of Cheddar and Bleu Cheese

Assorted Crackers

Sliced Cold Meats

Relishes and Pickles*

Benne Bits · Assorted Fancy Cookies

Crisp Sweet Green Tomato Pickles

Yield: 10-12 pints

These crystalized green tomatoes are not only delicious, but are beautiful as well. They make a very attractive party pickle or gift item.

NOTE: Soaking process should be done in covered bowl in refrigerator. Weight down tomatoes so they do not float. Tomatoes should be lifted daily to rotate those in bottom to top of bowl.

7 pounds small, firm, green
   tomatoes (silver dollar size)
lime water (2 cups pickling lime
   to 2 gallons water)
alum water (1 cup powdered alum
   to 2 gallons water)
1 tablespoon soda
ginger tea (3 teaspoons ground
   ginger to ½ gallon water)
7 pounds sugar
1 tablespoon mace (whole or
   ground)
1 tablespoon whole cloves
1 tablespoon whole allspice
½ gallon white vinegar
   (to cover sugar)

Slice tomatoes ¼ inch thick. Cover with lime water and soak 3 days. On fourth day drain and soak in clear water. On following three days soak in alum water. On eighth day rinse tomatoes in clear water. Drain. Place tomatoes in large kettle. Cover with water containing 1 tablespoon alum. Bring to boil. Remove kettle to sink and add 1 teaspoon soda. (Solution will foam.) Drain tomatoes. Boil in ginger tea <u>4 minutes.</u> Drain and set aside. Combine sugar, spices and vinegar. Boil until thick. Add tomatoes and boil 4 minutes. Layer hot tomatoes very carefully in sterilized jars. Cover with syrup. Seal while hot.

Heath Merrill Rushin (Mrs. Emmett)

Curry Slices

Yield: 3 pints

8 cups (2½ pounds) cucumbers,
   thinly sliced
1 medium onion, thinly sliced
1 tablespoon plain salt
2 cups cider vinegar
1½ cups sugar
1 tablespoon curry powder
2 teaspoons mixed pickling
   spices
1 teaspoon celery seed
1 teaspoon mustard seed
½ teaspoon pepper
1 green pepper, cut in thin strips

Place cucumbers and onion in large bowl. Sprinkle with salt and cover with ice water. Let stand three hours. Drain well. Combine remaining ingredients in large kettle and heat. Add cucumbers and onions. Heat just to boiling. Seal in sterilized jars.

Irene D. Howell

Lemon Yellow Artichoke Pickles

Yield: 12 pints

An old family recipe from Charleston, South Carolina.

½ bushel artichokes
2 pounds Bermuda onions,
   sliced thin
6 lemons, sliced thin
12 hot peppers or ¼ teaspoon
   red pepper
1 large can Coleman's dry
   mustard
2 ounces celery seed
2 ounces turmeric
1 tablespoon allspice
1 tablespoon mace
1 tablespoon whole black pepper
1½ cups salt
3 pounds brown sugar
1 gallon vinegar

Thoroughly clean and dry artichokes. Mix together all ingredients in 3-gallon crock. Stir well each day for one week. Pickles are ready to eat on the eighth day.

Gail Rabai (Mrs. John)

Aunt Josie's Sweet Chunk Pickles

Yield: 9 pints

Spices can be changed according to taste.

7 pounds cucumbers
2 cups pickling lime
8 cups vinegar
7½ cups sugar
1 tablespoon salt
1 teaspoon celery seed
1 teaspoon whole cloves
1 teaspoon mixed pickling spices
cinnamon buds (optional)
1 cup raisins (optional)

Wash and slice cucumbers in ¼-inch slices. Dissolve lime in 2 gallons water. Place cucumbers in stone jar or enamel container. Cover with lime solution; let stand 24 hours. Rinse well and cover with clear water; let stand 3 hours. Drain well and cover with solution of vinegar, sugar, salt and spices. Let stand overnight in solution. The next day boil 40 minutes. Pack while hot. Cinammon buds may be added, if available. If using raisins, the above can be cooked 35 minutes and then add raisins. Cook additional 5 minutes. If raisins are omitted, an extra cup of sugar added to vinegar solution will make pickles quite sweet.

Harry McDaniel

Refrigerator Pickles

Easy. Ready to eat in 3 to 5 days.

Yield: 1 gallon

4 cups sugar
4 cups vinegar
½ cup salt
1⅓ teaspoons turmeric
1⅓ teaspoons mustard seed
1½ teaspoons celery seed
2 large onions, sliced
12 (or more) cucumbers, sliced

Mix sugar, vinegar, salt, turmeric, mustard seed and celery seed. Let stand overnight. Pack cucumbers and onion slices in jars or container. (May use large Tupperware bowl.) Cover with vinegar mixture. Do not seal, but cover with lid and store in refrigerator. Will keep about one month.

Pat Sanderlin (Mrs. Charles W.)

Company Best Pickles

Yield: 7 pints

10 medium cucumbers
8 cups sugar
2 tablespoons mixed pickling spices
5 teaspoons salt
4 cups cider vinegar

Cover whole cucumbers with boiling water. Allow to stand 24 hours. Drain. Repeat procedure three times. The fifth time drain and slice into ½-inch pieces. Combine sugar, spices, salt and vinegar. Bring to boil and pour over cucumbers. Let stand two days. On third day bring to boil then pack and seal in sterilized pint jars.

"Sam" Doud (Mrs. Harry)

Kosher Dill Pickles

Quick method.

Yield: 7-8 pints

30-40 medium cucumbers, cut lengthwise
1 quart vinegar
1 quart water
¾ cup sugar
½ cup non-iodized salt
7-8 cloves garlic
7-8 hot peppers
14-16 fresh dill sprigs or
10-12 teaspoons dill seed

Wash and drain cucumbers. Combine vinegar, water, sugar and salt; simmer 15 minutes. Pack cucumbers into jars, leaving ½-inch head space. Put 1 clove garlic, 1 hot pepper and 2 sprigs dill (or 1½ teaspoons dill seed) in each jar. Cover with boiling hot vinegar mixture. Adjust lids. Process in boiling water bath 15 minutes.

Estelle Coleman (Mrs. Charles)

153

Crisp Pickles

Yield: 1 quart

A delicious party pickle. Easy!

1 quart kosher dill pickles
3 cups sugar
1-3 cloves garlic

Drain off pickle juice and reserve. Slice pickles. Cover with sugar and let stand. Sugar will dissolve and make a liquid. When it does, put pickle slices, liquid and garlic back in jar. If not enough liquid to fill jar, add some of the reserved juice. Chill.

Ida Hammond

Okra Pickles

Yield: 1 pint

tender untrimmed okra, enough to fill one pint jar
1 teaspoon mustard seed
1 pod hot pepper
1 clove garlic (peeled)
½ teaspoon salt
white vinegar, enough to pour over and cover okra

Wash okra; pack in sterilized pint jar. Add mustard seed, pepper, garlic and salt. Bring vinegar to boiling point and pour over okra. Seal. Allow to stand two weeks. Chill and serve.

Charles Newton

Squash Pickles

Yield: 12 pints

4 quarts squash, sliced thin
6 medium onions, sliced thin
¼ cup salt
5 cups sugar
1½ teaspoons celery seed
1½ teaspoons mustard seed
1 teaspoon turmeric
3 cups white vinegar

Cover squash, onions and salt with crushed ice and let stand 3 hours. Drain. Add remaining ingredients and let come to a boil. Put into pint jars and seal.

**Frances Arrington Elyea
(Mrs. George D.)
RHS President 1981-82**

Zucchini Pickles

Yield: 6-7 pints

Recipe can also be made with cucumbers.

- 7 pounds zucchini squash, sliced
- 2 cups pickling lime
- 2 quarts vinegar
- 4 pounds sugar
- 6 slices lemon
- 1 teaspoon cloves
- 1 tablespoon mixed pickling spices
- 1 stick cinnamon
- 2 tablespoons salt

Dissolve lime in 2 gallons cold water. Add zucchini slices. Let stand 24 hours. Drain and wash. Soak zucchini in ice water 5-6 hours. Drain. Combine vinegar, sugar, lemon and spices which have been tied in a cloth. Bring to boil. Pour syrup over zucchini. Let stand 24 hours. Boil slowly one hour. Seal in sterile jars while hot.

Estelle Coleman (Mrs. Charles)

Pickled Vegetables

Yield: 3 pints

- 3 cloves garlic
- 1½ teaspoons dill
- 1½ teaspoons peppercorn
- 1½ teaspoons salt
- 3 pieces chili pepper
- cauliflower flowers
- bell pepper, thin strips
- carrots, thin strips
- 2 cups vinegar
- 2 cups water
- ½ cup sugar

Wash 3 pint jars. Put into each jar 1 garlic clove, ½ teaspoon dill, ½ teaspoon peppercorn, ½ teaspoon salt and 1 piece chili pepper. Pack mixed raw vegetables into jars. Combine vinegar, water and sugar; boil. Pour boiling mixture over vegetables and seal. Refrigerate after opened.

Martha Coursey (Mrs. Bob L.)

Aunt Elva's Hot Pepper Relish

Yield: 5-6 pints

- 4 pounds onions (white or yellow)
- 75 pods chili peppers (half red, half green)
- 2 cups sugar
- 3 tablespoons salt
- 3 cups white vinegar

Grind onions and peppers together (use a food processor). Combine sugar, salt and vinegar in a pot and bring to a boil. Add onion and pepper to mixture. Cook 5 minutes. Pour into hot jars and seal.

Dr. Wendell Phillips

Good Gift Vegetable Relish

Yield: 1½ quarts or
24 (¼ cup) servings

Makes a delightful salad and doubles as a great relish for gift giving occasions. Prepare 24 hours ahead.

1 (17 ounce) can LeSueur peas
1 (12 ounce) can Green Giant
  white shoe peg corn
1 (17 ounce) can French style
  green beans
1 medium onion, chopped
1¼ cups celery, chopped
1 (2 ounce) jar chopped pimiento,
  drained

Drain well the canned vegetables. Place in large bowl and add onion, celery and pimiento. Mix. Toss with dressing.

Dressing

½ cup corn oil
½ cup vinegar
¾ cup sugar
½ teaspoon salt
½ teaspoon pepper

Dressing: Heat ingredients to boiling. Cool to warm. Add to vegetables and toss lightly. Store in refrigerator. Drain and reserve marinade just before serving. Use reserved marinade to restore any leftovers. Juices from vegetables make delightful broth. Keeps two months in refrigerator.

Hazel McDaniel (Mrs. Harry A.)

Mama Jones' Relish

Yield: 6-8 pints

1 gallon ripe tomatoes
4 cups sugar
6 onions, chopped
3 pods bell pepper, chopped
  and seeds removed
1 quart white vinegar
hot peppers to taste, chopped
  and seeds removed

Peel tomatoes by dipping in boiling water. Combine all ingredients in non-aluminum Dutch oven. Bring to boil over medium heat. Lower heat; cook two hours. Pour into hot pint jars. Seal.

Blanche Lantz (Mrs. W. E.)

BREADS

Dot Beebe

**GOULDING HOUSE
GOULDING PLACE
Circa 1867**

GOULDING HOUSE
Goulding Place

Goulding House was built upon a wooded knoll at the far end of Goulding Place in 1867 for Dr. Francis R. Goulding, minister, chaplain, author, and inventor, after his retirement to Roswell.

The unpretentious simplicity of the story-and-a-half home places it in the style of "Plantation Plain." Dr. Goulding chose the homesite for its elevation and view, its rolling, wooded terrain and spring-fed brooklets, a sylvan setting for writing his adventure stories for which he was famous.

Though he invented a sewing machine several years before Elias Howe's, Dr. Goulding failed to have his invention patented. At the time, he wrote in his diary, "Having satisfied myself about this machine, I laid it aside that I might attend to other and weightier duties."

The Goulding home was restored with the commitment to return it to its original condition and preserve the character of the lovely structure. The rooms are large, but not overwhelming, as with the Greek Revival homes. The delicate wood and plaster work is simple and unadorned, as is the trim of windows and doors. Balusters are plain rectangular pickets with smooth, round hand-railings, accentuating the grace of the stairway.

The brick is Flemish bond, the symmetrical windows, shuttered. From the broad back veranda is a breath-taking view of the ancient woodlands and the misty Blue Ridge foothills.

———

THANKSGIVING DINNER AT GOULDING HOUSE

Baked Hen
Corn Bread Dressing with Gravy*

Green Beans   Sweet Potato Soufflé
Mixed Turnip and Mustard Greens
Cranberry Sauce
Hot Rolls
Lemon Meringue Pie

Iced Tea   Coffee

Corn Bread Dressing

Serves 8
400°oven

Distinctively Southern stuffing to accompany baked chicken or turkey.

2 cups corn bread, crumbled
(bread made with corn meal,
buttermilk and 1 egg)
1½ cups homemade biscuits,
crumbled
3 eggs
⅓ cup finely diced onion
¼ cup finely diced celery
3½ to 4 cups chicken broth
½ cup melted butter
salt and pepper to taste

Combine all ingredients and mix well. Place in 9 x 13-inch casserole dish and bake 30 minutes at 400°. Makes enough dressing to serve with a 3½ to 4 pound hen.

**Mrs. J.I. Wright
by Mary Wright Hawkins**

Magnolia Ledge Crisp Corn Pones

Serves 3
350°, 400° oven

1 cup self-rising meal
2 tablespoons cooking oil
1 cup (less 1 tablespoon) boiling
water

Mix all ingredients thoroughly. Divide into six patties (1 heaping tablespoon each, approximately one-half inch thick). Place in hot greased iron skillet or pan. Bake at 350° for 15 minutes and then at 400° for 15 minutes (until brown and crisp).

Frances Boggs (Mrs. Gilbert H., Jr.)

Apple Muffins

Yield: 8-10
400° oven

1 egg
½ cup sugar
4 tablespoons melted butter
2 cups flour
4 teaspoons baking powder
½ teaspoon salt
1 cup milk
1 cup chopped apple
½ teaspoon cinnamon
2 tablespoons sugar

Beat egg; add sugar and butter. Add dry ingredients, milk and apple. Mix. Pour into greased muffin tins. Mix cinnamon and sugar and sprinkle over top of muffins. Bake at 400° for 20 minutes.

Nan Warren (Mrs. James P., Jr.)

Spiced Bran Muffins

Yield: 4 dozen large
or 8 dozen small,
400° oven

Batter can be refrigerated for up to 6 weeks.

3 cups all bran cereal
1 cup boiling water
½ cup salad oil
2½ cups flour
1⅓ cups sugar
1 teaspoon salt
2 beaten eggs
2 cups buttermilk
1 teaspoon soda
heavy dash cinnamon, ginger and
    nutmeg
1 cup white raisins (optional)

Combine 1 cup cereal, boiling water and oil. Combine remaining 2 cups cereal and all other ingredients. Add oil mixture. If raisins are used, soak in boiling water, drain and add. Spoon mixture into muffin pans sprayed with Pam to two-thirds capacity. Bake at 400° for 15 minutes. Do not overbake.

Wilma Deuel DuVal

Ham Muffins

Yield: 1 dozen
400° oven

1½ cups flour
2 teaspoons baking powder
2 teaspoons sugar
¼ teaspoon salt
½ cup wheat bran
¾ cup ground, cooked ham
2 eggs
1 cup milk
3 tablespoons melted shortening

Sift flour, baking powder, sugar and salt together. Stir in wheat bran and ham. Beat eggs; add milk and melted shortening. Add to flour mixture and stir only until flour disappears. Fill greased muffin pans two-thirds full and bake at 400° for 20-25 minutes.

Mary Brannon (Mrs. Randall H.)

1929 Ice Box Rolls

Yield: 4 dozen
375° oven

Old recipe from North Augusta Chapter of Winthrop Daughters.

1 cup boiling water
¼ cup sugar
1 tablespoon Crisco
1 tablespoon butter
¼ cup lukewarm water
2 packages yeast
½ teaspoon sugar
1 egg
4 cups plain flour
1 teaspoon salt

Combine boiling water, ¼ cup sugar, Crisco and butter. Let cool until lukewarm. Combine ¼ cup water, yeast and ½ teaspoon sugar. Add to first mixture. Add egg, flour and salt. Beat well. Put in refrigerator. Make rolls as needed. Let set 1-2 hours before baking at 375° for 20-25 minutes (until golden).

Sue C. Rowland (Mrs. Henry)

Alabama Ice Box Rolls

Yield: 32
400° oven

Dough will keep in refrigerator several days.

½ cup shortening
¼ cup sugar
¾ teaspoon salt
½ cup boiling water
1 egg, beaten
1 teaspoon lemon extract
1 envelope yeast dissolved in
   ½ cup cold water
3 cups flour

Place shortening, sugar and salt in bowl. Pour boiling water over. Let cool. Add egg, lemon extract and dissolved yeast. Add flour and mix well. Turn into greased bowl, cover and refrigerate overnight. Divide dough into 2 parts. Keep 1 part in refrigerator. Roll other into 16-inch circle. Brush with melted butter and cut into 16 wedges. Roll up each wedge beginning at wide end. Place on oiled pan with point underneath. Roll other half of dough in same way and repeat procedure. Let stand in warm place until double in bulk and very light (4-5 hours). Bake at 400° for 10-15 minutes.

Marian Steele (Mrs. Ed L.)

French Bread Rolls

Yield: 2-2½ dozen
375° oven

Dough can be kept in refrigerator one week.

½ cup milk
½ cup softened margarine
⅓ cup sugar
1 teaspoon salt
1 package dry yeast
¼ cup very warm water
3 eggs
3½ cups all-purpose flour
egg white

Scald milk. Combine margarine, sugar and salt. Cream until fluffy. Sprinkle yeast into warm water, stirring until dissolved. Add yeast mixture, milk, eggs and flour to creamed mixture. Beat vigorously 2 or more minutes with wooden spoon. Cover and let rise for 2 hours. Beat 2 more minutes. Cover tightly with Saran wrap and aluminum foil. Refrigerate overnight. Punch dough down. Pinch off pieces and make rolls. Snip top of rolls with scissors. Brush with egg white and let stand an hour. Bake at 375° for 15 to 20 minutes.

Jean McFarland (Mrs. John)

161

Janice's Rolls

Yield: 2-2½ dozen
400° oven

2½ cups self rising flour
2⅔ tablespoons sugar
½ teaspoon soda
½ cup shortening
1 cup buttermilk
1 package yeast dissolved in
   2 tablespoons lukewarm water

Mix flour, sugar, soda. Cut in shortening. Add buttermilk and dissolved yeast. Place in refrigerator and let rise 1-2 hours. When ready to roll out, flour rolling surface and hands. Place dough on surface and turn over two or three times. Can be cut with large cutter or glass and folded over as Parkerhouse rolls, or cut two and stack together for biscuits. Bake at 400° approximately 15 minutes.

Sylvia Patrick (Mrs. Trummie)

Short Breads - Party Biscuits

Yield: 3-4 dozen
350° oven

2 sticks margarine
8 ounces sour cream
2 cups sifted self-rising flour

Melt margarine. (Do not let bubble.) Cool slightly. Add sour cream, mixing well. Slowly add flour. Spoon heaping teaspoonful into ungreased 2-inch muffin tins. Bake 20-25 minutes at 350°. May be prepared one hour before baking.

Sara M. Smith

Whole Wheat Angel Biscuits

Yield: 3-4 dozen
400° oven

Dough may be chilled before baking or baked biscuits frozen for later use.

2 packages dry yeast
2 tablespoons lukewarm water
2 cups whole wheat flour
3 cups all-purpose flour
2 teaspoons baking powder
1 teaspoon salt
1 teaspoon baking soda
3 tablespoons sugar
1 cup shortening
2 cups buttermilk

Dissolve yeast in lukewarm water. Mix together dry ingredients and cut in shortening. Add yeast and buttermilk to dry mixture. Knead dough until it holds together. Roll or pat dough to half-inch thickness. Cut with biscuit cutter and fold in half. Bake at 400° for 15 to 20 minutes.

Etha L. Bearden

Blackberry Spice Muffins

Yield: 4 dozen
400° oven

Three generation favorite of the Pratt Family. To a girl at school away from family and friends how much fun to receive big baskets of wild blackberry muffins from home. Heath Rushin fondly recalled the days when a train conductor or bus driver did not mind handling fragile extra baggage like baked goods covered with a cloth and tucked in baskets.

¾ cup butter or Crisco
2 cups sugar
4 eggs, beaten
3 cups flour
1 teaspoon soda
1 teaspoon cinnamon
1 teaspoon cloves
1 teaspoon allspice
½ cup buttermilk
1 glass blackberry wine
   (½ - ¾ cup)
1 cup blackberry jam (do not
   use preserves)

Cream butter; add sugar and beaten eggs. Sift together flour, soda and spices. Add alternately flour mixture and liquids. Stir in blackberry jam. Mix thoroughly. Pour into greased muffin tins. Bake at 400° for 25 minutes.

Heath Merrill Rushin (Mrs. Emmett)

Mexican Corn Brunch Bread

Serves 12
350°, 300° oven

Like eating cake. Even good served cold at a picnic.

1 cup butter
1 cup sugar
4 eggs
1 (4 ounce) can green chilies,
   seeded and chopped
1 (1 pound) can cream style
   corn
½ cup shredded Monterey Jack
   cheese
½ cup shredded cheddar
   cheese
1 cup flour
1 cup yellow corn meal
4 teaspoons baking powder
¼ teaspoon salt

Preheat oven to 350°. Cream butter and sugar. Add eggs one at a time, mixing well. Add chilies, corn and cheeses; mix well. Sift together flour, corn meal, baking powder and salt. Add to corn mixture. Pour into greased and floured 9 x 13-inch pan. Put in oven and reduce heat to 300°. Bake 1 hour. Serve warm.

Jeanne Bump (Mrs. Gerald J.)

Cream Cheese Braids

Yield: 4 loaves
375° oven

1 cup sour cream
½ cup sugar
1 teaspoon salt
½ cup melted butter or margarine
2 packages dry yeast
½ cup warm water (105°-115°)
2 eggs, beaten
4 cups all-purpose flour

Heat sour cream over low heat; stir in sugar, salt and butter. Cool to lukewarm. Sprinkle yeast over warm water in large mixing bowl and stir to dissolve. Add sour cream mixture, eggs and flour. Mix well, cover and refrigerate overnight. The next day, divide dough into four parts and roll each into 12 x 8 - inch rectangle on well floured board.

Cream Cheese Filling

16 ounces cream cheese, softened
¾ cup sugar
1 egg, beaten
1/8 teaspoon salt
2 teaspoons vanilla

Combine all ingredients for cream cheese filling (makes 2 cups). Spread one-fourth filling on each rectangle and roll up, jelly roll fashion, beginning at long sides. Pinch edges together and fold ends under slightly. Place on greased baking sheets, seam side down. Slit each roll at 2-inch intervals about two-thirds through to resemble a braid. Cover and let rise in warm draft-free, place until doubled in bulk (about 1 hour). Bake at 375° for 12-15 minutes. Spread with glaze while warm.

Glaze

2 cups powdered sugar
4 tablespoons milk
2 teaspoons vanilla

Glaze: Combine all ingredients in small bowl. Mix well. Yield: about 1 cup.

Burma Denny (Mrs. J. B.)

Sour Cream Corn Bread

Serves 9-12
400° oven

1 cup self-rising corn meal
2 eggs
1 teaspoon sugar
1 cup cream style corn
1 cup commercial sour cream
½ cup salad oil

Combine all ingredients, mixing well. Pour into greased 9-inch pan, or greased muffin pan. Bake at 400° for 20-30 minutes.

Ruby Ezzard (Mrs. Thomas M.)

Cheese Onion Bread

Yield: 1 loaf
350° oven

½ cup chopped onion
1 tablespoon melted fat
1 beaten egg
½ cup milk
1½ cups Bisquick
1 cup grated cheese
1 tablespoon poppy seeds
  (optional)
2 tablespoons melted butter

Cook onion in fat until tender, not brown. Combine egg and milk; add Bisquick and stir only until dry ingredients are moist. Add onion and ½ cup cheese. Place in greased 9 x 5 x 2 - inch loaf pan. Top with remaining cheese, poppy seeds and melted butter. Bake at 350° for 30 minutes.

Wanda Bardin (Mrs. Charles)

Cinnamon Bread

Yield: 2 loaves
375° oven

1 cup milk
4 cups flour
1 teaspoon salt
¼ cup sugar
1 cup soft butter
1 package yeast
¼ cup warm water
3 egg yolks, beaten
1½ cups sugar
1½ teaspoons cinnamon

Scald milk; set aside to cool. Stir flour, salt and ¼ cup sugar in large bowl. Cut in butter with pastry blender to look like meal. Dissolve yeast in water. Mix yolks, yeast and milk together. Add to flour mixture. Beat well with wooden spoon. Chill overnight. Divide dough in half and roll each into 13 x 8 - inch rectangle. Brush with melted butter. Mix 1½ cups sugar and cinnamon. Sprinkle over dough. Roll jelly roll style. Place in 2 greased pans and cover. Allow to rise 2 hours. Dough will not double. Bake one hour at 375°. After 35 minutes, if browning too quickly, cover with brown paper. Remove from pan while hot.

Glaze

1 cup powdered sugar
1½ teaspoons vanilla
1½ teaspoons butter
1 or 2 tablespoons water

GLAZE: Combine glaze ingredients and frost bread.

Pat Spencer (Mrs. Bill)

Dilly Bread

Yield: 1 loaf
350° oven

1 package dry yeast
¼ cup warm water
1 cup low-fat cottage cheese,
   heated to lukewarm
2 tablespoons sugar
1 teaspoon salt
1 tablespoon minced onion
2 teaspoons dill seed
¼ teaspoon baking soda
2½ cups all-purpose flour
1 tablespoon margarine

Soften yeast in warm water and combine with cottage cheese. Add all other ingredients except flour. Gradually mix in flour to form stiff dough; beat well. Let rise in warm place about 60 minutes or until doubled in bulk. Punch dough down and put in well-oiled 2-quart round casserole dish or 9 x 5-inch loaf pan. Cover and let rise about 40 minutes. Bake at 350° for 40-50 minutes. Brush with melted margarine while still hot. Cool 5 minutes before removing from pan.

Sherry Wier (Mrs. T. E.)

Hog Heaven Bread

Yield: 3 loaves
350° oven

This bread has complete protein.
3 cups whole wheat flour
1 cup rye flour
½ cup brown sugar or honey
2 tablespoons dry yeast (3 if you
   grind your own flour)
1 tablespoon salt
1½ cups water
¾ cup milk
4 tablespoons butter
2-3 cups unbleached flour

Mix wheat flour, rye, sweetener, yeast and salt. Warm milk, water and butter to about 80° and add to dry ingredients. Mix well and add enough unbleached flour to make stiff dough. Knead about 10 minutes. Put to rise in greased bowl, covered with a towel, near stove (at least 80°). Punch down and put in 3 greased (1 pound) coffee cans. Let rise again. Bake at 350° about 40 minutes. Cool on wire racks (upside down in cans).

Judy B. Raiford

Grapenut Bread

Yield: 2 loaves
325° oven

Tastes better the second day!

1 cup grapenuts
2 cups buttermilk or sour milk
2 eggs, beaten
1 cup sugar
½ teaspoon salt
1 teaspoon baking soda in ¼ cup hot water
4 cups flour
2 teaspoons baking powder
1 cup raisins (optional)

Soak grapenuts in buttermilk 30 minutes. Add eggs, sugar, salt and dissolved baking soda to grapenut mixture. Sift flour and baking powder into mixture. Add raisins. Stir until well mixed. Pour into 2 loaf pans. Bake at 325° for 50-60 minutes.

Marian Steele (Mrs. Ed L.)

Authentic Shaker Lemon Bread

Yield: 1 loaf
350° oven

⅓ cup shortening
1⅓ cups sugar
2 eggs
1½ cups sifted flour
1½ teaspoons baking powder
¼ teaspoon salt
½ cup milk
½ cup English walnuts
grated rind and juice of 1 lemon

Beat together shortening and 1 cup sugar until light and fluffy. Add eggs, one at a time, beating well after each one. Stir dry ingredients together and add alternately with milk to sugar mixture, beating well after each addition. Add nuts and lemon rind. Turn batter into greased loaf pan. Bake at 350° for 50-60 minutes. Blend remaining ⅓ cup sugar and lemon juice. Pour over bread while hot.

Jackie Williams, (Mrs. Walton)
Nova Goolsby (Mrs. George)

One-Two-Three-Four Wheat Bread

Yield: 2 loaves
325° oven

Traditional Mormon recipe. Hearty and faintly sweet.

1 tablespoon baking soda
2 cups brown sugar
3 cups cultured buttermilk
4 cups wheat flour

Sift baking soda with flour to prevent lumps. Mix by hand with other ingredients. Do not use electric mixer. Pour into 2 well greased bread pans and bake at 325° for one hour.

Sue Danbom (Mrs. Bob)

Maundy Thursday Bread

Yield: 3 loaves
350° oven

1½ cups scalded milk
½ cup butter or margarine
2 tablespoons salt
½ cup sugar or honey
2 yeast cakes
½ cup lukewarm water
2 eggs, beaten
8-9 cups all-purpose flour

Pour scalded milk over butter, salt and sugar. Cool. Dissolve yeast in lukewarm water and let stand until it bubbles (about 5 minutes). Add yeast and beaten eggs to cooled milk. Gradually add flour, beating thoroughly. (Do not add more flour than necessary to make easily handled dough. If fingers come away clean, enough flour has been used.) Turn out on floured board and knead until smooth and elastic. Place in greased bowl, cover, and let rise until doubled in size (about 1½ hours). Punch down and turn out on floured board. Shape into 3 loaves and place in greased 8-inch loaf pans. Let rise in warm place until doubled in size (about 1½ hours). Bake at 350° for 40 minutes. Bread is done if it has pulled away from side of pan and sounds hollow, if thumped.

Darby Butler (Mrs. J. L.)

Spoonbread

Serves 6
350° oven

Fourth generation recipe from the Williams family.

1⅓ cups fresh yellow cornmeal
1⅓ teaspoons salt
1⅓ cups cold milk
2 cups hot milk
3½ tablespoons butter
3 eggs, slightly beaten

Mix cornmeal and salt. Stir into cold milk. Add to hot milk in medium pot and cook on low heat until mixture thickens, stirring constantly. Remove from heat; add butter. Add a little hot mixture to eggs, and then stir eggs into pot of hot mixture. Mix well. Pour into 2-quart baking dish. Bake at 350% for 45 minutes or until firm in center and lightly browned.

Mickey Cox (Mrs. Ralph)

Pumpkin Bread

2 eggs
½ cup vegetable oil
1½ cups sugar
1 cup pumpkin
⅓ cup water
1¾ cups flour
1 teaspoon soda
1 teaspoon salt
¼ teaspoon baking powder
¼ teaspoon cloves
¼ teaspoon allspice
¼ teaspoon nutmeg
¼ teaspoon cinnamon
½ cup chopped nuts
⅓ cup light brown sugar
1 teaspoon cinnamon

Yield: 1 medium loaf or 2 small loaves
350° oven

Beat eggs; add oil and 1½ cups sugar. Blend pumpkin and water; add to egg mixture. Sift next eight ingredients. Stir into pumpkin mixture. Add nuts. Pour into greased medium loaf pan or 2 small loaf pans. Mix together brown sugar and cinnamon. Sprinkle over top of loaf. Bake at 350° for 1 hour for medium loaf and 45 minutes for 2 small loaves.

Marva L. Mapp (Mrs. C. A.)

Zucchini Bread

3 eggs
2 cups sugar
1 cup oil
2 cups zucchini squash, unpeeled, grated
½ cup chopped nuts
½ cup raisins
3 cups flour
1 teaspoon salt
1 teaspoon soda
½ teaspoon baking powder
1½ teaspoons cinnamon
1½ teaspoons nutmeg
1 teaspoon vanilla

Yield: 2 loaves
350° oven

Beat eggs until light and fluffy. Add sugar, oil, zucchini and mix well. Mix all dry ingredients together and add to egg mixture. Add vanilla; mix. Pour into two (9½ x 5½ x 2¾ - inch) loaf pans. Bake at 350° for 55 minutes to 1 hour.

Lu Brune (Mrs. Pat H.)

Yeast Bread

Yield: 1 loaf
375° oven

1½ tablespoons sugar (may use ½ tablespoon honey as part of sugar)
1¼ teaspoons salt
3 tablespoons shortening
½ cup warm water
1 package active dry yeast, dissolved in ½ cup warm water
1½ cups unbleached flour
1½ cups whole wheat flour

Stir sugar, salt and shortening in warm water until melted. Cool to lukewarm. Stir in dissolved yeast. Add 1½ cups flour and beat until smooth. Stir in most of remaining flour and turn out on floured board. Knead until dough is smooth and elastic (8-10 minutes). Add more flour while kneading, if necessary. Put dough in greased bowl and lightly grease top. Cover bowl with damp cloth and set in warm, draft free place to rise until doubled in bulk (about 30 minutes). Punch down dough and squeeze out air bubbles. Pat or roll into 6 x 10-inch rectangle. Starting with narrow end, roll tightly, jelly roll fashion, sealing dough about every half turn. Seal very well. Place in greased baking pan, cover with damp cloth, and allow to rise to double size in warm draft-free place (about 45 minutes). Bake at 375° for about 50 minutes (until top and sides are brown). Remove from pan and cool on rack.

Marguerite Cauble (Mrs. Mark)

Corn Waffles

Serves 6

Serve with creamed chicken.

1 (8 ounce) package corn muffin mix
2 eggs
1 cup milk
1 tablespoon salad oil

Empty corn muffin mix into bowl. Add eggs and ½ cup milk. Mix until smooth. Stir in remaining milk and salad oil. Let stand 5 minutes. Bake until steaming in preheated waffle baker set at medium heat. (Corn waffles bake longer than plain waffles.)

Martha Stovall

PIES
and
CAKES

Marguerite Cauble

ROSWELL PRESBYTERIAN CHURCH
MIMOSA BOULEVARD
Circa 1840

ROSWELL PRESBYTERIAN CHURCH

The first families to settle in Roswell were people of strong religious faith, leaders in Presbyterian churches in Savannah and Darien and other coastal towns of Georgia. Their first thoughts in the new settlement, after establishing their homes, was to build their church.

Dr. Nathaniel Pratt, pastor of the Darien Presbyterian Church, was asked to come to Roswell in 1839 to help organize the church and become its first minister. He served the church for 39 years. He and his wife, Catherine Barrington King, daughter of Roswell King, built the home, Great Oaks, across from the church.

A lovely columned house of worship, the Roswell Presbyterian Church was erected in 1840 on land donated by the King family, the first public building in the town. Seventeen slave members worshipped from the balcony. A two-room school, The Academy, was built on adjacent property.

During the Civil War, the church became a hospital for Union soldiers, most of whom were suffering from exposure to the July heat. Services were held on Sundays for the soldiers, though the pews and organ had been removed to make room for the litters. A church member hid the communion silver, and the pulpit Bible was removed and was missing for almost a century. The building, however, was unharmed and has remained in use through the years. A larger sanctuary was built adjacent to the original building in 1978. Items of interest during the war years and other memorabilia are on display in the church History Room.

The Roswell Presbyterian Church is listed on the National Register of Historic Places.

DINNER ON THE GROUNDS AT THE HISTORIC ROSWELL PRESBYTERIAN CHURCH

Favorite Dishes Brought by Church Members
and Served on Tables Under the Trees

Fried Chicken	Roast Beef	Baked Ham
	Chopped and Molded Salads	
Potato Salad		Coleslaw
Vegetable Dishes		Meat Casseroles
	Pickles and Preserves	
Biscuits		Corn Bread
	Pies* and Cakes	
	Plenty of Iced Tea	

Chess Pie

Serves 6-8
325° oven

Great Southern favorite found at all kinds of social gatherings.

1½ cups sugar
1 tablespoon flour
½ teaspoon nutmeg
3 eggs, beaten
1 teaspoon vanilla
1 tablespoon corn meal
1 tablespoon vinegar
1 stick margarine or butter
1 unbaked pie shell

Sift together sugar, flour and nutmeg; add to beaten eggs. Stir in vanilla, meal and vinegar. Melt butter slightly and add to mixture. Pour into unbaked pie shell. Bake at 325⁰ about 40 minutes (until brown).

Ruby Ezzard (Mrs. Thomas M.)

Calypso Pie

Serves 10

From the Fox and Hounds Restaurant.

14-15 Hydrox cookies
¼ cup butter
½ gallon coffee ice cream
fudge sauce
whipped cream
chopped pecans or almonds

Crush cookies and mix with butter. Pat into 9-inch pie pan. Soften ice cream and whip. Pour into crust. Top with fudge sauce. Add high layer of whipped cream. Scatter nuts over top. Can be frozen and kept for weeks. Remove from freezer 30 minutes before serving.

Liz Meadow (Mrs. Jack)

Chocolate Walnut Pie

Serves 8
350° oven

Rich and elegant.

3 large eggs
1½ cups sugar
6 tablespoons butter, melted
2 teaspoons vanilla
¾ cup flour
1½ cups semi-sweet chocolate chips
1½ cups chopped walnuts
1 unbaked pie shell, chilled
whipped cream or vanilla ice cream
chopped walnuts
chocolate shavings
crème de cocoa

Break eggs into bowl and whip lightly. Continue whipping and add sugar. Whip in melted butter, then vanilla. Stir in flour, then chocolate chips and 1½ cups nuts. Fill pie shell. Bake 40 to 45 minutes (until filling is fairly firm and crust is light brown). Chill. Serve with whipped cream or vanilla ice cream. Garnish with chopped walnuts, chocolate shavings and a spoonful of crème de cocoa.

Public House Restaurant
Roswell Square

Chocolate Pie with Meringue Crust

Yield: One pie
300° oven

3 egg whites
1/8 teaspoon salt
¼ teaspoon cream of tartar
¾ cup sugar
½ cup pecans
½ teaspoon vanilla
4 ounces sweet cooking chocolate
3 tablespoons water
1 tablespoon brandy
2 cups heavy cream

Beat egg whites until foamy. Add salt and cream of tartar; beat. Add sugar gradually, continuing to beat until very stiff peaks form. Fold in nuts and vanilla. Pile into lightly greased 8-inch pie pan, forming a nest by pushing meringue up sides of pan. Bake 50 minutes at 300⁰. Cool. Melt chocolate and water in top of double boiler. Cool; add brandy. Whip 1 cup heavy cream; fold into chocolate mixture. Pour into meringue shell and chill several hours. When ready to serve, top with remaining whipped cream.

Pat Majure (Mrs. James C.)

Chocolate Chip Pie

Yield: One pie
350° oven

4 tablespoons butter
1 cup sugar
½ cup plain flour
2 eggs, beaten
1 cup semi-sweet chocolate chips
1 cup chopped pecans
1 teaspoon vanilla
1 unbaked pie shell

Melt butter and set aside to cool. Sift sugar and flour together. Stir in eggs and add remaining ingredients. Pour into pie shell. Bake at 350⁰ for 30 minutes. Serve warm with ice cream.

Betty Townsend (Mrs. Alto B.)

French Mint Pie

Serves 6-8

Rich but delicious. Found at the Craftwood Inn in Manitou Springs, Colorado.

2 squares unsweetened chocolate
1 cup powdered sugar
1 stick butter
2 eggs
¼ teaspoon mint flavoring
9-inch graham cracker crust

Melt chocolate and set aside to cool. Beat sugar and butter until smooth and add unbeaten eggs, one at a time. Continue beating and add chocolate and mint flavoring. Spread into graham cracker crust. Place in refrigerator and chill several hours.

Evie Brundrett (Mrs. G. A.)

Graham Cracker Cream Pie

Serves 6
350° oven

1¼ cups graham cracker crumbs
¼ cup melted butter
¾ cup sugar (or brown sugar for butterscotch pie)
2 tablespoons flour
2 tablespoons cornstarch
½ teaspoon salt
1½ cups milk
3 egg yolks
1 teaspoon vanilla
2 egg whites
4 tablespoons sugar

Mix crumbs and butter. Blend well. Reserve about 1/8 cup mixture to sprinkle on top of meringue. Press remaining into pie pan. Combine sugar, flour, cornstarch and salt in saucepan. Scald milk and add slowly to dry ingredients. Put mixture over medium heat until it begins to thicken, stirring constantly. Gradually add egg yolks and let mixture come to a boil, continaully stirring. Remove from heat. Add vanilla. Let cool. Beat egg whites with sugar for meringue. Pour cooled cream filling into graham cracker crust. Spread meringue over filling and seal edges. Sprinkle reserved crumbs over meringue and brown in 350° oven for 12-15 minutes. Let cool before serving.

Sarah Robertson (Mrs. Donald)

Grandmother's Graham Cracker Pie

Yield: One pie
300° oven

20 graham crackers, crushed
½ cup butter, melted
½ cup sugar
3 eggs, separated
2 cups milk
¼ cup sugar
2 tablespoons cornstarch
2 tablespoons vanilla

Mix cracker crumbs, butter and sugar. Reserve ½ cup. Press mixture into 9-inch pie pan. Mix egg yolks, sugar and cornstarch. Add milk. Cook over medium heat until just bubbling. Remove from heat; add vanilla. Pour into crust. Beat egg whites until peaks form. Spread on top of pudding. Sprinkle on reserved crumbs. Bake at 300° for 20-30 minutes.

Jean Moll (Mrs. Donald R.)

Georgia Cracker Pie

Serves 6-8
325° oven

3 egg whites
1 cup sugar
1 teaspoon vanilla
20 Ritz crackers, crushed fine
1 cup pecans, broken
whipped cream or Cool Whip
½ teaspoon maple flavoring

Beat egg whites until frothy. Slowly add ½ cup sugar. Beat until stiff. Add vanilla. Mix ½ cup sugar with cracker crumbs and nuts. Fold into whites. Pour into greased pie pan. Bake 30 minutes at 325°. When cool, top with whipped cream mixed with maple flavoring.
Clarece Martin (Mrs. P. L.)

Key Lime Pie

Serves 6-8
300° oven

An authentic recipe from Key West.
1 (8 or 9-inch) deep dish pie shell
4 large eggs
1 can Eagle Brand condensed
   milk
⅓ cup **fresh** lime juice

Bake pie shell according to instructions on wrapper. Set aside to cool. Separate 3 eggs. Beat whites until stiff peaks form. Add remaining egg, whole, to yolks and beat until thick. Add condensed milk. Beat until thick. Add lime juice and beat again. Fold whites into milk mixture. Pour into cooled pie shell and bake at 300° for 12 to 15 minutes. Chill in refrigerator before serving.
Harry Doud

Lemon Cake Pie

Yield: One pie
350° oven

1 cup sugar
3 tablespoons margarine
pinch of salt
3 tablespoons flour
3 egg yolks
juice and grated rind of one
   lemon
1 cup milk
3 egg whites, beaten
1 unbaked pie crust (deep dish)
whipped cream

Cream sugar, margarine and salt. Add egg yolks. Stir in flour, milk, lemon juice, and rind. Beat egg whites and fold into mixture. Pour into pie crust and bake at 350° for 45 minutes. Serve with whipped cream, if desired.
Ellie Brazee (Mrs. John)

Pecan Pie

Yield: One pie
425°, 325° oven

1 cup dark Karo syrup
3 eggs, beaten
½ cup sugar
1 teaspoon vanilla
piece of butter, size of walnut
1 cup pecans
unbaked pie shell

Mix together all ingredients and pour into pie shell. Bake 5 to 10 minutes at 425° to set pastry. Reduce heat to 325° and bake about 45 minutes until set.
Helene Moorman (Mrs. J. W., Sr.)

Angel Pecan Pie

Yield: One pie
350° oven

3 egg whites
1 cup sugar
1 teaspoon baking powder
1 cup Ritz cracker crumbs
1 cup chopped pecans
1 teaspoon vanilla

Beat egg whites until stiff. Mix in sugar and baking powder. Combine crumbs and pecans; fold into meringue. Fold in vanilla. Place in 9-inch pie plate. Cover sides and bottom of plate to make crust. Bake at 350° for 30 minutes. Cool. Add filling.

Filling
1 cup whipping cream
2 tablespoons sugar
1 teaspoon vanilla
¼ teaspoon almond flavoring
¼ cup pecan pieces

Filling: Whip cream with sugar, vanilla and almond flavoring until peaks form. Spoon into cooled shell. Sprinkle nuts over top. Chill.
Nancy Rittenburg (Mrs. John)

Rhubarb Custard Pie

Yield: One pie
350° oven

3 eggs
2 cups sugar
3 tablespoons milk
¼ cup flour
¼ teaspoon nutmeg
4 cups raw diced rhubarb
1 tablespoon butter
2 pie crusts

Beat eggs slightly. Stir in remaining ingredients and pour into a pastry lined pie pan. Dot with butter. Cover with a full top crust or lattice crust. Bake 50 to 60 minutes at 350°.
Mabel Lehman (Mrs. Ted)

Tom and Jerry Pie

Serves 6

3 egg yolks
¾ cup sugar
1/8 teaspoon salt
⅔ cup water
⅓ cup bourbon
1 tablespoon gelatin
¼ cup water
3 egg whites, stiffly beaten
1 baked 9-inch pie shell
whipped cream
nutmeg

Beat egg yolks, salt and sugar. Add ⅔ cup water and bourbon. Put in top of double boiler and cook until slightly thickened, stirring constantly. Soak gelatin in ¼ cup water and add to hot mixture. Cool and beat until thick and frothy. Fold in stiffly beaten egg whites. Pour into baked pie shell. Place in refrigerator to congeal. Top with sweetened whipped cream and sprinkle with nutmeg.
Mrs. Bernard P. Wolff

Grandma's Banana Fritters

Serves 4

For variation use peaches, pineapples, strawberries or any fruit in place of bananas.

1 cup all-purpose flour
¼ teaspoon salt
1 teaspoon baking powder
1 tablespoon sugar
1 beaten egg
¼ cup milk
1 tablespoon cooking oil
1 cup mashed bananas
powdered sugar (optional)

Combine flour, salt, baking powder and sugar in bowl. Mix together egg, milk, oil and bananas. Lightly stir into dry ingredients. Do not over mix. Drop from teaspoon into deep cooking oil heated to 365° (or when an inch square of bread browns in 60 seconds). If teaspoon is dipped into hot fat before dipping into fritter batter, the batter will slip off the spoon more easily and the fritters will have a more uniform shape. Fry until brown and cooked in center (3 to 5 minutes). Drain on paper towel. Sprinkle with powdered sugar, if desired.
Ella Mae Carter (Mrs. Robert R.)

French Apple Cake

Yield: Tube cake
350° oven

1½ cups salad oil
2 cups sugar
2 eggs
1 teaspoon vanilla
1 teaspoon baking powder
1 teaspoon cinnamon
½ teaspoon salt
3 cups plain flour
½ cup nuts
3 cups peeled, chopped apples
  (red delicious)

Mix first seven ingredients. Add 2 cups flour and beat with electric mixer. Fold in remaining 1 cup flour, apples and nuts. Spoon mixture into greased and floured tube pan or sheet pan. Bake 1¼ hours at 350⁰. Serves 12.
Rose Wing (Mrs. George)

Kentucky Mountain Carrot Cake

Yield: Tube cake
325° oven

2 cups sugar
2 cups sifted flour
1½ teaspoons baking powder
1 teaspoon salt
1½ teaspoons nutmeg
1½ cups salad oil
4 eggs, separated
1½ cups grated raw carrots
1¾ cups chopped walnuts

Sift all dry ingredients together in large mixing bowl. Add oil, egg yolks, carrots and nuts. Mix all well. Beat egg whites until stiff and gently fold into batter. Pour into greased tube pan. Bake at 325⁰ for 1½ to 1¾ hours. Optional: While hot, pour glaze over cake and let stand about 1 hour.

Glaze
1 cup sugar
½ cup buttermilk
1 teaspoon light corn syrup
2 tablespoons rum
2 teaspoons grated lemon rind

Glaze: Combine all ingredients and blend well. Pour over hot cake.
Louise Coleman (Mrs. Frank S.)

Cherry Cheese Cake

Yield: 9x13-inch cake
350° oven

¼ pound butter
1 cup flour
1½ tablespoons sugar
16 ounces cream cheese
2 cups powdered sugar
2 teaspoons vanilla
1 pint whipped cream
Comstock fruit pie filling

Mix butter, flour and sugar. Press into bottom of 9x13-inch pan. Bake at 350⁰ for 25 to 30 minutes. (Watch, as it burns easily.) Beat cream cheese, powdered sugar and vanilla. Fold in whipped cream. Pour into cool shell and top with pie filling.
Diane Guesman (Mrs. Richard)

Easy Lime Cheesecake

Yield: 2 (9-inch) or
1 (12x9-inch) cheesecake

Excellent when necessary to prepare one or two days before serving.

1 (3 ounce) package lime Jell-O
1 cup hot water
8 ounces cream cheese, softened
1 cup sugar
½ tablespoon vanilla
3 tablespoons lemon juice
1 (13 ounce) can evaporated milk, chilled
2 (9-inch) graham cracker crusts, or crust to cover bottom of (9x12-inch) baking dish

Dissolve Jell-O in hot water. Refrigerate until cool only . With electric mixer beat cheese until soft; add sugar and blend. Stir in vanilla. Blend in Jell-O, small amounts at a time. Add lemon juice and mix well. Refrigerate mixture while you whip evaporated milk until stiff. Fold cheese mixture into whipped milk. Pour into crust(s) and refrigerate at least 3-4 hours before serving.
Barbara Durrett (Mrs. Thomas J., III)

Hot Milk Cake

Yield: 8-inch cake
350° oven

3 eggs, well beaten
1½ cups sugar
1½ cups flour
¼ teaspoon salt
¾ cup milk
2 tablespoons butter or margarine
1½ teaspoons baking powder

Add sugar to eggs; beat well. Add flour, salt and baking powder sifted together. Heat milk and butter together to boiling point. Remove from heat and pour into cake mixture. Stir until smooth and pour into well greased 8x8-inch pan. Bake at 350⁰ for 40 minutes.
Willa Todd Moore

Harvey Wallbanger Cake

**Yield: Bundt cake
350° oven**

1 package orange cake mix
1 package vanilla pudding
4 eggs
½ cup cooking oil
½ cup orange juice
½ cup Galliano
2 tablespoons vodka

Beat all ingredients on low speed for ½ minute, then medium speed for five minutes. Pour into greased and floured Bundt pan and bake at 350⁰ for 45-50 minutes. Cool in pan 10 minutes. Remove to rack and top with glaze while still warm. Serves 10.

Glaze

1 cup sifted confectioners' sugar
1 tablespoon orange juice
1 tablespoon Galliano
1 tablespoon vodka

Glaze: Mix all ingredients and pour over warm cake.
Yvonne Lambert (Mrs. Paul V.)

Fruit Cocktail Cake

**Yield: 2-quart cake
300° oven**

1 (1 pound, 14 ounce) can fruit cocktail, less ¼ cup (well drained)
¼ cup rum
1 tablespoon soft butter
½ cup finely chopped walnuts
¼ cup flaked coconut
¼ cup brown sugar
1 cup sugar
1 egg
1¼ cups flour
1 teaspoon baking soda
¾ teaspoon salt
whipped cream

Soak fruit in rum 15 minutes. Drain well. Rub butter on inside of 2-quart mold. Combine nuts, coconut and brown sugar; press into buttered mold. Beat granulated sugar and egg together; stir in fruit cocktail and dry ingredients together. Mix until completely moistened. Spoon into mold. Bake at 300⁰ for 1 hour and 20 minutes. (Check after 1 hour.) Cool 10 minutes. Invert on serving plate. Scrape any remaining sugar mixture in pan onto cake. Serve warm or cold with whipped cream.
Anita Stong (Mrs. Stanley)

181

Japanese Fruit Cake

Yield: 3-layer cake
350° oven

You may opt to ice the whole cake with the filling recipe.

1 cup butter
2 cups sugar
4 eggs
3¼ cups flour
1 teaspoon baking powder
1 cup (scant) water or milk
1 teaspoon vanilla
1 teaspoon cinnamon
1 teaspoon allspice
½ teaspoon cloves
¼ pound raisins, chopped fine

Cream butter and sugar. Beat in eggs. Sift together flour and baking powder; stir in alternately with water or milk. Add vanilla and mix well. Pour off ⅓ of batter into round cake pan. To remaining batter add spices and raisins. Divide into 2 round cake pans. You will have 3 layers (two dark, one light). Bake at 350° about 30 minutes for light layer and about 40 minutes for dark layers.

Filling

juice of 2 lemons
grated rind of 1 lemon
1 good-size coconut, grated
1 (8 ounce) can crushed
    pineapple, undrained
2 cups sugar
1 cup boiling water
2 tablespoons cornstarch

Filling: Mix all ingredients except cornstarch in saucepan. Dissolve cornstarch in ½ cup cold water. Bring first mixture to boiling and add dissolved cornstarch. Continue to cook, stirring constantly, until mixture drops in a lump from the spoon. Cool; spread between layers. (Good as icing, too.)

Fluffy Icing

½ cup water
1 cup sugar
1 teaspoon vinegar
2 tablespoons white corn syrup
2 egg whites
½ teaspoon vanilla

Fluffy Icing: Mix water, sugar, vinegar and syrup in saucepan. Boil, without stirring, until it gives a long thread.Beat egg whites until stiff. Beat in vanilla. Slowly pour boiled mixture over egg whites and beat until cool and stiff enough to hold its shape. Spread over cake.

Haden Coleman (Mrs. Woodrow)

French Pastry Cake

The frosting makes this cake!
5 eggs, separated
1½ cups sugar
½ cup water
¾ teaspoon baking powder
1½ cups sifted cake flour
¼ teaspoon almond flavoring
¾ teaspoon vanilla
¾ teaspoon cream of tartar

Beat egg yolks until light. Add sugar and water; blend well. Add baking powder, flour, almond and vanilla flavorings. Beat egg whites; add cream of tartar and continue beating until stiff, but not dry. Gently fold egg whites into cake mixture. Bake in ungreased angel food pan at 325⁰ for 50-60 minutes. Cool. To frost, slice through cake to make 4 layers. Frost each layer, top and sides of cake. Refrigerate.

Frosting
3 squares Baker's unsweetened
**   chocolate**
3 cups powdered sugar
½ pound unsalted butter
5 eggs
1 teaspoon vanilla

Frosting: Melt chocolate; cool. Cream butter and sugar. Stir in melted chocolate. Add eggs one at a time, beating well. Add vanilla and mix well. Let stand in cool place ½ hour before frosting cake.
JoAnn Rieger (Mrs. Thomas B.)

Pecan Cream Cake

Rich, rich, rich — but worth it!
6 eggs, separated
1½ cups sugar
2 teaspoons baking powder
2 tablespoons flour
3 cups pecans, ground
2 cups whipping cream

Beat egg yolks; add sugar and beat well. Set aside. Sift flour, baking powder and nuts. Beat egg whites until stiff. Fold nut and flour mixture into egg whites. Fold all into egg yolk mixture. Blend well. Pour into 3 (9-inch) pans. Bake at 350⁰ for 20 minutes. Cool. Whip cream and spread between layers and on top of cake.
Beverly Shelton

Roasted Pecan-Cream Cake

Yield: 3-layer cake
350° oven

5 eggs
½ cup butter
½ cup vegetable shortening
2 cups sugar
1 teaspoon soda
1 cup buttermilk
2 cups plain flour, sifted 2 times
3½ ounces coconut
1 cup chopped roasted pecans
1 teaspoon vanilla
1 teaspoon coconut flavoring

Separate eggs and beat whites until stiff. Set aside. Cream butter, shortening and sugar. Add egg yolks, one at a time, beating well after each addition. Dissolve soda in buttermilk; add alternately with flour. Beat well. Add coconut, nuts and flavorings. Fold in stiffly beaten egg whites. Pour into 3 greased and floured 9-inch cake pans. Bake 25 minutes at 350°. Cool; ice.

Cream Cheese Icing

8 ounces cream cheese, softened
½ cup butter
1 pound powdered sugar
1 teaspoon almond flavoring

Icing: Combine ingredients and beat well. Spread between layers and on top of cooled cake.
Bob Hancock

Brown Sugar Pound Cake

Yield: Tube cake
350° oven

Mrs. C. W. Reid collected pound cake recipes and shared this favorite with friends.

½ pound butter or margarine
½ cup vegetable oil
1 pound brown sugar
1 cup white sugar
5 large or 6 small eggs
3 cups plain flour
1 teaspoon baking powder
1 teaspoon salt
1 cup milk
2 tablespoons vanilla

Cream butter and oil. Add sugars. Cream until fluffy and light. Add eggs, one at a time, beating well after each. Sift flour, baking powder and salt together. Add to sugar and egg mixture alternately with milk and vanilla. Bake at 350° for 1 hour and 15 minutes in 10-inch tube pan.

Glaze

1 cup confectioners' sugar
6 tablespoons cream
½ cup nuts
2 tablespoons butter

Glaze: Mix all ingredients and drizzle over top while cake is hot.
Margaret Harris (Mrs. William)

Chocolate Pound Cake

Yield: Tube cake
325° oven

3 cups sugar
2 sticks margarine
½ cup vegetable shortening
5 eggs
½ cup cocoa
¼ teaspoon salt
½ teaspoon baking powder
3 cups flour, sifted 3 times
1 teaspoon vanilla
1 cup + 2 tablespoons milk

Cream sugar, margarine and shortening. Add eggs, one at a time, and beat until smooth. Sift together dry ingredients. Add to egg mixture alternately with milk and vanilla. Pour into greased and floured tube pan and bake at 325° for 1 hour 45 minutes.

Dot Beebe (Mrs. Philip)

Pound Cake

Yield: Tube cake
300° oven

8 medium or 10 small eggs
6 tablespoons sugar
1 pound butter
2⅔ cups sugar
3½ cups flour, sifted
8 tablespoons coffee cream or Carnation
1 teaspoon vanilla or almond flavoring

Separate eggs. Whip whites with 6 tablespoons sugar. Place in refrigerator. Cream softened butter and add sugar gradually. Add egg yolks two at a time. Stir in flour and cream alternately. Add flavoring. Fold in beaten egg whites (this is important). Bake in greased tube pan 1½ hours at 300°.

Evelyn W. Callaway (Mrs. Lee)

Cream Cheese Pound Cake

Yield: Tube cake
325° oven

3 sticks margarine
8 ounces cream cheese
3 cups sugar
dash salt
1½ teaspoons vanilla
6 large eggs
3 cups cake flour, sifted

Cream margarine, cheese and sugar until light and fluffy. Add salt and vanilla; beat well. Add eggs one at a time, beating well after each addition. Stir in flour. Spoon mixture into greased and floured 10-inch tube pan. Bake at 325° about 1½ hours. Serve plain or with fresh berries.

Gail Turner (Mrs. Joseph)

Berry Pound Cake

Yield: Bundt cake
350° oven

Serve as coffee cake or dessert. Freezes well.

1 package yellow cake mix
1 cup sour cream or fruit flavored
  yogurt
4 eggs
1 cup chopped cranberries
½ cup chopped nuts

Combine all ingredients and beat at low speed two minutes. Pour into greased Bundt pan. Bake at 350⁰ for 35 to 45 minutes. Cake is done when toothpick inserted in center comes out clean.

Alice McMillan (Mrs. Cliff)

Chocolate Fudge Cake and Icing

Yield: 2-layer cake
350° oven

½ cup butter, softened
1 (16 ounce) package dark brown
  sugar
3 eggs
3 (1 ounce) squares unsweetened
  chocolate, melted
2¼ cups sifted cake flour
2 teaspoons baking soda
½ teaspoon salt
1 cup sour cream
1 cup hot water
1½ teaspoons vanilla

Cream butter. Gradually add sugar, beating well. Add eggs, one at a time, beating well after each addition. Add chocolate and mix well. Combine flour, baking soda and salt; gradually add to chocolate mixture alternately with sour cream, beating well after each addition. Add water, mixing well. Stir in vanilla. Batter will be thin. Pour evenly into two well greased and floured 9-inch cake pans. Bake at 350⁰ for 45 minutes or until cake tests done. Let cool in pans 10 minutes. Remove layers and place on wire rack to complete cooling. Spread frosting between layers and on top and sides of cake.

Chocolate Frosting

4 (1 ounce) squares unsweetened
  chocolate
½ cup butter
1 (16 ounce) package powdered
  sugar, sifted
½ cup milk
2 teaspoons vanilla

Frosting: Combine chocolate and butter. Place over low heat until melted, stirring constantly. Combine sugar, milk and vanilla in medium mixing bowl; mix well. Set bowl in ice water and stir in chocolate mixture. Beat at high speed of portable mixer until spreading consistency (about 2 minutes).

Dot Ringler (Mrs. Arthur H.)

Chocolate Ice Box Cake

Yield: 13x8-inch cake
350° oven

First Layer
1½ sticks margarine, melted
½ cup chopped nuts
1½ cups flour

First layer: Mix and press into 13x8-inch pan. Bake at 350⁰ for 15 to 20 minutes.

Second Layer
4 ounces cream cheese, softened
1 cup whipped topping
(buy 9 ounce size)
4 ounces sour cream
1 cup sifted powdered sugar

Second layer: Mix well and spread on cooled crust.

Third Layer
2 packages chocolate fudge
instant pudding
3 cups milk

Third layer: Mix well, beating until thick. Spread on top of cheese layer.

Fourth Layer
whipped topping
nuts

Fourth layer: Spread remainder of 9-ounce whipped topping over third layer. Sprinkle with nuts. Let set overnight in refrigerator. Keeps well.
Hazel R. Iseman (Mrs. L. J.)

Mississippi Mud Cake

Yield: 13x9-inch cake
350° oven

2 sticks butter or margarine
½ cup cocoa
2 cups sugar
4 eggs, slightly beaten
1½ cups all-purpose flour
pinch salt
1½ cups chopped nuts
1 teaspoon vanilla
miniature marshmallows
chocolate frosting

Melt butter and cocoa together. Remove from heat; stir in sugar and beaten eggs. Mix well. Add flour, salt, chopped nuts and vanilla. Mix well. Spoon batter into greased and floured 13x9x2-inch pan. Bake at 350° for 35-40 minutes. Sprinkle marshmallows on top of warm cake. Cover with favorite chocolate frosting.
Lu Brune (Mrs. Pat H.)

$300 Chocolate Cake

Yield: 9x12-inch cake
325° oven

2 cups sugar
2 cups flour
1 cup water
1 stick butter or margarine
1 cup Wesson oil
4 tablespoons cocoa
½ cup buttermilk
2 eggs, beaten
1 teaspoon baking soda
1 teaspoon vanilla
dash salt

Icing
4 tablespoons milk
4 tablespoons cocoa
1 stick margarine or butter
1 teaspoon vanilla
pinch salt
1 box confectioners' sugar

Mix sugar and flour in large bowl. In saucepan mix water, butter, oil and cocoa. Bring to boil; boil one minute, stirring constantly. Pour over sugar and flour mixture; stir well. Add buttermilk, eggs, baking soda, vanilla and salt. Mix well. Pour into greased and floured 9x12-inch pan. Bake at 325⁰ for one hour. Ice while hot.

Icing: Mix all ingredients except sugar in saucepan. Bring to boil. Add sugar and beat well. Pour over hot cake.

Carolyn Parker (Mrs. J. Edwin)

Chocolate Cream Cake

Yield: 1 loaf cake
325° oven

1 cup boiling water
2 squares (2 ounces) unsweetened chocolate
½ cup butter or margarine
1 teaspoon vanilla
1¾ cups brown sugar, firmly packed
2 eggs
1¾ cups + 2 tablespoons all-purpose flour, unsifted
1 teaspoon baking soda
¼ teaspoon salt
½ cup sour cream

Pour water over chocolate in bowl. Let stand until cool. Cream butter and vanilla; add brown sugar and blend well. Add eggs, one at a time, beating well after each addition. Pour measured flour into square of waxed paper. Add baking soda and salt; stir to blend. Add to creamed mixture; mix well. Blend in sour cream and melted chocolate. Pour into greased, waxed paper lined, 9x5x3-inch loaf pan. Bake 1 hour 15 minutes at 325⁰, or until cake pulls away from sides of pan. Cool on rack 10 minutes. Turn cake out of pan and remove waxed paper. Ice with chocolate fudge frosting, if desired.

Alice McMillan (Mrs. Cliff)

Sausage Cake

Yield: Tube cake
350° oven

Takes the place of fruit cake and keeps well. May be prepared several days ahead.

1 pound mild pork sausage,
  uncooked
1 pound brown sugar
1 cup lukewarm coffee
1 teaspoon soda
2½ cups flour
1 teaspoon cinnamon
½ teaspoon cloves
½ teaspoon nutmeg
½ teaspoon mace
½ teaspoon allspice
1 teaspoon salt
1 heaping teaspoon baking
  powder
1 cup seeded raisins
1 cup black walnuts
cooking sherry

Mix sausage and sugar with large spoon or hands. (Do not use electric mixer). Dissolve soda in coffee and add to mixture. Sift together flour, spices, salt and baking powder. Add to sausage mixture. Bring raisins to boil in small amount of water. Add to sausage mixture. Stir in nuts. Pour into greased and floured tube pan and bake at 350⁰ for 45-50 minutes. Cool about 10 minutes. Remove from pan and sprinkle with sherry. Wrap in a cloth until cake is at room temperature. Frost with Caramel Icing and place English walnuts on top.

Caramel Icing

½ cup butter
3½ cups sugar
2 cups dark Karo syrup
1 teaspoon vinegar
1 cup milk
1 teaspoon vanilla

Icing: Melt butter in heavy saucepan. Remove from heat and add 3 cups sugar. Stir well. Add syrup, vinegar and milk. Place over heat and stir. Meanwhile, caramelize ½ cup sugar by heating it in heavy iron skillet and stirring until sugar becomes brown liquid. Bring syrup mixture to boiling and add caramelized sugar. Cool until soft ball forms in water. Remove from heat; cool. Add vanilla and beat until spreading consistency.
Mildred W. Kelley

189

Sponge Cake

Yield: Tube cake
350° oven

Delicious served with side dishes of strawberries or other fruit and whipped cream.

6 large eggs, separated
¾ cup sugar
½ cup orange juice
1½ cups all-purpose flour, sifted
1 teaspoon baking powder
½ cup sugar

Add ¾ cup sugar to egg yolks and beat 2 minutes. Add alternately orange juice and mixture of flour and baking powder. In separate bowl beat egg whites with ½ cup sugar until peaks form. Fold gently into first mixture. Spoon into ungreased tube pan. Bake at 350⁰ one hour, or until toothpick comes out clean. Turn pan upside down immediately. Remove cake when completely cool. Serves 12 or more.
Marcia Bauman

Tomato Cake

Yield: 3-layer cake
350° oven

2 cups sugar
1¼ cups shortening
4 eggs
3 cups sifted all-purpose flour
1 teaspoon soda
1 teaspoon salt
2 cups finely diced tomatoes

Filling
1 cup sugar
½ cup butter
1 teaspoon vanilla
1 teaspoon cinnamon
1 cup finely diced tomatoes

Icing
3 cups confectioners' sugar
¼ cup butter
3 tablespoons milk

Cream sugar and shortening until light and fluffy. Add eggs, one at a time, alternating with mixed dry ingredients and tomatoes. Pour into 3 greased and floured 9-inch cake pans. Bake at 350⁰ for 25-30 minutes. Cool.

Filling: Mix all ingredients in saucepan and cook on low heat until thick. Cool and spread between layers of cooled cake.

Icing: Cream sugar and butter. Add milk. Beat until smooth. Ice top and sides of cake.
Mable Kirk Morrow

Mandeltorte (Almond Torte)

Yield: Tube cake
325° oven

Every German has a sweet tooth and this is a favorite of all.

1 cup sifted all-purpose flour
¾ cup sugar
1½ teaspoons baking powder
½ teaspoon salt
1 teaspoon ground cinnamon
1 teaspoon orange peel
4 eggs
3/8 cup cold water
¼ cup oil
1 teaspoon vanilla
¼ teaspoon cream of tartar
1 cup finely chopped toasted
  almonds
Chocolate Fluff Frosting
½ cup toasted slivered almonds
  for garnish

Sift together flour, sugar, baking powder, salt, cinnamon and orange peel into large bowl. Make well in center. Separate eggs, reserving one yolk for Chocolate Fluff Frosting. Beat remaining 3 yolks well with water. Add oil, yolk mixture and vanilla to well in center of dry ingredients. Beat all 4 egg whites with cream of tartar until stiff peaks are formed. Gradually pour batter over egg whites and fold in. Fold chopped almonds in last. Turn into ungreased 9-inch tube pan. Bake in slow oven (325⁰) 50-55 minutes. Cool. Ice with Chocolate Fluff Frosting and garnish with almonds. Serves 10.

Chocolate Fluff Frosting

2 squares unsweetened baking
  chocolate
3 tablespoons butter
½ pint whipping cream
¼ teaspoon salt
1 tablespoon instant coffee
½ teaspoon orange peel
1 teaspoon vanilla
3 cups sifted powdered sugar

Frosting: Melt chocolate and butter together over very low heat. Blend in ¼ cup cream, salt, coffee, orange peel and vanilla. Beat in egg yolk, reserved from cake, and sugar. Whip remaining cream until stiff. Fold into chocolate mixture.

Chris Spielmann (Mrs. Robert J.)

191

Carrot Torte

Yield: 2-layer cake
325° oven

4 eggs, separated
¼ cup sugar
¾ cup sugar
1 cup grated carrots
1 lemon rind, grated
½ cup flour
1 teaspoon baking powder
½ teaspoon cinnamon
½ teaspoon mace
pinch salt
¼ cup nuts
whipped cream

Beat egg whites with ¼ cup sugar. Beat egg yolks with ¾ cup sugar. Combine beaten whites and yolks, carrots and lemon rind. Fold in flour, baking powder, spices and salt. Mix in nuts. Pour into two 8-inch greased pans. Bake at 325⁰ for 25 minutes. Remove cakes from pans. Spread whipped cream between layers. Cut and serve, topped with any remaining whipped cream.
Glenna Florence (Mrs. T. J.)

Orange Cranberry Torte

Yield: Tube cake
350° oven

2¼ cups flour
1 cup sugar
¼ teaspoon salt
¼ teaspoon baking powder
1 teaspoon baking soda
1 cup coarsely chopped walnuts
  or pecans
1 cup chopped dates
2 eggs, beaten
1 cup buttermilk
¾ cup salad oil
1 cup fresh cranberries
grated rind of 2 oranges
1 cup orange juice
1 cup sugar
whipped cream (optional)
hard sauce (optional)

Sift together flour, sugar,. salt, baking powder and soda. Add nuts and dates. Stir in eggs, buttermilk and oil. Fold in cranberries and orange rind. Pour into 10-inch tube pan. Bake at 350⁰ for one hour. Let cool in pan. Combine orange juice and sugar. Place cake on rack over a platter. Pour mixture over cake and drippings over cake again. Serve with whipped cream flavored with rum or brandy, or fluffy hard sauce.
Helen Gutknecht (Mrs. Edgar E.)

Almond Coffee Cake

Serves 16-18
350° oven

Pastry
½ cup butter
1 cup all-purpose flour
2 tablespoons water

Batter
½ cup butter
1 cup water
1 teaspoon almond extract
1 cup flour
3 eggs

Glaze
3 ounces cream cheese, softened
1 teaspoon vanilla or almond
  extract
2 cups powdered sugar
slivered almonds

Pastry: Cut butter into flour and sprinkle with water. Blend quickly with fork. Divide into two parts. On 11x14-inch ungreased cookie sheet, pat dough into two (3x14-inch) rectangles. Set aside.

Batter: Combine butter and water, bring to boil. Add extract and remove from heat. Beat in flour. Add eggs one at a time. Spread on pastry. Bake at 350⁰ for 50-60 minutes.

Glaze: Blend all ingredients except almonds. Spread on cool cake. Sprinkle almonds on top. NOTE: Cake freezes well.
Patsy Turner (Mrs. William)

Cayman Surprise

Yield: 9x13-inch cake
350° oven

Cake
1 (16 ounce) can crushed
  pineapple, undrained
2 cups flour, unsifted
2 cups sugar
2 teaspoons baking soda
2 eggs
2 teaspoons vanilla
¾ cup crushed nuts

Cake: Blend all cake ingredients and pour into greased 9x13-inch pan. Bake at 350⁰ for 45 minutes.

Topping
1 (8 ounce) package cream cheese
1¾ cups soft butter
1 teaspoon vanilla
2 cups confectioners' sugar

Topping: While cake is still hot, blend all ingredients with electric mixer and spread over top of cake.
Connie Kulp (Mrs. Samuel)

193

Fruited Orange Ring Brunch Cake

Yield: Bundt cake
350° oven

3 cups Bisquick
1¼ cups buttermilk
¾ cup sugar
1 teaspoon baking soda
3 tablespoons margarine,
  softened
3 eggs
1 tablespoon grated orange rind
1 teaspoon vanilla
1 cup raisins, chopped
1 cup pecans, chopped
1 cup glazed fruit, chopped

Orange Glaze
1 cup powdered sugar
3 tablespoons margarine or
  butter, melted
2 teaspoons grated orange peel
1 - 2 tablespoons orange juice

Place first 8 ingredients in large mixing bowl and beat on low speed 4 minutes, scraping bowl occasionally. Beat in raisins, pecans and glazed fruit. Pour into greased and floured Bundt pan. Bake 50-55 minutes at 350°. (Toothpick inserted in center should come out clean when done.) Cool 10 minutes and remove from pan. Cool completely and drizzle with Orange Glaze. Garnish with finely shredded orange peel, if desired.

Orange Glaze: Combine all ingredients and beat until smooth. (Amount of orange juice depends upon desired consistency.)
Josephine Wills (Mrs. William)

Roswell Coffee Cake

Yield: 9x12-inch cake
350° oven

1 cup margarine
2 cups sugar
2 eggs
1 cup sour cream
1 teaspoon vanilla
2 cups cake flour
1 teaspoon baking powder
¼ teaspoon salt
⅓ cup brown sugar
1 teaspoon cinnamon
½ cup pecans

Cream margarine and sugar with eggs. Fold in sour cream and vanilla. Add flour, baking powder and salt. Pour into greased 9x12-inch cake pan. Mix brown sugar, cinnamon and pecans. Sprinkle over batter. Bake at 350° for 55 minutes. Cool completely before removing from pan.
Connie Kulp (Mrs. Samuel)

Moravian Sugar Cake

Serves 12
375° oven

Tender, moist coffee cake served on special occasions in Moravian homes. Known as the cake with "puddles" on top!

- 1 cake yeast or 1 package dry granular yeast
- ½ cup lukewarm water
- 1 cup hot unseasoned mashed potatoes
- 1 cup granulated sugar
- 4 tablespoons soft butter
- ½ cup shortening
- 1 teaspoon salt
- 1 cup potato water
- 2 eggs, beaten
- flour
- butter
- brown sugar
- cinnamon

Soak yeast in lukewarm water. Combine mashed potatoes, granulated sugar, 4 tablespoons butter, shortening and salt. Let cool. Add yeast mixture and potato water. Let rise in warm place until spongy. Add eggs and enough sifted flour to make soft dough. Let rise until double in bulk. Punch down on lightly floured board. Spread out evenly in greased flat baking pan (15x10x1-inch or 2 cake pans). When "light", use fingers to make holes and fill with pieces of butter and brown sugar. (Don't stint one bit on either!) Dust with cinnamon. Bake at 375° for 20 minutes (until golden brown). Cut into squares. Serve hot or cold.

Nancy Rittenburg (Mrs. John)

Macaroon Cupcakes

Yield: 24 cupcakes
300° oven

- 1 cup sugar
- ¾ cup sifted flour
- ½ teaspoon baking powder
- ½ teaspoon salt
- 6 egg whites
- ⅓ cup sugar
- ½ teaspoon cream of tartar
- ½ teaspoon vanilla
- ½ teaspoon almond extract
- 1 (3½ ounce) can coconut flakes

Sift together one cup sugar, flour, baking powder and salt. Set aside. Beat egg whites until soft peaks form. Slowly add ⅓ cup sugar and cream of tartar; beat until stiff. Add vanilla and almond extract. Fold in sifted dry ingredients about 2 tablespoons at a time. Fold in coconut flakes. Fill paper-lined cupcake pans ⅔ full. Bake at 300° for 40 minutes.

Barbara Garrison (Mrs. Gary)

FOOD OF FRIENDSHIP

A generous serving of love, laughter and camaraderie enhances the flavor of any cup of coffee or favorite meal. Doc Staples was so good at dishing up an atmosphere of congeniality that people in the habit of dropping by his drug store on Canton Street soon found themselves members of a sociable Coffee Club. For over twenty years affable folks could be found congregating around the table in the front of the store enjoying Tina Green's grits and gravy and the food of friendship. The crowd of regulars included preachers, politicians, merchants, housewives, construction workers and journalists. Special occasions were celebrated with informal parties and a large bulletin board covered with notes and announcements provided news of absent members.

A friendly face could usually be found at Stribling's Drug Store with its fancy marble soda fountain and Coca Cola served up in "real" Coke glasses! According to Aubrey Morris, folks could pick up some neighborly conversation and news of the day along with their sodas, aspirin and notions.

There was a time young people met the gang at the Rock Bait Inn, a quaint old store and filling station that used to mark the corner at Norcross and Alpharetta Streets. Rose Polatty thought Cokes and hot dogs never tasted so good as they did then on the way home from classes at Roswell High School.

Festive social gatherings might occasionally be found on the square and maybe a little ice cream or freshly baked pie! Juanita Mitchell remembered the Teddy Roosevelt Centennial Celebration in October 1958. Amid music and speeches from the bandstand, churches and civic organizations set up booths and wagons to display their homemade delicacies for sale. An array of relishes, preserves, and five-cent dill pickles was as colorful as the ladies costumed in their nineteenth century dresses and sunbonnets.

Picnics have always been a marvelous opportunity to share good food, good friends, good times. Hembree Springs, Lover's Rock overlooking Vickery Creek and the Chattahoochee River banks have beckoned convivial parties since the earliest days of the Colony and perhaps years before that. In 1853 a young Mittie Bulloch described a picnic following an excursion on horseback up Brush Mountain. "... the gentlemen had spread planks and carriage cushions were arranged for us to rest on and at about 4 o'clock we had our dinner. Sandwiches, chicken wings, bread and cheese disappeared miraculously. Tom (King) had a fire built and we had nice hot tea and about 6 o'clock we commenced our return."

COOKIES, SMALL CAKES and CANDY

Fran Eubanks

MINTON HOUSE
NORCROSS STREET
Circa 1849

MINTON HOUSE
Norcross Street

Major John Minton brought his wife, Rosina Fabian, and family to Roswell from their home in Midway, Georgia, in 1849, to join the King family and other friends from the coast. Major Minton spent his life as a soldier, a veteran of five wars.

When he was only twenty, he was decorated for gallant conduct by General Andrew Jackson. He was the only man from Liberty County to aid Texas in her struggles with Mexico. People said at the time he "lacked sense." When he was sixty-four, he enlisted in Roswell as a private in the Confederate army and was wounded in the Battle of Manassas. He never fully recovered, though he lived another productive ten years in Roswell.

Minton House was built soon after the Mintons arrived in 1849, an unpretentious, story-and-a-half home of brick set in Flemish bond. Slender columns support the gently sloping roof, and each of the four upstairs bedrooms has its own dormer window and fireplace. The unadorned simplicity on the exterior of Minton House prevails throughout the interior. Floors are random width, hand-hewn planks, and the hearths are of polished creek stone. Simple mantel shelves are of golden heart-pine. The framing and trim were carved from lumber off the place. The bricks were baked on the site, of clay dug from creek and river banks and molded by hand.

The charming cottage is a reflection of the unassuming but stalwart character of its original owner.

CHRISTMAS DINNER AT MINTON HOUSE

Baked Country Ham
Candied Sweet Potatoes

Butterbeans   Green Beans

Celery, Olives and Relishes
Hot Yeast Rolls

Old Fashioned Tea Cakes*   Pound Cake

Coffee

Old Fashioned Tea Cakes

Yield: 50-60
350° oven

Children's favorite "cake-cookie" baked at Minton House.

½ cup butter
¾ cup sugar
1 egg
½ teaspoon vinegar
1 teaspoon soda
½ teaspoon salt
2⅓ cups all-purpose flour

Cream butter and sugar; add egg, beating well. Combine vinegar and soda; add to creamed mixture. Mix in flour and salt. Chill. Roll out on dough board to about ¼ inch thickness. Cut with medium (2½-inch) biscuit cutter. Bake on greased cookie sheet 10-15 minutes at 350°. Tea cakes should be lightly browned.

Clyde Lackey (Mrs. Dennis)
by Mary Henry (Mrs. Lamont)

My Grandmother's Tea Cakes

Yield: 70-80
375° oven

½ cup butter
½ cup Crisco
1 cup sugar
1 egg
2½ cups flour
½ teaspoon soda
2 tablespoons milk
1 teaspoon vanilla

Cream butter, Crisco and sugar until fluffy. Add egg and mix well. Stir in dry ingredients. Mix until smooth. Blend in milk and vanilla. Mix well. Dough will be very stiff. Divide in half. On floured wax paper, roll each half into log about 1½ - 2 inches in diameter. Cut off slices about ¼ inch thick; place on greased cookie sheets. Bake 10 minutes at 375°. Remove from cookie sheets immediately.

Tulah Vatalaro (Mrs. R. J.)

Potato Chip Cookies

Yield: 40-50
350° oven

1 pound butter or margarine
1 cup sugar
3 cups all-purpose flour
2 teaspoons vanilla
⅔ cup chopped nuts (optional)
2 cups crushed potato chips
powdered sugar

Cream together butter and sugar. Blend in flour gradually, mixing well. Stir in potato chips and nuts. Drop by teaspoonful on greased baking sheet. Bake 12 minutes at 350°. Cool; roll in powdered sugar.

Laura Mulvihill

199

Grandma Sweeny's Sugar Cookies

Yield: 8-10 dozen
375° oven

My mother, Esther Sweeny Jackson, was euphoric when recalling the sugar and ginger cookies made in a dishpan by her grandmother in Pennsylvania. My southern antecedents would have called them "tea cakes" or "gingercakes".

1 pound butter
1 pound sugar
3 eggs
8 cups flour
1 teaspoon baking soda (rather rounding)
pinch salt
1 cup buttermilk
1 whole nutmeg, grated, or
   1 teaspoon ground nutmeg

Cream butter and sugar until fluffy. Add eggs, beating well after each addition. Combine soda, salt and flour; add to creamed mixture alternately with buttermilk. Beat in nutmeg. Refrigerate over night. (Freezing dough improves flavor. Keeps indefinitely.) Roll out on floured board to about ¼ inch thick. Cut with 2 or 3-inch cutter. Bake on greased cookie sheet 10 minutes at 375°.

**Rose Jackson Polatty
(Mrs. George J., Sr.)**

Bakestone Cakes

Yield: several dozen

Old, old Welsh recipe. Name comes from cooking on a soapstone which is like a griddle, but called a bakestone.

4 cups flour, unsifted
1 cup sugar
3 teaspoons baking powder
¼ teaspoon salt
½ teaspoon nutmeg
1 cup shortening
1 cup currants or raisins
3 eggs
¼ cup milk

Blend first 6 ingredients as for pie crust. Add currants, eggs and milk. Roll out ¼ inch thick. Cut into 2-inch rounds. Bake on ungreased pancake griddle on top of stove or on electric griddle set at 325°. Bake slowly over low heat. Turn to bake evenly. Keep well in tin box or freeze beautifully. To serve, warm in toaster oven. Wonderful for breakfast, tea or with a glass of sherry.

Emma Ball (Mrs. Robert B.)

Easy Caramel Nut Refrigerator Cookies

Yield: 6-8 dozen
350° oven

Dough may be frozen until ready to bake.

1¼ cups butter
1 cup white sugar
1 cup brown sugar (packed)
2 eggs
1½ teaspoons vanilla
1 cup chopped walnuts or
   pecans
4½ cups all-purpose flour
1 teaspoon baking soda
1/8 teaspoon salt

In large saucepan melt butter. Add sugars, beating until well blended. Remove from heat. Add eggs, one at a time, beating well after each addition. Beat in vanilla and stir in nuts. Sift together flour, soda and salt. Add gradually to butter mixture, blending well. Divide dough into 2 parts. Place each part on large sheet of Saran Wrap and form into roll about 2 inches in diameter. Chill until firm. (At this point, dough may be frozen. Before baking, thaw slightly.) Cut rolls in ¼ inch slices (or thinner). Place on greased cookie sheets. Bake at 350° for 9-10 minutes. Remove from pan with spatula and cool on wax paper.

Delores Lotze

Happiness Cookies

Yield: 5 dozen
350° oven

½ pound butter or margarine
6 tablespoons sugar
1 teaspoon almond or vanilla
   extract
1 (3½ ounce) can coconut or
   1 cup fresh grated coconut
2¼ cups all-purpose flour
powdered sugar

Cream butter. Add all other ingredients; mix well. (Use hands, if necessary.) Divide dough into thirds. Roll into logs on floured, waxed paper. Freeze until ready to bake. Thaw just enough to slice into ¼-inch rounds. Bake on foil covered pans 15 to 20 minutes at 350°. Bottoms should be lightly brown, top barely brown. Sprinkle with powdered sugar.

Elizabeth S. Mills (Mrs. George)

Chocolate Crinkle Cookies

Yield: 5 dozen
350° oven

½ cup butter
2 cups granulated sugar
4 squares (4 ounces) unsweetened chocolate, melted
3 eggs
2 teaspoons vanilla
2 cups flour
2 teaspoons baking powder
½ teaspoon salt
½-1 cup confectioners' sugar

Cream butter and sugar. Beat in chocolate. Add eggs one at a time. Stir in vanilla. Sift together flour, baking powder and salt; add to chocolate mixture. Chill dough 2-3 hours. Roll into small balls (about 1 teaspoon dough) and roll in confectioners' sugar to coat. Bake 2 inches apart on ungreased cookie sheet for 10-12 minutes at 350°. Do not overbake.

Beth Benson

Alice's Date-Filled Cookies

Yield: 2-3 dozen
375° oven

Children love them and they are fun to make!

1 pound dates, chopped
¾ cup water
½ cup sugar
1½ cups brown sugar
1 cup butter or margarine
2 eggs
3 cups all-purpose flour
1½ cups minute rolled oats
1 teaspoon vanilla
1 teaspoon cream of tartar
1 teaspoon soda in 1 tablespoon
water
confectioners' sugar

Boil dates, water and ½ cup sugar about 5 minutes (until mixture is smooth). Set aside to cool. Mix next eight ingredients with electric beater. Dough will be quite thick. Chill for better handling. Divide dough in half. Roll each half into a rectangle 1/8 inch thick. Using 2-inch cookie cutter, cut as many rounds as possible. Place half the rounds on greased cookie sheet. Make small mounds of date mixture on this half. Place remaining rounds over date mixture and gently seal around sides with fork. Bake 10 to 12 minutes at 375° (until light brown). Roll in confectioners' sugar while warm, not hot. Cookies keep well.

Lizanne Abreu (Mrs. Peter M.)

Date Nut Fingers

Yield: 12 dozen

1 cup chopped dates
1 cup chopped pecans
1 cup sugar
½ cup butter or margarine
1 tablespoon light corn syrup
1 egg, well beaten
2 cups Rice Krispies cereal
¼ teaspoon almond extract
½ teaspoon vanilla
confectioners' sugar

Combine first 6 ingredients in 1½ to 2-quart saucepan. Cook over medium heat 10 minutes, stirring constantly. Do not overcook. Remove from heat; stir in cereal and flavorings. Cool. Mixture will be sticky. Dust hands with confectioners' sugar. Form into finger size rolls. Roll in confectioners' sugar until well coated.

Kathleen Burch (Mrs. J. C. Horton)

Chocolate Cookies

**Yield: 50
300° oven**

Soft drop cookie. Children love them!

½ cup shortening
1½ cups sugar
2 eggs
2 squares unsweetened
  chocolate, melted
1 cup thick sour cream
1 teaspoon vanilla
2¾ cups flour
½ teaspoon soda
½ teaspoon salt
½ teaspoon baking powder
nuts (optional)

Cream shortening and sugar; add eggs, melted chocolate, sour cream and vanilla. Sift flour, soda, salt and baking powder together and add to chocolate mixture. Add nuts, if desired. Drop dough by teaspoon on greased baking sheet. Bake 8-10 minutes at 300°.

Evie Brundrett (Mrs. G. A.)

Oatmeal Drop Cookies

Yield: 6-8 dozen

No bake cookies.

2 cups sugar
½ cup cocoa
1 stick margarine
½ cup milk
1 teaspoon vanilla
3 cups quick Quaker Oats
½ cup coconut
½ cup chopped pecans or
  walnuts

Mix sugar, cocoa, margarine, milk, and vanilla. Bring to a boil; cook one minute, stirring. Add oats, coconut and nuts. Mix well and drop by teaspoonful onto wax paper.

Claudine Washington (Mrs. James P.)

Oatmeal Cookies

Yield: 6-8 dozen
350° oven

½ cup butter
½ cup shortening
1 cup white sugar
1 cup brown sugar
2 eggs, beaten
2 cups flour
2 teaspoons soda
1 teaspoon baking powder
1 teaspoon salt
1 teaspoon vanilla
2 cups rolled oats (1 minute
    Oats)
1 cup flaked coconut
½ cup pecan pieces

Cream together butter, shortening and sugars. Beat in eggs. Sift together flour, soda, baking powder and salt. Add to butter mixture, mixing well. Add vanilla. Fold in oats, coconut and pecans. Dough will be very thick. Form into balls the size of a hickory nut. Place on greased cookie sheet. Do not flatten. Bake 8-10 minutes at 350°.

Jinny Welch (Mrs. William)

Nutmeg Logs

Yield: 4 dozen
350° oven

Unusual flavor. A treat with coffee, tea or eggnog.

1 cup butter, softened (or ½ cup
    butter, ½ cup margarine)
2 teaspoons vanilla
2 teaspoons rum flavoring
¾ cup sugar
1 egg
3 cups sifted all-purpose
    flour
¼ teaspoon salt
1 teaspoon nutmeg

Cream butter with flavorings. Beat in sugar, then egg. Sift flour with salt and nutmeg. Add to butter mixture; mix well. On sugared board shape dough into "snakes" ½ inch in diameter. Cut into 3-inch lengths. Bake on buttered cookie sheets at 350° for 12-15 minutes. Cool on rack. Frost and sprinkle with nutmeg.

Frosting

⅓ cup butter
1 teaspoon vanilla
2 teaspoons rum flavoring
2 cups confectioners' sugar,
    sifted
2 tablespoons light cream or
    3 ounces cream cheese

Frosting: Cream butter with flavorings. Beat in confectioners' sugar and cream. Frost cookies. Mark tops with fork tines.

Joan Brown (Mrs. John)

Scottish Shortbread Fingers

Yield: 3 dozen
350°, 300° oven

As good as those at Harrods! Time to season improves flavor.

1 cup butter (<u>not</u> margarine)
¾ cup (4X) confectioners' sugar, packed
1¾ cups all-purpose flour
¼ cup rice flour (may use all-purpose flour)

Cream butter. Add sugar gradually. Blend well. Do not overwork. Mix flours together; sift into creamed mixture, mixing quickly and lightly. Cover with wax paper. Refrigerate 30 minutes to chill. Roll dough ½ inch thick on lightly floured board, using part confectioners' sugar with flour. Cut into fingers 2¼ inches long by ¾ inch wide. (May be cut into cookies no larger than 1½ inches in diameter.) Prick surface of dough with prong of fork. Using spatula, place on ungreased cookie sheet. Bake 5 minutes in pre-heated 350° oven. Reduce heat to 300°. Bake 20-25 minutes (until light in color, <u>not</u> brown). Cool on rack. Place in covered tin box in cool place. Refrigerate or freeze.

Carolyn Warthen (Mrs. Gerald)

Ginger Cream Cookies

Yield: 3 dozen
350° oven

Pratt family favorite. Outstanding!

¾ cup shortening
1 cup sugar
4 tablespoons molasses
1 egg, well beaten
2 cups all-purpose flour
1 teaspoon baking soda
1 teaspoon nutmeg
1 teaspoon cloves
1 teaspoon ginger
1 teaspoon cinnamon
granulated sugar

Cream together shortening and sugar. Add molasses and beaten egg. Sift together dry ingredients; add to sugar mixture and mix until smooth. Put dough in refrigerator about an hour. Form into balls the size of a walnut. Roll in granulated sugar. Bake on greased cookie sheet 15 minutes at 350°.

Carolyn Pratt

205

The Big Cookie

Yield: As the cookie crumbles!
350°-375° oven

Try to let this cookie age at least one day!

1 cup peeled almonds (blanched
   or unblanched)
2⅔ cups all-purpose flour
1 cup sugar
pinch salt
1 teaspoon grated lemon peel
1 stick plus 2 tablespoons butter
1 stick margarine, room
   temperature
2 tablespoons lemon juice
1 tablespoon Grand Marnier

Grind almonds in food processor (or blender) until coarsely ground. Mix with flour, sugar, salt and lemon peel. With pastry blender, cut in butter and margarine until crumbly. Sprinkle lemon juice and Grand Marnier over mixture. Lightly toss together until blended. Mixture will be crumbly. Spread into buttered and floured 12-inch pizza pan. Pat lightly. Bake 15 minutes at 350°-375°. Reduce heat to 300°-325° and bake 20 minutes. Turn cookie around several times to assure even baking. Let cool in pan on a rack and when thoroughly cool, wrap well. Break into chunks to eat.

Marian David (Mrs. John H., Jr.)

Christmas Fruit Cookies

Yield: 4 dozen
350° oven

½ cup butter
¾ cup brown sugar
1 egg
½ teaspoon vanilla
1 cup flour
½ teaspoon salt
½ teaspoon baking soda
½ teaspoon cinnamon
1 cup chopped nuts (filberts)
1 cup chopped walnuts
¼ pound candied cherries,
   chopped
1 pound dates, chopped
¾ cup chopped candied
   pineapple
¼ cup flour

Cream butter and sugar in electric mixer until fluffy. Beat in egg and vanilla. Sift dry ingredients together and add to egg mixture, mixing well. Set aside. Combine fruits, nuts and ¼ cup flour. Add to batter, mixing well. Drop by teaspoon onto greased cookie sheet. Bake 12 minutes at 350°.

Hazel Iseman (Mrs. L. J.)

206

Christmas Wreaths

Yield: 2 dozen

32 large marshmallows
6 tablespoons butter
½ teaspoon vanilla
½ teaspoon almond extract
about 1 teaspoon green food
  coloring
4 cups cornflakes
red cinnamon candies

Melt marshmallows and butter in large saucepan over low heat. Mix in flavorings and food color. Add cornflakes and stir gently to coat. Place pan in large pot of hot water and stir occasionally. Butter hands and shape mixture into wreaths on wax paper. Sprinkle on candy to decorate. Cool thoroughly before removing from wax paper. Yield depends on size of wreaths.

Ruth Anderson

Snappy Turtle Cookies

350° oven

1½ cups sifted all-purpose flour
¼ teaspoon soda
¼ teaspoon salt
½ cup butter or margarine
½ cup firmly packed brown
  sugar
1 egg, whole
1 egg yolk
¼ teaspoon vanilla
1/8 teaspoon maple flavoring
pecan halves (about 1 cup)
1 egg white

Sift together flour, soda and salt. Set aside. Cream butter; add sugar gradually, beating well. Add egg and egg yolk, beating well. Blend in flavorings. Add dry ingredients gradually, mixing well. Arrange pecan halves in groups of three, round side up, on greased baking sheets to resemble head and hind legs of turtle. Mold dough into balls using rounded teaspoonful for each. Dip bottom of ball in egg white and press onto nut halves. Bake 10-12 minutes at 350°. Do not over bake. Cool. Ice with chocolate frosting.

Chocolate Frosting

2 squares (4 ounces) semi-sweet
  chocolate
¼ cup milk
1 tablespoon butter
1 cup sifted confectioners' sugar

Frosting: In top of double boiler over boiling water combine chocolate, milk and butter. Stir until chocolate melts and mixture is smooth. Remove from heat; add confectioners' sugar, beating until frosting is smooth and glossy.

Louise Donaldson (Mrs. Herschel)

207

Waffle-Baked Cookies

Yield: 60
waffle baker

Recipe originated in France and is sometimes referred to as French cakes. Taste like fresh pound cake!

1 pound butter
2¼ cups sugar
8 eggs, beaten
3¾ cups flour
½ teaspoon salt
1 tablespoon vanilla

Cream butter and sugar. Add beaten eggs. Stir in flour, salt and vanilla. Mix well. Drop by rounded tablespoons on waffle baker. They cook rather quickly. Serve plain or sprinkle with powdered sugar while still warm.

Eva Corder (Mrs. J. B.)

Apple Butter Bars

Yield: 3 dozen
350° oven

1½ cups plain flour
1 teaspoon baking soda
1 teaspoon salt
2½ cups quick cooking oats
1½ cups sugar
1 cup butter or margarine, melted
1½ cups apple butter

Sift flour, soda and salt together in large bowl. Add oats and sugar. Stir in butter and mix well. Press half of mixture in bottom of greased 13 x 9 x 2-inch baking pan. Top with apple butter. Sprinkle with remaining crumb mixture. Press gently with spoon. Bake 55 minutes at 350°. Cool. Cut into bars.

Carol Bentley

Brer Rabbit Gingerbread

Yield: 15 squares
350° oven

This is the original Brer Rabbit molasses recipe. It was used at Bulloch Hall for open hearth cooking demonstrations. Adapts well to food processor too!

½ cup butter or shortening
½ cup sugar
1 egg, beaten
1 cup molasses or cane syrup
2½ cups all-purpose flour
1½ teaspoons soda
1 teaspoon cinnamon
1 teaspoon ginger
½ teaspoon salt
1 cup hot water

Cream together butter and sugar. Add beaten egg and molasses, beating well. Sift dry ingredients together. Add to butter mixture with hot water. Beat until smooth. Batter will be soft. Pour into greased 9 x 12 x 2-inch pan. Bake 35 minutes at 350°.

**Frances Coleman Rucker
(Mrs. Malcolm)**

Glenda's Plantation Squares

Yield: 2 dozen
350° oven

1 box yellow cake mix
1 egg
1 stick margarine, melted
8 ounces cream cheese
2 eggs
1 box confectioners' sugar

In large mixing bowl, using wooden spoon, blend together cake mix, 1 egg and melted margarine. Put into 9 x 12-inch ungreased pan. In small bowl, with electric mixer, blend well cream cheese, 2 eggs and confectioners' sugar. Pour mixture over first layer. Bake 40 minutes at 350°.

Carolyn Sparks (Mrs. Don)

Graham Cracker Crunch Cookies

Yield: 4-5 dozen
325° oven

48 Keebler graham crackers
1 cup pecans, chopped
1 stick margarine
1 stick butter
½ cup sugar

Break graham crackers apart along lines as they come from the box. Place on greased cookie sheets close together. Sprinkle with nuts. In saucepan combine margarine, butter and sugar. Bring to boil and cook 3 minutes. Pour over crackers. Bake 11 minutes at 325°. Remove from oven. Allow to cool about 10 minutes. Separate into bars. Cool on wax paper. Store in air tight container in refrigerator.

Marguerite Nesbitt

Lemon Squares

Serves 10-15
350° oven

½ cup butter
1 cup all-purpose flour
¼ cup confectioners' sugar
2 eggs, beaten
2 tablespoons lemon juice
1 teaspoon grated lemon rind
½ teaspoon baking powder
1 cup sugar
2 tablespoons flour

Combine butter, flour and sugar. Press into 9-inch square baking pan. Bake 15 minutes at 350°. Cool. Beat together eggs, lemon juice, lemon rind, baking powder, sugar and flour. Pour over cooled crust. Bake 25 minutes at 350°. Cool.

Lucy Yankee (Mrs. Paul)

Hello Dollies

Yield: 20-24 squares
350° oven

1 stick margarine
1 cup graham cracker crumbs
1 (6 ounce) package chocolate
chips
1 (3½ ounce) can coconut
1 cup chopped pecans
1 can Eagle Brand condensed
milk

Blend margarine and crumbs well. Press into bottom of 9 x 9-inch baking pan. Layer remaining ingredients over crust in order listed. Bake 30 minutes at 350°. Cool. Cut into squares.

Margaret Harris (Mrs. William)

Dream Bars

Yield: 15-20
300°, 350° oven

Crust
½ cup brown sugar, packed
½ cup butter, softened
1 cup all-purpose flour

Crust: Thoroughly combine brown sugar, butter and flour. Press into ungreased jelly roll pan. Bake 10 minutes at 300°. Remove from oven.

Topping
1 cup brown sugar, packed
1 teaspoon baking powder
2 tablespoons flour
½ teaspoon vanilla
½ teaspoon salt
2 eggs
1½ cups shredded coconut
1 cup chopped pecans

Topping: Combine brown sugar, flour and baking powder. Beat eggs, adding vanilla and salt. Add eggs to brown sugar mixture. Stir in coconut and chopped nuts. Pour over baked crust. Bake at 350° for 20 minutes. Cool and cut into bars.

Carol Frey (Mrs. William E., Sr.)

Chocolate Balls

Yield: 115

1 stick margarine
2 boxes powdered sugar
1 (3½ ounce) can coconut
1 can Eagle Brand milk
2 cups pecans, finely
chopped
1½ teaspoons vanilla
¾ cake paraffin
8 ounces semi-sweet chocolate

Melt margarine. Add powdered sugar, coconut, milk, pecans and vanilla. Mix thoroughly. Chill. Make into small balls. Chill well. Melt together semi-sweet chocolate and paraffin in top of double boiler over hot water. Let cool a little. Dip balls into mixture. Place on wax paper.

Martha C. Mansell

Toffee Square Cookies

Yield: 40 large or
80 medium squares
325° oven

Nuts can be tinted any color to fit a special occasion.

1 cup softened butter
1 cup granulated sugar
1 egg yolk
1 teaspoon vanilla
2 cups all-purpose flour
½ teaspoon baking soda
1 teaspoon cinnamon
1 (12 ounce) package semi-sweet
chocolare chips
1 cup pecans, chopped medium
fine

Cream butter. Add sugar, egg yolk and vanilla; beat well. Sift dry ingredients together. Add to egg mixture. Place batter in greased 11 x 16-inch pan. Press flat into pan with wet hands. Bake 30 minutes at 325°. Remove from oven and spread chocolate chips evenly over batter. Return to oven for 5 minutes to melt chips. Spread like frosting. Sprinkle chopped nuts on top. Cut into squares while hot. Remove from pan when cool.

Sue Danbom (Mrs. Bob)

Two-Tone Fudge

Yield: 2½ pounds

2 cups firmly packed brown
sugar
1 cup granulated sugar
1 cup evaporated milk
½ cup butter
1 (7 ounce) jar marshmallow
creme
1 teaspoon vanilla
1 (6 ounce) package (1 cup)
butterscotch flavored morsels
1 cup coarsely chopped walnuts,
divided
1 (6 ounce) package (1 cup) semi-
sweet chocolate morsels

Combine sugars, evaporated milk and butter in saucepan. Bring to full boil over moderate heat, stirring constantly. Boil ten minutes, stirring occasionally. Remove from heat. Add marshmallow creme, vanilla and stir until mixture is smooth. To 2 cups of hot mixture, add butterscotch morsels and ½ cup walnuts. Stir until morsels are melted and mixture is smooth. Pour evenly into greased 9-inch square pan. To remaining hot mixture add chocolate morsels and ½ cup walnuts. Stir until morsels are melted and mixture is smooth. Pour evenly over butterscotch mixture. Chill until firm.

Bette Tate (Mrs. Logan C., Jr.)

211

Kentucky Bourbon Balls

Yield: about 60

about 60 pecan pieces the size
of ¼ of a pecan
2 tablespoons butter
⅓ stick butter
1 pound box powdered sugar
about ¼ cup bourbon (depending
on humidity)
3 tablespoons shaved paraffin
1 large package semi-sweet
chocolate bits or 8 ounces
semi-sweet chocolate

Toast pecan pieces lightly in 2 tablespoons butter. Drain on paper towel. Mix ⅓ stick butter and powdered sugar. Add bourbon slowly until you can roll in little balls. Put toasted nut in center of each ball. Refrigerate on cookie sheet which is covered with wax paper for 30 minutes. Melt chocolate and paraffin in top of double boiler. Dip each ball rapidly with fork into chocolate and put back on wax paper. Refrigerate until cool. Keep in air tight container in refrigerator.

Beth Hamilton (Mrs. Robert)

Two Minute Fudge

Yield: 32 squares
Microwave oven

1 box confectioners' sugar
½ cup cocoa
¼ teaspoon salt
¼ cup milk
1 tablespoon vanilla
1 cup chopped nuts (optional)
1 stick butter or margarine

In glass or ceramic bowl (not metal) mix together sugar, cocoa, salt, milk and vanilla. Blend in nuts, if desired. Place stick of butter on top of mixture. Microwave on high for two minutes. Remove from oven and beat until smooth. Pour into 8 x 4 x 3-inch pan lined with waxed paper. Chill 30 minutes to 1 hour. Cut into squares.

Laura Mulvihill

Dot's Candy Squares

Yield: 4 dozen

1 cup butter or margarine
1 cup peanut butter (crunchy or
smooth)
1 (16 ounce) package powdered
sugar, sifted
1½ cups graham cracker crumbs
1 (12 ounce) package semi-sweet
chocolate morsels, melted

Melt butter in medium saucepan. Remove from heat and stir in peanut butter, powdered sugar and graham cracker crumbs. Press mixture into 13 x 9 x 2-inch ungreased baking pan; spread melted chocolate morsels evenly over top. Chill 30 minutes. Cut into 1½-inch squares.

Dot Ringler (Mrs. Arthur)

Caramels

1 cup butter
2 cups light brown sugar
1 cup light Karo syrup
pinch (about 1/8 teaspoon) salt
pinch (about 1/8 teaspoon) cream
   of tartar
1 can Eagle Brand condensed milk
1 teaspoon vanilla

**Yield: 2 pounds
Candy thermometer**

Melt butter in heavy 2-quart pan. Add syrup and brown sugar, then milk, salt and cream of tartar. Quickly bring to boil, stirring constantly. Cook until candy thermometer reaches 246° (continue to stir). Remove from heat and stir in vanilla. Pour into buttered 9-inch square glass pan. Cool thoroughly. Cut in squares. Squares may be wrapped individually in wax paper.

Sarah Robertson (Mrs. Donald)

Buttermilk Pralines

3 cups granulated sugar
1 cup buttermilk
1 stick butter or margarine
1 level teaspoon baking soda
1 tablespoon white Karo syrup
1 teaspoon vanilla
1 cup chopped pecans

Yield: 30-40

Mix first five ingredients in large saucepan (should be fairly high because soda causes mixture to boil up). Bring to boil, stirring occasionally. Lower heat to medium, stirring occasionally, until soft ball forms in cold water. Remove from heat and cool 2-3 minutes. Add vanilla and beat with electric mixer until mixture begins to thicken. Add pecans and mix well. Drop quickly by teaspoons on wax paper. Cool. Yield depends on size.

Harold H. Smith

Swedish Nuts

½ pound (1½ cups) blanched
   almonds
½ pound (2 cups) walnut halves,
   or 1 pound pecan halves
2 egg whites
1 cup sugar
dash salt
½ cup butter or margarine

**Yield: 3-3½ cups
325° oven**

Toast nuts at 325° until light brown. Beat egg whites until stiff, adding sugar and salt. Fold nuts into meringue. Melt butter in 15½ x 10½ x 1-inch jelly roll pan. Spread nut mixture over butter. Bake at 325° about 30 minutes, stirring until nuts are coated with brown crust and no butter remains in pan. Cool.

Fran Eubanks

213

Peanut Brittle

Yield: 2 pounds
Candy thermometer

2 cups sugar
1 cup white Karo syrup
½ cup water
2 cups raw Spanish peanuts
  (do not use salted or roasted)
½ teaspoon salt
1 teaspoon butter
1 teaspoon vanilla
1½ teaspoons baking soda

Place sugar, syrup and water in large heavy saucepan. Cook over medium heat, stirring until mixture reaches 250° and sugar is dissolved. Add raw peanuts, salt and butter. Cook until peanuts begin to brown, skins pop and syrup turns yellow brown (325°). Remove from heat; quickly stir in vanilla and soda. Mixture will foam. Pour quickly onto 4 buttered cookie sheets. Do not spread out on sheets. As soon as you can slip a knife under edges of mixture, carefully pull candy out thin toward edges of pan. Work quickly in pulling process so candy will be pulled thin before it sets. Let cool and divide as desired.

Helen Gutknecht (Mrs. Edgar)

DESSERTS

Jo Rudolph

**NAYLOR HALL
CANTON STREET
Circa 1840**

NAYLOR HALL

The original portion of this imposing two-storied home was built in the 1840's by Barrington King for Hugh Proudfoot, an Englishman who came to Roswell to be the bookkeeper for the Roswell Manufacturing Company. He was said to have been related to Englishmen Peter and Francis Minhinnet, carpenter and stone-mason during construction of the mills and early homes.

The original clapboard cottage, like other early cottages in town, consisted of two main rooms downstairs and two up, with one central fireplace for heating and cooking. The cottage is now contained within the framework of the present structure.

Hugh Proudfoot and his wife, Euphemia, had one servant, and farmed 148 acres of land. Their two baby daughters, fathered in his middle years, died in infancy. In the spring of 1861, though in his late sixties, he joined the Roswell Guards to fight for the Southern cause. Hugh Proudfoot, his wife, and baby daughters are buried in the Roswell Methodist Cemetery, on land he gave to the Methodist Church.

The restoration of the home was begun in the 1920s and furthered by a number of owners. Included in the additions were a columned portico with pedimented roof and one-story wings at either side. Twelve-pane, double-hung windows across the front give light and ventilation to the lofty interior. The imposing white-columned home sits well back from the street and commands an arresting vista through ancient towering oaks.

———

MOTHER'S DAY BRUNCH AT NAYLOR HALL

Frozen Mandarin Orange Salad
Asparagus Quiche
Angel Biscuits
Banana Pudding*

Iced Tea with Lemon Wedges   Coffee

Banana Pudding

Serves 12

A favorite at historic Naylor Hall.

3 cups milk
1 family size instant vanilla
  pudding mix
1 (9 ounce) frozen whipped
  topping
1 can sweetened condensed milk
1 large box vanilla wafers
about 8 bananas, peeled and
  sliced

Beat milk and pudding mix. Blend in whipped topping and condensed milk. Alternate wafers, bananas and pudding mixture in large dish ending with pudding mixture on top. Refrigerate.

Terry Wilcoxon (Mrs. Jerry)

Bread Pudding Supreme

Serves 8
350° oven

2¾ cups whole milk
3 slices of bread, crust removed
¼ cup butter
1½ cups sugar
3 eggs, beaten
1 teaspoon vanilla
nutmeg
whipped cream (optional)

Scald milk in top of double boiler. Add bread (torn into small pieces), butter and sugar. Cool to room temperature. Add beaten eggs and vanilla. Beat all until bread disintegrates. Pour into greased 1-quart casserole. Place casserole in large pan of hot water. Bake about 1 hour at 350° until top is light brown. Sprinkle with nutmeg or serve with whipped cream.

Laura Roberts Wing (Mrs. Henry)

Caramel Pudding

1½ cups brown sugar
2 cups boiling water
1 heaping tablespoon butter
1 cup granulated sugar
1 cup all-purpose flour
2 teaspoons baking powder
½ teaspoon ground cloves
½ teaspoon ground nutmeg
1 cup raisins
¾ cup milk

Combine brown sugar, water and butter. Bring to a boil, stirring constantly, until butter is melted and sugar is dissolved. Pour into greased 1½-quart casserole. Sift together sugar, flour, baking powder and spices. Stir in raisins; add milk, mixing well. Pour over brown sugar mixture. Do not stir. Bake at 350⁰ for 45 minutes. Cool.

Pauline Dwiggins

Mamma's Caramel Pudding

I remember my grandmother, who lives at Holbrook Campground in Cherokee County, serving this pudding to me as a child.

1 can Eagle Brand condensed
   milk
nut meats for garnish
whipped cream for garnish
fruits for garnish

Remove paper wrapping from can of milk. Place unopened can in boiling water to cover and keep at boiling point 2½ hours, being careful to keep can covered with water. Remove from water; chill thoroughly. To serve, remove top and bottom of can and push contents out of can whole. Cut in slices and garnish with nut meats, whipped cream or fruits.

Nancy Phillips (Mrs. Wendell)

Holiday Snow Pudding

Serves 8

1 (3 ounce) package lime Jell-O
¾ cup boiling water
1 cup sweetened pineapple juice
3 egg whites

Dissolve Jell-O in water. Add pineapple juice. Cool. When mixture thickens slightly, beat egg whites until stiff and fold into Jell-O mixture. Refrigerate until set. Spoon Holiday Sauce over each serving.

Holiday Sauce

3 egg yolks
1 tablespoon flour
½ cup sugar
1¼ cups milk, scalded
¼ teaspoon vanilla
¼ teaspoon orange extract
1 (5 ounce) bottle red maraschino cherries, drained and finely chopped

Holiday Sauce: Beat egg yolks, gradually adding mixed flour and sugar. Slowly pour in hot milk, beating constantly. Cook in double boiler over hot (not boiling) water until mixture coats a spoon. Stir constantly. Remove from heat and stir in vanilla, orange extract and cherries. Refrigerate several days, if possible.

Sara Newton (Mrs. Charles)

Persimmon Pudding

Serves 10-12
350° oven

Gather ripe persimmons each day when they fall from the tree. Squeeze through 2 layers of cheesecloth to remove seeds. When you have 4 cups of pulp, proceed with the pudding.

4 cups persimmon pulp
3 eggs, separated
½ cup sugar
2 cups whole milk
2 cups sifted, unbleached all-purpose flour
1 medium sweet potato, grated
¼ cup butter, melted
whipped cream

Add well beaten egg yolks to persimmon pulp. Beat well. Add sugar gradually, beating well. Add milk, flour and grated sweet potato alternately, beating well after each addition. If needed, add more flour to make a medium stiff batter. Add butter; blend. Beat egg whites until stiff and fold into persimmon mixture. Pour into greased 12 x 7-inch glass casserole. Bake 50 minutes at 350°. Serve with whipped cream or topping of your choice.

Laura Galbraith

Scandinavian Pudding

Serves 8

1 package unflavored gelatin
½ cup cold water
5 eggs, separated
¾ cup sugar
juice of one lemon
1 teaspoon grated lemon rind
   (or to taste)
pinch salt
whipped cream
maraschino cherries or toasted
   almonds

Soak gelatin in water 5 minutes. Dissolve over boiling water. Cool to lukewarm. In large mixing bowl beat egg yolks well. Add sugar a little at at a time, beating constantly. Add lemon juice and rind; continue beating. Add cooled gelatin mixture and beat again. Add salt to egg whites; beat until stiff. Fold into yolk mixture. Pour into 1½-quart compote bowl. Chill until firm. Serve with whipped cream and maraschino cherries or finely ground toasted almonds as a garnish.

Mamie Burleigh

Charlotte Russe

Serves 12-14

2 eggs, separated
2 tablespoons sugar
pinch salt
1¼ cups milk
1¼ tablespoons unflavored
   gelatin
¼ cup cold water
½ pint whipping cream
3 tablespoons confectioners'
   sugar
¾ teaspoon vanilla
1 box lady fingers

Beat egg yolks. Add sugar and salt; mix well. In double boiler scald milk and gradually add to egg yolk mixture. Cook over hot water, stirring constantly until mixture thickens. Soften gelatin in water. Add to milk mixture; strain. Beat egg whites until stiff and fold into milk mixture. Set pan in larger pan of ice water and stir, scraping down sides and bottom until mixture thickens. Whip cream until stiff, adding confectioners' sugar and vanilla while beating. Fold whipped cream into milk mixture. Split lady fingers in half lengthwise. Line bottom and sides of chilled bowl (about 9-inch) with fingers turned crust side out. Pour complete mixture into bowl and chill.

R.E. Blouin (Mrs. M. R.)

Cool Lemon Dessert

Serves 12
350° oven

1 cup unsifted flour
½ cup margarine, softened
⅓ cup chopped pecans
8 ounces cream cheese
1 cup confectioners' sugar
2 cups frozen whipped topping
2 (3 ounce) packages instant lemon pudding
4 cups milk

Combine flour, margarine and nuts. Press into 9 x 13-inch pan. Bake 12-15 minutes at 350° until light brown. Cool. Mix cream cheese, confectioners' sugar and 1 cup topping. Spread over crust. Mix lemon pudding as directed on package using 4 cups milk. Pour over cheese layer. Place in refrigerator about 1 hour. Top with remaining topping. Chill until ready to serve.

Mary Hood

Strawberry Whip and Soft Custard

Serves 10-12

Whip

2 cups sliced, fresh strawberries
½ cup sugar
1 envelope (1 tablespoon) unflavored gelatin
1 cup cold water
2 cups boiling water
2 (3 ounce) packages strawberry flavored gelatin

Whip: Mix strawberries and sugar. Set aside. Soften unflavored gelatin in cold water. Pour boiling water over strawberry gelatin. Stir in unflavored gelatin until dissolved. Chill until gelatin begins to set. Whip until light and fluffy. Fold in strawberries. Pour into mold. Chill until firm. Serve with soft custard and additional berries.

Soft Custard

1 cup milk
1 tablespoon sugar
1 tablespoon flour
1 egg, beaten
1 tablespoon butter
1 teaspoon vanilla

Soft Custard: Scald milk. Mix flour and sugar; add to milk. Continue cooking over moderate heat, stirring constantly until mixture coats spoon. Pour a little of hot mixture into beaten egg, stirring constantly. Return egg mixture to milk mixture. Cook about 5 minutes. Remove from heat; add butter and vanilla, stirring to melt and mix butter; cool. Serve over strawberry whip.

Lucille Couch (Mrs. George M.)

Elegant Cheese Squares

Serves 12-15
375° oven

2 cups graham cracker crumbs
½ cup butter, softened
6 tablespoons sugar
16 ounces cream cheese,
  softened
1 cup sugar
¼ teaspoon salt
1 cup milk
2 teaspoons lemon juice
2 teaspoons brandy
3 cups Cool Whip, thawed
mint leaves

Combine crumbs, butter and 6 tablespoons sugar. Mix well and press firmly over bottom and sides of 9 x 13-inch baking dish. Bake at 375° for 8 minutes. Cool. Beat cream cheese until smooth and fluffy. Add 1 cup sugar gradually, beating constantly. Add salt. Blend in milk, lemon juice and brandy. Fold in Cool Whip and mix well. Spoon into crumb lined pan. Chill at least 3 hours. Cut into squares. Garnish with mint leaves.

Connie Lindstrom (Mrs. Kelsey)

Pumpkin Dessert

Serves 20
350° oven

Crust
one box yellow cake mix
½ cup melted butter
1 egg, beaten

Crust: Reserve one cup cake mix. Combine remainder of cake mix with melted butter and egg. Pat firmly into greased 9 x 13-inch pan.

Filling
3 cups pumpkin pie mix
2 eggs
⅔ cups milk

Filling: Mix and stir until smooth. Pour over crust.

Topping
1 cup reserved cake mix
1 teaspoon cinnamon
¼ cup cold butter
¼ cup sugar

Topping: Combine with pastry blender and sprinkle on top of filling. Bake at 350° for 45-50 minutes. Serve with whipped cream or vanilla ice cream.

Jan Coombs (Mrs. Robert E.)

Chocolate Caramel Fingers

Yield: 25-30
340° oven

Base
1 stick butter, softened
¼ cup sugar
¾ cup flour

Cream butter and sugar. Beat in flour, mixing well. Spread evenly in 1½-quart (8 x 10-inch) greased baking pan. Bake 30 minutes at 340°.

Filling
1 stick butter
¼ cup sugar
3 tablespoons light Karo syrup
⅔ cup Eagle Brand condensed milk

Filling: Combine all ingredients in saucepan and cook about 25 minutes (until thick and golden brown). Stir often. Pour over base. Cool until set.

Topping
4 ounces semi-sweet chocolate
⅓ cup butter

Topping: Melt together in top of double boiler. Pour on top of filling. Chill. Cut into very thin (¼ inch) strips.

Elaine Toney

Chocolate Eclair Dessert

Serves 12

2 packages instant vanilla pudding
3 cups milk
1 (9 ounce) Cool Whip
graham crackers (less than 1 box)

Combine pudding and milk. Blend in Cool Whip. Arrange layer of graham crackers in 9 x 15-inch pan. Pour half the pudding mixture over crackers. Place another layer of crackers. Pour remaining mixture and top with another layer of crackers.

Frosting
2 ounces unsweetened chocolate
1 tablespoon light Karo syrup
1 tablespoon vanilla
3 tablespoons margarine
1½ cups confectioners' sugar
3 tablespoons milk

Frosting: Combine all in double boiler; heat and stir until smooth. Spread evenly over crackers. Refrigerate overnight.

Pat Mortimer (Mrs. Ed)

Chocolate Eclairs

Yield: 12
375° oven

Shells

1 cup water
½ cup butter or margarine
1 cup sifted all-purpose flour
1/8 teaspoon salt
4 eggs, room temperature

Shells: In saucepan bring water and butter to a boil. Remove from heat; add flour and salt all at once, beating constantly with wooden spoon until mixture leaves sides of pan in smooth ball (about 1 minute). Start oven heating to 375°. To flour mixture add eggs, one at a time, beating well with spoon after each addition. Drop batter 1 heaping tablespoon at a time onto ungreased cookie sheet (12 puffs in all). Bake 40 minutes. DO NOT PEEK! Puffs will be high and golden. Remove with spatula to wire racks away from drafts. Refrigerate. To fill, cut off top one-third of puff and remove interior with a spoon.

Filling

1 package Jell-O instant vanilla
  pudding
1 teaspoon vanilla

Topping

½ cup chocolate chips
1 tablespoon water
¼ cup white corn syrup

Filling: Mix pudding according to package directions, adding 1 teaspoon vanilla.

Topping: Melt chocolate chips with water in top of double boiler. Stir in corn syrup. Cool. Drizzle over filled puffs. Serve cold.

Anne Bishop

Milky Way Ice Cream

Yield: 5 quarts

6 Milky Way bars (regular size)
2 cups milk
6 eggs, beaten
1½ cups sugar
2 (13 ounce) cans evaporated milk
2 teaspoons vanilla
additional milk to fill freezer

Melt Milky Way bars in 2 cups milk in top of double boiler. Beat eggs and sugar together in large bowl. Add Milky Way mixture to eggs; stir. Add evaporated milk and vanilla; blend well. Chill in refrigerator 2 hours. Pour into 5-quart freezer and fill to within 2 inches of top with milk. Freeze as with any ice cream.

Nancy Phillips (Mrs. Wendell)

Orange Alaska

Elegant!

6-8 fresh, heavy skinned attractive oranges
1 cup orange sherbet, softened
1 cup orange yogurt
¼ cup fresh orange juice
¼ cup Cointreau or Grand Marnier
1 teaspoon grated orange rind
fresh orange or lemon leaves

Cut circular or zig zag slice from stem end of each orange. (Leave ⅔ to ¾ of the orange.) Scoop out pulp and strain juice, reserving it for next step. Combine orange sherbet and yogurt, stirring until thoroughly blended. Add orange juice, liqueur and orange rind. Mix well. Spoon into orange shells and place in muffin tin. Spread top of each orange shell with meringue, completely covering sherbet and bringing meringue well down over the edges; freeze. Just before serving preheat broiler to 500°. Slip oranges under broiler just until meringue turns golden. (Not more than 3 minutes!) Watch constantly. Serve at once on bed of fresh, glossy citrus leaves.

Meringue
2 egg whites
¼ teaspoon cream of tartar
3 tablespoons sugar
¼ teaspoon vanilla

Meringue: Beat egg whites until frothy; add cream of tartar, continue to beat until soft peaks form. Gradually add sugar and vanilla. Beat until stiff and glossy.

Carolyn Warthen (Mrs. Gerald)

Cream Cheese Tarts

16 ounces cream cheese
¾ cup sugar
1 teaspoon vanilla
2 eggs
1 box vanilla wafers
paper cupcake liners (2½-inch diameter)
1 can blueberry or cherry pie filling
1 tablespoon brandy or rum (optional)

Combine cream cheese, sugar, vanilla and eggs; beat until smooth. Line 24 muffin cups with paper liners. Place 2 vanilla wafers in bottom of each cup. Fill cups ⅔ full of cream cheese mixture. Bake 15-20 minutes at 350°. Cool thoroughly. Add brandy or rum to pie filling, if desired. Top tarts with pie filling. Refrigerate.

Olivia Allen

Pecan Tarts

Yield: 24
350° oven

Crust
1 stick margarine, room
 temperature
3 ounces cream cheese
1 cup unsifted all-purpose flour
dash salt
24 paper tart cups
24 pecan halves

Filling
¾ cup brown sugar
2 tablespoons margarine, room
 temperature
1 large egg
24 pecan halves

Crust: Beat margarine and cream cheese together until thoroughly mixed. Cut in flour as in pie dough. Form dough in 24 balls about 1 inch in diameter and press into small paper tart cups bringing dough up sides to edge of each cup. Crumble ½ pecan into each cup.

Filling: Blend all ingredients together and place a teaspoonful in each tart cup. Top with pecan half. Bake 20 minutes at 350°.

Carol Hoskinson (Mrs. C. Richard)

Schaum Tart

Serves 12-24
250° oven

9 large or 10 small egg whites
¼ teaspoon salt
½ teaspoon cream of tartar
2 cups sugar
1 teaspoon vanilla
1 teaspoon almond extract
1 teaspoon vinegar
whipped cream
fresh strawberries, blueberries
 or peaches

Add salt to egg whites and beat until stiff. Beat in cream of tartar. Add sugar gradually, beating well. Beat in vanilla and almond extract. Add vinegar and beat until very stiff. Pour into 9½-inch spring form pan. Bake 50-60 minutes at 250°. Tart will rise an inch or more above pan and should be light brown on top. Cool before removing pan. Top with whipped cream and fresh fruit.

R.E. Blouin (Mrs. M. R.)

NOTES

FOUNDERS' CEMETERY
Sloan Street

Founders' Cemetery is the burial site of a number of Roswell's early settlers and members of their families. Unmarked gravestones of faithful servants and tiny graves of settlers' children bespeak of the hardships suffered. From the peaceful graveyard can be heard the sounds of the waterfall and nearby mill village.

Mark Collis

INDEX

ORDER FORMS

Please send me _____ copies of THE HISTORIC ROSWELL COOK BOOK at $7.95 per copy, plus $1.25 per copy postage and handling. Georgia residents add 4 per cent ($.32) sales tax per book.

Enclosed is my check or money order for $_____ .

NAME: _____

STREET: _____

CITY: _____ STATE: _____ ZIP _____

Make checks payable to The Historic Roswell Cook Book

        Mail to: **The Historic Roswell Cook Book**
                         Roswell Historical Society, Inc.
                         P.O. Box 274
                         Roswell, Georgia 30077

Please send me _____ copies of THE HISTORIC ROSWELL COOK BOOK at $7.95 per copy, plus $1.25 per copy postage and handling. Georgia residents add 4 per cent ($.32) sales tax per book.

Enclosed is my check or money order for $_____ .

NAME: _____

STREET: _____

CITY: _____ STATE: _____ ZIP _____

Make checks payable to The Historic Roswell Cook Book

        Mail to: **The Historic Roswell Cook Book**
                         Roswell Historical Society, Inc.
                         P.O. Box 274
                         Roswell, Georgia 30077

Please send me _____ copies of THE HISTORIC ROSWELL COOK BOOK at $7.95 per copy, plus $1.25 per copy postage and handling. Georgia residents add 4 per cent ($.32) sales tax per book.

Enclosed is my check or money order for $_____ .

NAME: _____

STREET: _____

CITY: _____ STATE: _____ ZIP _____

Make checks payable to The Historic Roswell Cook Book

        Mail to: **The Historic Roswell Cook Book**
                         Roswell Historical Society, Inc.
                         P.O. Box 274
                         Roswell, Georgia 30077